UNIVERSITY OF WASHINGTON
PUBLICATIONS IN HISTORY

# DAVID LLOYD

## COLONIAL LAWMAKER

BY ROY N. 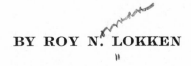 LOKKEN

UNIVERSITY OF WASHINGTON PRESS

SEATTLE

1959

*This book is published with assistance
from a grant by the Ford Foundation.*

*To my parents*

# Preface

David Lloyd was without honor among eighteenth- and nineteenth-century historians of colonial Pennsylvania. Robert Proud scarcely mentioned him, and his only observation concerning Lloyd was that "his political talents seem to have been rather to divide than to unite. . . ." Mrs. Deborah Logan, a descendant of James Logan, quoted Proud's estimate of Lloyd in her collection of the correspondence of James Logan and William Penn. She added that, although Lloyd was an able lawyer and judge and excellent in his private relationships with people, his political policy was such "that may suit the crafty politician, but must ever be disclaimed by the Christian statesman."

Not until the twentieth century did historians recognize the significance of Lloyd as a historic personage. Biographical sketches appeared, but none of them were satisfactory. Edward Channing, in Volume II of his *A History of the United States,* mentioned the inadequacy of existing memoirs of Lloyd. Since Channing's day, such historians of colonial Pennsylvania as Wayland F. Dunaway have tended to write of Lloyd as a precursor of Thomas Jefferson and Andrew Jackson. Some of them, however, have fallen into the error of "presentism" by depicting Lloyd as a democrat fully adapted to a nineteenth-century or twentieth-century frame of reference. Others have presented Lloyd as a seventeenth-century republican, accepting uncritically an inaccurate comment by Mrs. Logan, that Lloyd was a soldier in Cromwell's army during the English Civil War.

The editors of the *Dictionary of American Biography* expressed
doubt that a balanced biography of Lloyd could be written because of the nature of the source materials but mentioned the
late Burton Alva Konkle's unpublished manuscript, David Lloyd
and the First Half Century of Pennsylvania. Konkle's manuscript was the first full-length biography of Lloyd written, but
it has remained unpublished because of its many deficiencies.
David Lloyd flourished during a relatively neglected period
of American history. For historians the colonial period has too
long meant the eve of the American Revolution--those years between the end of the Seven Years War and the opening shots at
Concord and Lexington during which the rationalizations of revolution were being formed and crystallized. The years between
the English Revolution of 1689 and the middle of the eighteenth
century were long ago abandoned to the antiquarian and the genealogist, except insofar as textbook writers have skipped over
them lightly in their hurry to get to what they considered the
heart of the matter, after 1763. Yet the heart of the matter
seems rather to belong to the neglected period than to the years
following the Peace of Paris. After all, American institutions
and political and legal concepts were in large part not the product of the rationalizations of Otis and Jefferson and John Adams, but of the efforts of the colonists to solve their immediate
problems in a manner conducive to their own best local interests. When those efforts took the form of political opposition
to proprietors and Crown officers, they in no way involved a
desire to disrupt the relations between the colonies and the
homeland. The essential spadework of revolution was performed
by men who did not dream of revolution.
It was during the years of Lloyd's active life that such char-
acteristically American institutions as the supreme court with
exclusively appellate jurisdiction and such modern legal concepts as fee simple became a part of the American heritage.
Without them the war of the revolution, when it came, would
have amounted to little more than aimless bloodshed. The work
of such men as David Lloyd made the achievements of Jefferson, Washington, and the Adamses meaningful.
The biographer of a relatively obscure colonial figure does
not have available to him the vast collections of personal papers
which render so enjoyable the task of a biographer of Thomas

Jefferson or Abraham Lincoln. He finds his data in widely scattered sources, and many of his data consist of indirect references to his subject. In preparing this biography I have obtained most of my materials from the manuscripts room of the Historical Society of Pennsylvania, and I have also availed myself of the resources at the library of the American Philosophical Society, the Free Library of Philadelphia, Friends Historical Library at Swarthmore College, and the collections at Friends Bookstore in Philadelphia. Moreover, I corresponded extensively with libraries, historical societies, and individuals in Pennsylvania, England, and Wales. I owe a debt of gratitude to more people than it is practical to name in this brief preface, but I wish to extend a special word of appreciation to Professor Max Savelle of the University of Washington and Professor Douglass Adair of Pomona College for their patient guidance and helpful counsel. At one time or another I have received financial assistance from the Patriotic Service Committee of the National Society of the Colonial Dames of America and from Mr. Fred T. Haley of Tacoma, Washington. To them go my most sincere thanks.

Madison, Wisconsin　　　　　　　　　　　　　　Roy N. Lokken
May, 1959

## Note on Chronology

England did not adopt the Gregorian (New Style) Calendar until 1752. Hence, the chronology throughout this book is Old Style, that is, the English variation of the Julian Calendar. In the Old Style Calendar, the year begins on March 25 instead of January 1. Before 1700 the difference between the New Style and the Old Style Calendars was 10 days; after 1700 it was 11 days.

# Contents

# Illustrations

DAVID LLOYD, COLONIAL LAWMAKER

A page from David Lloyd's notebook

# 1. "A Sober and Ingeneous Man"

Early in the summer of 1686, David Lloyd and his wife Sarah boarded the *Amity* at London for the strange new world west of the western horizon. The whole tenor of his life, at least since he had gone to work in the London offices of William Penn's lawyers several years earlier, seemed oriented in the direction of the English colonies in North America. Penn, second only to George Fox in the hearts of English Quakers, had, in 1681, acquired from his friend, Charles II, a vast proprietary on the Delaware River west of West New Jersey, north of Maryland, and south of New York. To this proprietary James, Duke of York, had subsequently added the three Lower Counties of New Castle, Sussex, and Kent on the west shore of Delaware Bay south of Pennsylvania and east of Maryland.

Lloyd's legal duties from 1683 to 1686 had been devoted to transactions involving this vast new colony. Lloyd's earliest work for Penn had included drawing up deeds, warrants, and other conveyances to first purchasers of Pennsylvania land.[1] Also he had begun a notebook in 1683 in which he had painstakingly copied and annotated, sometimes in Latin, sometimes in English, sometimes in a Gothic chirography, sometimes in his usual rounded penmanship, acts of Parliament of principal interest to Penn and himself, among them laws governing *quo warranto* proceedings.[2]

The *quo warranto* laws were particularly apropos. James II was following the policy established by his late brother, Charles II, of strengthening the monarchial power by institut-

ing *quo warranto* proceedings against corporations in the kingdom and against the charters of troublesome colonies in North
America to render them more dependent on the Crown. Only
recently James II had revoked the corporation charter of Connecticut, following by only two years the forfeiture of the corporation charter of Massachusetts Bay, which had long exhib-
ited autonomous tendencies. Pennsylvania, fledgling province
though it was, was also displaying autonomous tendencies by
1686, and Penn was having difficulty keeping a tight rein on his
colonists.[3] The Quakers who colonized and governed Pennsylvania had many enemies in the English government, and Penn,
in spite of his long personal friendship with the King, feared,
as he informed the Pennsylvania colonists later in the year,
losing his proprietary charter as the result of *quo warranto*
proceedings which might be instituted because of reported disturbances in Pennsylvania.[4] The danger was particularly great
because Pennsylvania lacked men trained in English law, and in
1686 the province had no attorney general capable of safeguard-
ing proprietary interests. For that reason Penn had, on April
25, 1686, given Lloyd his commission as Attorney General of
Pennsylvania.[5]

Penn's selection of Lloyd to bear the responsibility of protecting his legal interests and charter rights in Pennsylvania
indicated the high regard that the Proprietor had for him. In
the letter of introduction, which Lloyd carried among his effects, Penn commended him to the colonists as "a sober and
ingeneous man, bred & of use to you."[6] Lloyd was not a Quaker,
but Penn could depend on his loyalty. Certainly there was nothing in Lloyd's demeanor at this time to indicate that in only
a few years the two men would be bitter opponents, and that
their enmity would occur after Lloyd's conversion to the Quaker faith.

Although Lloyd was not a Quaker, he did not share the prejudice against Quakers which had been widespread in England
ever since George Fox had first undertaken his hazardous ministry. The entries in Lloyd's notebook reveal his keen interest
in the fate of the Quakers in England during 1685 and 1686.
Hundreds of Quakers had suffered imprisonment after the revo-
cation of the Declaration of Indulgence in 1673, and many more
had endured economic reprisals because of their religious pro-

fession. After James II had ascended the throne, Penn had successfully used his influence on the erstwhile Duke of York to obtain from him a general pardon, dated March 15, 1685/86, which had resulted in the release of more than one thousand Quakers from English prisons. Lloyd had copied the pardon into his notebook. [7]

Lloyd had reasons other than his associations with Penn for his interest in the general pardon of imprisoned Quakers because the pardon aroused memories of the sufferings of Quakers in the vicinity of his birthplace, Manafon, [8] a tiny hamlet which nestled on the bank of the river Rhiw in the cold and mountainous uplands of Montgomeryshire in northern Wales. Lloyd's birth in 1656[9] had come at a time of great religio-political upheavals, religious persecution, and militant religious nonconformity. A king had been beheaded, and a Puritan Republic had been established. The Republic had rapidly metamorphosed into the Protectorate of Oliver Cromwell. Lloyd's fourth birthday had seen the demise of the Protectorate and the ascension of Charles Stuart, the good-natured and sensual son of the beheaded king, to the throne at Whitehall. The Stuart Restoration had signaled the victory of the Church of England in its long struggle against the Presbyterian and Independent churches, and religious nonconformity had been driven to the wall. Yet, during this period the courage and independence of the religious nonconformist in England and Wales had been asserted most splendidly. Such valiant itinerant nonconformist preachers as Vavasor Powel had suffered great hardships to carry the gospel to isolated Welsh farmers who had possessed, as yet, no Bible. George Fox and thousands of his followers, who were called Quakers because they were said to tremble at the word of the Lord, had endured imprisonment and merciless persecution for their belief that all wars were unlawful, that the worship of God was purely an inner, spiritual experience, that no Christian should swear an oath even though required to do so by the state, and that opposition to capital punishment for crimes affecting property only was a Christian duty.

David Lloyd's parents had not adopted the Quaker faith, but their relatives, members of the landed gentry, at nearby Dolobran Hall had. [10] There Charles Lloyd, oldest in a family of

three sons and one daughter, and since his father's death the
head of the household, had greeted the Stuart Restoration by
erecting a Quaker meetinghouse near Dolobran Hall. Charles
had possessed every advantage that a young Welshman could
desire--family, social position, and wealth. His family boasted
an ancestry extending back to the kings of Dyfed in southern
Wales and the marriage of the "Fair Maid of Kent, " the grand-
daughter of Edward I, to Edward, the "Black Prince" of
Wales. [11] Charles had succeeded his father as a Justice of the
Peace of Montgomeryshire and had appeared certain to be
elected High Sheriff of the county, a very important office in
those days. Yet he had tossed position and influence aside to
follow the dictates of his conscience. His younger brother
Thomas had also entered the Society of Friends in 1661 and
had interrupted his education at Jesus College, Oxford, where
Charles and another brother John had been graduated earlier, because his conscience had rebelled against the persecution of Quakers at that institution. By 1662 both Charles and
Thomas had been active in Quaker meetings at Dolobran and
nearby communities.

Indignant social retaliation against the nonconformist Lloyds
of Dolobran Hall had been swift. Charles, who had just been
elected High Sheriff of Montgomeryshire, had been removed
from office and imprisoned at Welshpool because he had refused to swear the oaths of allegiance and supremacy, and he
had remained a prisoner there throughout most of David Lloyd's
boyhood, until 1672. [12]

The imprisonment of Charles Lloyd, however, had not daunt-
ed his brother Thomas. In spite of the Conventicle Act of 1669,
which Parliament had intended as a means of destroying religious nonconformity by outlawing all religious assemblies except those in the Church of England, Thomas Lloyd had led
Quaker meetings at Meifod, the home of David Lloyd's paternal grandfather, and Dolobran, where Thomas Lloyd was later
remembered as having been "very Charitable To the Poor, &
Compassionate To those in affliction. "[13] Soon Thomas Lloyd
too was imprisoned. Released from imprisonment in 1672,
Thomas and Charles Lloyd had again become active in Quaker meetings at Meifod and Dolobran and had even gone so far
as to debate the tenets of their religious profession with the

Anglican bishop of St. Asaph. [14] Their sufferings because of their religion had made a lasting impression on David Lloyd. The Lloyds of Dolobran also had a stake in the Quaker colony toward which David Lloyd and his wife were beginning their journey. Charles and Thomas Lloyd were extensive purchasers of Pennsylvania land, as the record of conveyances issued to them, some by David Lloyd when he was working in Penn's law offices, indicated. [15] Thomas Lloyd had sailed to Pennsylvania with Penn on the *Welcome* in 1682, a member of the first shipload of Quakers to migrate to the colony which Penn had intended to be a sanctuary for Quakers and the persecuted of all religious faiths. When Penn had returned to England in 1684, he had left the government of the colony in the hands of Thomas Lloyd, whose education, background, and position of leadership among Quakers had made him an ideal choice for President of the Provincial Council. Thomas Lloyd still held that position in 1686, and it was he to whom David Lloyd would present his credentials upon arrival in Philadelphia. They would be the only representatives in Pennsylvania of the Lloyds of Dolobran, Manafon, and Meifod. Charles Lloyd, because he was the head of the family, remained at the ancestral home in Dolobran, Wales. [16]

There was another Lloyd in America, but his bones rested beneath the soil of Maryland. This was David Lloyd's brother Ralph. David, Ralph, and their sister Jane, who remained in England, had not enjoyed the advantages of their relatives at Dolobran Hall. Born of obscure, lower-class parents, David Lloyd and his brother and sister had not received the benefits of a formal education beyond, probably, the grammar schools maintained by the Church of England in the larger towns near Manafon. [17] David had been fortunate to receive his legal training in the office of Sir George Jeffreys, the brilliant Welsh lawyer who was later to become the Chief Justice of England and one of the most controversial figures in English history.[18] While studying law, David Lloyd had married Sarah, a girl five years younger who had come from Cirencester, Gloucestershire. [19] Ralph Lloyd, however, had sought his fortune in America.

Ralph had evidently indentured himself for a term of years as a servant to buy passage to Maryland. After his term of serv-

ice had ended, he bought from his master 5,000 acres of land
for £20. Consequently, Ralph had had every opportunity to
raise himself from his former servile state to a position of independence and influence in his New World community. He
had not been so fortunate, however. He had fallen in love with
a woman whose name is not revealed in the sources. At first
she had returned his love but finally had jilted him to marry
another man. Ralph had nevertheless continued to love her,
and she had encouraged him even after her marriage. The
affair had gone to the extent of Ralph's having willed nearly
his entire estate to her.

The sources do not show the cause of Ralph's death, but they
indicate that the terms of his will were carried out. When David
and Jane Lloyd had learned of the will, they determined to challenge it. They had written to James Harrison, Penn's land
agent who lived at Pennsbury, the Proprietor's estate in Pennsylvania, for a true copy of the will. David and Jane Lloyd
had expected that their brother's jilter would deal fairly with
them. To make sure, David had asked Harrison to give him
a more detailed account of Ralph's estate and an estimate of
what his own share of the estate ought to be. If the Maryland
woman proved intractable, David Lloyd had intended to give
a letter of attorney to "A kinsman of mine that coms to maryland [probably Thomas Lloyd] And leave him to Examine the
matter. . . ." He had added that if the Maryland woman "make
Expedition and send us something Considerble I shall not trouble my Self with useing Any other meanes. . . ." He had threatened that otherwise he would "turne it over to such that will
torment her sufficiently with law."[20]

If David Lloyd ever succeeded in wresting from his brother's
jilter any portion of the landed estate which she had inherited,
existing sources say nothing about it. All evidence indicates
that when the *Amity* began its long voyage across the Atlantic, David and Sarah Lloyd possessed little more than the
lawyer's professional skill and salary. There is not even evidence that they owned a single share in The New Mediterranean
Sea Company, which David Lloyd was to represent in America.
Lloyd's ability as an attorney and his commission as Attorney
General of Pennsylvania had brought him to the attention of Dr.
Daniel Coxe, Sir Matthias Vincent, and Major Robert Thomp-

son, partners in The New Mediterranean Sea Company. Coxe, the leader of the partnership, who had been speculating in West New Jersey properties for several years, was a doctor of physic, a member of the Royal Society in London, and a former physician to Charles II. He and his partners dreamed of establishing a fur-trading empire which would extend from the settled portions of Pennsylvania far back into the western wilderness. To this end they had, on April 20, 1686, purchased from Penn 30, 116 acres of Pennsylvania land, and ten days later they had appointed David Lloyd their agent to care for their lands in Penn's colony. [21] On June 7 Coxe, his partners, and other adventurers had formed The New Mediterranean Sea Company, and Penn had granted the new company 5, 000 acres on or near the Delaware and Susquehanna rivers and 95, 000 acres on or near a great lake, the "New Mediterranean Sea, " which appears to have been Lake Erie. The company had declared its intention of establishing a colony in the vicinity of the great lake. [22]

Eventually Coxe's ambitious project was to prove a failure, but that would not affect David Lloyd's fortunes. At least Lloyd's position with the new company gave him a salary. Whether or not Lloyd received an income from Penn at this time is not clear. If he did, when the *Amity* completed its voyage and docked at Philadelphia on July 15, 1686, Lloyd, although he possessed no land or other material wealth, was not entirely dependent on Penn.

# 2. Pennsylvania

When David and Sarah Lloyd disembarked at Philadelphia on July 15, 1686, they saw a bustling community of about 800 frame and brick houses concentrated on the Delaware River front. The houses were of a plain architecture, and they showed that their inhabitants preferred solid foundations, strong frames, and good cellars to ornamentation. Nevertheless, the influence of the English Renaissance was clearly in evidence. Many houses were also of a style that was later to be called American Georgian. Although most of the town's dwellings were small and modest in appearance, some houses were three stories high, and a few had balconies. [1]

Front Street, Philadelphia's main thoroughfare, extended along the bank of the Delaware River. Here the principal business of the town was conducted. Farmers from Bucks County, Chester County, and the rural area of Philadelphia County carted their produce along Front Street to the wharves on the Delaware River bank. At one or other of the three private docks, built by Quaker merchants in 1684, the farmers sold the product of their labor, chiefly grains, either to the Philadelphia merchants or directly to the captains of ships lying at anchor. A larger dock at the bank of Dock Creek, which emptied into the Delaware at Front Street, accommodated small vessels from the New Jerseys and New England laden with building timber and other imports. Below this dock was a low, sandy beach which the colonists employed as a public landing place for such imports as stones and logs that could not be unloaded safely

at the docks. Above the beach and its adjoining dock was Blue
Anchor Tavern, Philadelphia's central place of business. Although the tavern had been built in 1682 primarily as a drinking
house, social center for men, and hostelry, much of the waterfront's mercantile business was transacted within its walls.
Near the river bank on the west side of Front Street, just above
Mulberry (now Arch) Street, stood a newly erected meetinghouse where the great majority of Philadelphia Quakers wor-
shiped. [2]

Most of the peninsula between the Delaware and Schuylkill
rivers, on which Penn had originally intended to erect a city
with fronts on both rivers, remained in forest. The specifica-
tions, drawn in 1681 by Captain Thomas Holme, the province's
first Surveyor General, called for a square of ten acres in the
center of the city (where Logan Square is now located), and
at the angles of the square there were to be a meetinghouse,
an assembly or statehouse, a market house, a schoolhouse,
and several other public buildings. Only the meetinghouse,
constructed of brick, had been erected, but few Philadelphia
Quakers attended it because of its location in the woods and
its distance from their homes. [3]

Such was the physical aspect of Philadelphia which David
and Sarah Lloyd saw after they had left their ship and walked
for the first time in the streets of Penn's "City of Brotherly
Love. " In the streets they observed the heterogeneity of Philadelphia society. There were the English and Welsh Quakers
who formed the largest portion of the colony's population and
who were distinguishable because of the simplicity of their
dress, [4] their use of the unconventional pronouns "thee" and
"thou, " and their persistent refusal to remove their hats in
the presence of social superiors. More ostentatious in their
dress were the Swedes, a hardy and ingenious people who reputedly used hardly any other tool in building except an axe.
Finns and Dutch--along with the Swedes, the older inhabitants
of the region--also walked the streets of Philadelphia. Mostly
farmers, they were said to live well and to possess abundant
larders. [5] Irish, too, were on the streets. Like the Welsh, they
were, for the most part, descendants of good families, freeholders, and men of better than average education. [6] Also,
there were Germans from nearby Germantown, which had been

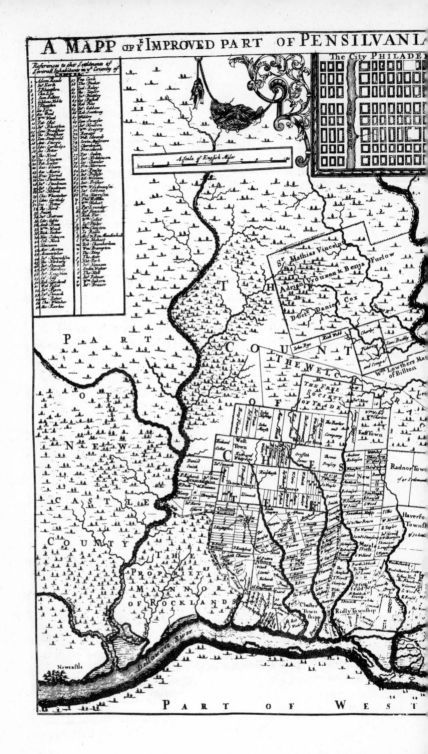

The State Historical Society of Wisconsin

Mapp of the Improved Part of Pensilvania in America, " in Carolo Allard and
rs, *A Miscellaneous Collection of 114 Maps of Various Parts of the World*
sterdam, *ca.* 1696)

settled in 1683 by Mennonites from Crefeld on the lower Rhine, led by Francis Daniel Pastorius, a lawyer and Mennonite minister from Frankfurt-am-Main. A few Negro slaves, chiefly house servants, and Indians of the friendly Delaware tribe mingled with the whites on the streets of Philadelphia.[7]

National, racial, and religious differentiations aside, the men whom David and Sarah Lloyd saw on the streets of Philadelphia on July 15, 1686, were merchants, tradesmen, workmen, artisans, and indentured servants. Although Philadelphia was chiefly a mercantile community, there was already an industrial life in the early stage of its development. The Free Society of Traders, a monopoly organized by adventurers in 1681, had a tannery, sawmill, glasshouse, and whalery in Philadelphia. Brickyards were in operation, and the Germans manufactured fine linen, which was sold at the annual fairs held in Philadelphia and at the biweekly markets. Ships and boats for the ocean and river traffic were under construction on the Philadelphia waterfront. Hence, a large portion of Philadelphia society consisted of carpenters, shoemakers, butchers, bakers, brewers, glovers, tanners, feltmongers, wheelwrights, millwrights, shipwrights, boatwrights, ropemakers, sailmakers, blockmakers, turners, and other skilled workmen.

Indentured servants made up a smaller proportion of the town's population. These were poor working people who had hired out their labor to obtain passage to America. Usually they worked four years or more for their masters, that is, their creditors, and were released from servitude with fifty acres of land, clothes, some tools, and perhaps a couple of cows with which to start farms of their own. It was a common saying in the seventeenth century that the poor were the hands and feet of the rich, and Penn encouraged immigrants to bring in servants by allowing them fifty acres of land for each servant they brought into the colony. David and Sarah Lloyd brought no servants with them, but many of the more prosperous colonists had. The servant system was regulated by the laws of the province, and servants, like slaves, were considered the personal property of the masters. Servants, to be sure, were on a higher social level than were the slaves, and they could eventually achieve freeman status. Nevertheless, they ranked lower than the workers and artisans.[8]

David and Sarah Lloyd spent their first few weeks in Philadelphia getting settled and adjusting themselves to their new surroundings. Life in the New World community was vastly different from the gayer life of London. Everyone's activity from dawn to dusk was severely regulated by the Philadelphia town government. The sound of a bell announced the beginning and end of the workday and the hours of meals. Curfew was at nine o'clock in the evening. Town officers went the rounds at that hour and made certain that the seven licensed ordinaries were not entertaining customers. No person was allowed in public houses after curfew except lodgers. To be sure, the want of a prison in Philadelphia rendered law enforcement difficult, and there were violations of the laws. Caves in the high bank along the Delaware River, originally used as homes in 1682 until houses had been built, were doing business as brothels and unlicensed drinking houses. Some colonists made a living by bootlegging and pimping. [9] Nevertheless, Philadelphia was as sober and well-regulated a town as any in the colonies, and from the point of view of a newcomer from London virtually devoid of legitimate entertainment. There were no theaters, no balls, no levees. Playacting and dancing were strictly forbidden. Social life was limited to the meetinghouse, the home, the Blue Anchor Tavern, and the drinking houses.

The food David and Sarah Lloyd ate in Philadelphia was Pennsylvania produce. The young province was already self-sufficient so far as food supplies were concerned and even produced foodstuffs for export. Practically all of Penn's domain was in forest, but the farmers clung to the fertile lands adjacent to the Delaware River, which separated Pennsylvania from West New Jersey; the Schuylkill River, a stream which flowed in a southeasterly direction from its source in the Appalachian Mountains in present-day Schuylkill County to enter the Delaware at Philadelphia; and their tributary creeks. The rich soil of the Delaware River Valley and the balanced climate belied the rumors then circulating in England that Pennsylvania land was barren and unproductive and that the climate was unbearably hot. [10] David Lloyd was not in Pennsylvania long before he concluded that the province would in time "certainly be the Grainary of America." [11] In the watershed of the Delaware River enough Indian corn and wheat were grown to supply the colonists' needs and to be exported to England and the West Indies as well. Lloyd wrote that the wheat was as good as any in England and that it sold for three shillings sixpence a bushel in Pennsylvania, a relatively good price which guaranteed the farmer a fair return for his labor. Farmers also raised barley, turnips, oats, carrots, parsnips, peas, hops, grapes, and other fruits for local sale and for their own larders. Some colonists entertained high hopes of raising tobacco for the export trade, and it was expected that good wine could be made from the wild grapes which grew in abundance. Lloyd tasted the grapes in William Penn's vineyard and found them good. [12]

During his first weeks in Pennsylvania David Lloyd noted the close relationship between the province's agriculture and commerce. Agriculture, based on the family-sized farm, was the foundation of Pennsylvania's economy. Farmers produced both for home consumption and for the intercolonial and trans-Atlantic trade. Philadelphia was a port of call for ships from England, Barbados, and Boston. Often ships which brought cargoes of immigrants to the province departed with cargoes of Pennsylvania-grown wheat and Indian corn. Lloyd noted that within two months after his arrival five ships from Bristol and one from Hull put in at Philadelphia with 260 passengers and that a ship from New England and two from Barbados stopped to pick up cargoes of corn. All the ships loaded and set sail for Barbados, except one which sailed north to New England. [13]

Pennsylvania's expanding economy indicated a prosperous future. As was the case everywhere in the colonies, however, money was scarce, and Pennsylvania colonists were experimenting with methods of attracting cash into the province. The first of these methods was in effect during David Lloyd's first weeks in Pennsylvania. The English money which Lloyd had brought with him increased 25 per cent in value in accordance with provincial law. The value of Spanish pieces of eight rose six shillings each in the province. [14] There were no uniform rates of exchange in England and the colonies, and there was no law prohibiting the revaluation of coin by colonial legislatures. The practice, however, was regarded with disfavor by the King's officers who were responsible for the enforcement of English laws of navigation and trade in the colonies, because it confused their accounts of customs duties collected in Pennsylvania ports. Penn was apprehensive lest tampering with the value of coin give offense to the King's officers. [15]

Pennsylvania colonists, however, were learning that the English mercantile system, in which the colonies acted at once as a source of raw materials and as a market for English manufactures, actually served to drain ready cash out of the colonies. Some less scrupulous Pennsylvanians had resorted to counterfeiting as an easy way to make up the deficiency, but provincial authorities had taken effective action to stamp out that practice. [16] The colonists needed good money, not bad money, and the Pennsylvania legislature revalued coin as a means of attracting good money into the province.

Because of the shortage of coin, Pennsylvania merchants were averse to paying customs duties on imports and exports. Penn had the right to collect customs duties for his own revenue, but when he was in the province from 1682 to 1684 he had indulged the merchants as a favor with exemption from such duties. After his return to England in 1684 the colonists had claimed the right not to pay customs duties to the Proprietor. In 1686 they objected even to paying the King's duties and grumbled about the restrictions laid upon them by the English laws of trade and navigation. [17] Such objections constituted a direct threat to Penn's charter, which specified that violation of the trade and navigation laws could result in the forfeiture of Penn's proprietorship of Pennsylvania to the Crown. [18] Penn lived in daily fear that the Crown would institute *quo warranto* proceedings against his charter because of, among other reasons, the unwillingness of the colonists to comply with acts of Parliament governing colonial commerce. This was a matter which concerned David Lloyd as the province's new Attorney General and as the Proprietor's legal representative in Pennsylvania. The young province, as Lloyd observed, had bountiful potentialities as a center of colonial trade, [19] but there were also internal dissensions which boded ill for the colony's relations with the Crown and with the Proprietor.

# 3. Defender of the Proprietary Interests

David Lloyd did not present his credentials to the Provincial Council until three weeks after his arrival. When he appeared in the Council room on August 5, 1686, his relative President Thomas Lloyd and only a few of the Council's eighteen members were present, as was normally the case even though the Pennsylvania Frame of Government, promulgated by Penn in 1683, required a quorum of twelve members at each Council meeting. After the President and Council had read the letter of introduction which David Lloyd had given them, the Attorney General took the tests required by provincial law and acts of Parliament, declaring his allegiance to the King and his fidelity to the proprietary and to the provincial government and promising the faithful performance of his office. [1]

At this meeting David Lloyd encountered the kind of problem which he would have to face as Penn's legal representative in Pennsylvania. One of the letters which Penn had given him to deliver to the Provincial Council contained matters which at once aroused the antagonism of the councilors. Penn recommended among other things that the colonists be taxed to pay the expenses of provincial government. He had been defraying the cost of governing Pennsylvania out of his own pocket, and partly for that reason he had gone deeply into debt. As he wrote to James Harrison, "I am £5,000 and more behind hand, than ever I received or saw for land in the province. . . ." [2] He had borrowed heavily from the steward of his estates in Ireland, Philip Ford, and he had been unable to repay Ford out of profits

realized in Pennsylvania. The merchants refused to pay the
Proprietor's customs duties, and Penn's proprietary agents
had failed to collect the quitrents--feudal dues of a shilling or
a bushel of wheat for every hundred acres--which every purchaser of land in the province owed annually to the Proprietor. [3]
Because money was in short supply, Penn's request for a "public supply," added to his efforts to collect quitrents and customs
duties from the colonists, angered some of the councilmen,
particularly those who were merchants. "What were we sent
for so far for so little?" they asked, as Penn was subsequently
informed. [4]

Shortly after this meeting of the Provincial Council, David
Lloyd endeavored to obviate the appearance of antiproprietary
sentiment among the colonists by impressing upon them the
fact that their powers in government were derived from the
Proprietor and that the Proprietor's powers in turn were derived from the King. Also, he advised that the courts in the
province were held by the King's authority in the Proprietor's
name. Penn himself believed that he governed on behalf of the
King, and David Lloyd officiated in the courts as the King's
Attorney as well as the Proprietor's. [5]

David Lloyd's defense of the Proprietor's interests soon won
for him the confidence of leading Philadelphia merchants and
members of the Provincial Council. One of the councilmen,
Phineas Pemberton, who was a close friend of Penn and a
highly efficient clerk of the county courts, deputy master of
the rolls, deputy register of deeds, and receiver of proprietary
quitrents in Bucks County, became, next to Thomas Lloyd,
David Lloyd's most intimate friend. [6]

David Lloyd's advice that the courts in Pennsylvania were
held by the King's authority in the Proprietor's name, however,
evoked the criticism of the colony's antiproprietary leader,
Dr. Nicholas More, who, according to Lloyd, denounced the
Attorney General's opinion "as a Lye."[7] More, the President
of the Free Society of Traders, had been a bitter and outspoken
critic of Penn ever since the promulgation of the Frame of
1683. In 1683 he had accused Penn, the Provincial Council,
and the Assembly of violating the King's charter and had declared that the Frame of 1683 would be considered treasonable
in England. [8] He resisted the tendency of the Assembly to imi-

tate the procedures of the House of Commons in England, and
in 1684 had called one assemblyman "a Person of a Seditious
Spirit. "[9] He had not only alienated the Assembly, but President
Thomas Lloyd and the Council as well, because of his declaration that he, as Chief Justice of the Supreme Provincial Court,
was not accountable to them. Patrick Robinson, the clerk of
the Philadelphia County courts and principal clerk of the Supreme Provincial Court, agreed with More, and his refusal
to obey the Assembly's order to produce the records of the
Supreme Provincial Court to facilitate the Assembly's investigation of More's judicial conduct had resulted in his being
designated by the Assembly "a publick Enemy to the Province
of Pennsylvania. . . . "[10] The President and Council subsequently expelled More from office on the basis of charges rendered against him by the Assembly. [11] They did not expel Robinson, but Robinson had decidedly alienated the friends of the
Proprietor who immediately looked around for a suitable successor.

They fixed upon David Lloyd. Upon the recommendation of
James Claypoole and Humphrey Morrey, Philadelphia merchants, and Dr. John Goodson, one of Penn's Commissioners
of Property, the President and Council appointed David Lloyd
to succeed Robinson in his county and Supreme Provincial Court
offices. [12]

By accepting these new appointments David Lloyd appeared
to be taking a stand in the controversy on the side of the opponents of Robinson and More, but it was only an appearance.
Lloyd, in fact, carefully avoided antagonizing Penn's critics.
The day after he had succeeded Robinson in the office of clerk
of the Philadelphia County courts the two men breakfasted together, and Lloyd thought Robinson "very kind. "[13] Moreover,
he contributed to a letter prepared by More for publication in
England to advertise the virtues of Pennsylvania and thereby
to induce people in England and the European continent to migrate to the province. [14] These incidents, of course, could be
explained as carrying out Penn's wishes to avoid factional controversies and to encourage activities which best promoted the
Proprietor's interests, but there were other indications that
Lloyd's defense of the proprietary interests was, at the most,
lukewarm.

To be sure, David Lloyd had defended the proprietary and royal prerogatives in the courts of Pennsylvania. Moreover, he endeavored to eliminate the vicious conditions which existed along the bank of the Delaware River fronting Philadelphia. Convinced that the only way to destroy the brothels and unlawful drinking houses was to evict the occupants of the caves in the river banks, he advised the Commissioners of Property to prosecute those colonists who refused to abandon the caves in which they lived.[15] That summed up Lloyd's total defense of the proprietary interests during 1686 and 1687.

David Lloyd took no action in matters which most deeply concerned Penn, particularly the persistent encroachments upon the Frame of 1683 by the Assembly. Ever since the Proprietor had returned to England in 1684, the colonists had evinced a tendency to go their own way, regardless of Penn's desires and original purposes. Penn had designed Pennsylvania to be a "Holy Experiment," embodying his conception of what a Christian commonwealth should be. The charter which Charles II had given him in 1681 allowed him, as was generally the case with English proprietary grants, considerable freedom in establishing a colonial government of his own choice. The only specific requirements in the royal charter were that freemen be permitted to participate in legislation and that colonial laws be consistent with the laws in England.[16] Accordingly, Penn had attempted to set up a political Utopia, based on the assumption that government, although man-made, is divinely ordained and "sacred in its institutions and end" and that its chief purpose was "to terrify evil-doers [and] to cherish those that do well."[17] In its mechanical aspects the provincial government, as established by Penn in a Frame which he prepared in England in 1682 and, when the colonists objected to that Frame, in another Frame which he granted in 1683, was based partly on Utopian political theory--probably James Harrington's *Oceana*[18]--and partly on colonial precedents. The legislature, as in the other colonies, was bicameral, consisting of the Council and house of representatives, or Assembly as the latter came to be known. All Council and Assembly seats were elective. Elections were annual, and the secret ballot, a Harrington device, was employed. Only freemen, that is, property owners--farmers and owners of large landed estates--and tax-

payers--merchants and other men of means who owned little or
no land--could vote and participate in government. The rotation
system, another Harringtonian idea, was in effect in the Council. One member from each county served three years, one
served two years, and the other served one year. Most of the
legislative and executive powers resided in the Governor and
Council, or, in the absence of a Governor, in the President
and Council. The Assembly's sole function, according to the
Frame of 1683, was to approve or disapprove legislation proposed by the Council. The Frame of 1683 expressed Penn's
conviction that government, to be secure, should have popular approval. [19]

The Assembly, however, had almost from the beginning developed its organization and functions beyond the limits set by
the Frame of 1683. Already it was imitating the procedures
of the House of Commons in England, and, although the Frame
provided for neither Speaker nor Clerk, there was a Speaker
from the beginning and a Clerk was appointed by the Assembly
annually after 1683. Moreover, the Assembly assumed for itself the right to debate every question before putting it to a
vote. Penn himself had set a precedent by permitting the Assembly to make proposals to the Governor and Council in matters pertaining to the welfare of the province and by holding
conferences with the Council on problems of state. What Penn
had granted as a benefaction the Assembly now claimed as a
right, and it demanded even greater privileges in legislation
and a more formal procedure in the conduct of bicameral conferences. [20]

Penn looked upon the Assembly's demands as further attempts by the popular legislature to challenge his prerogatives
as the King's Governor, and he believed that the colonists had
time and again forfeited their right to the Frame of 1683. Even
more important, he feared that the colonists' grasping for
power had resulted in violations of the King's charter and would
result in *quo warranto* proceedings against his title to Pennsylvania. He wanted all provincial laws passed since his return to
England in 1684 abrogated and the Assembly compelled to observe the letter of the Frame of 1683. [21]

The records are eloquent in their silence as to David Lloyd's

position on the privileges which the Assembly had assumed
and on the laws which the Assembly had passed. Lloyd never
appeared before the Council to complain of the Assembly's
encroachments upon the Frame of 1683 or to urge the abrogation
of provincial laws passed before 1684. He supported in open
court the Proprietor's authority as the King's deputy in the
judiciary of the province, but he never upheld Penn's prerogative as the King's Governor in the provincial legislature.
He did not even remonstrate to the Council against the publication by provincial authorities of official papers which contained no mention of the Proprietor's or of the King's name,
thereby, in effect, denying recognition to any sovereign power
above themselves, although Penn himself complained of that
practice. [22]

David Lloyd's evident indifference to Penn's wishes as far
as the Assembly and the provincial laws were concerned reflected the attitude of his relative Thomas Lloyd. In February, 1686/87, Penn commissioned Thomas Lloyd to head a
board of five commissioners, any three of whom he authorized
to act collectively as Deputy Governor of Pennsylvania and the
Lower Counties, and he instructed the board to abrogate all
laws passed after August, 1684, and to dismiss the Assembly.
He instructed the board, furthermore, to inspect the past
proceedings of the Council and Assembly and to inform him
"in what they have broke the Bounds or Obligations of their
Charter [i. e., the Frame of 1683], " to call a new Assembly,
and to forbid "any Parlies or open Conferences between the
Provincial Council & the Assembly, but One . . . Propose,
& let the other consent or dissent according to Charter." Penn
reserved to himself a veto power in legislation and ordered
that the new Assembly should pass new laws in such a manner
"as to avoid a greater Inconveniency, which I foresee, " that
is, *quo warranto* proceedings. [23]

Thomas Lloyd took no more action to defend Penn's charter
from *quo warranto* proceedings than had David Lloyd. Thomas
Lloyd and the board he headed ignored Penn's instructions.
They made no effort to abrogate the laws of the province, to
dismiss the Assembly, and to call a new Assembly which would
have no powers other than those Penn had specifically granted

in the Frame of 1683.[24] Both David and Thomas Lloyd appeared
unconcerned that Penn might lose his charter because of *quo
warranto* proceedings.

On May 30, 1687, the King-in-Council initiated *quo warranto*
proceedings against Penn's charter, and against charters which
had been granted to the Proprietors of Carolina and the Bahama
Islands as well.[25] Penn, in an evident effort to propagandize
his cause to the colonists whose indifference was reflected in
the records of the Council and Assembly, published for distribution among the colonists a book, entitled *The Excellent Privilege of Liberty and Property Being the Birthright of the Freeborn Subjects of England,* which contained copies of the Magna
Charta, Edward I's Confirmation of the Charters, the Statute
*de tallagio non concedendo,* and other related documents, along
with his charter and the Frame of 1683. In the preface of this
anthology Penn expressed his hope that the book might

> . . . raise up noble resolutions in all the Freeholders . . . not to give
> away anything of Liberty and Property that at present they do (or of
> right as loyal English subjects ought to) enjoy, but take up the good
> example of our ancestors, and understand that it is easy to part with
> or give away great privileges, but hard to be gained if once lost.[26]

The book constituted a reminder to the colonists of their English heritage and of the privileges which Penn had granted them
in the Frame of 1683, and Penn's purpose in publishing it was
obviously to warn the colonists of what they were in danger of
losing if the Crown revoked his charter. But Penn never intended that the colonists should have the right to arrogate to themselves rights and privileges which were not theirs by virtue of
their English heritage and which he had not specifically granted
them. Thomas Lloyd and the Board of Commissioners believed
that the colonists had such a right, as did the members of
the Council and Assembly. David Lloyd's lukewarm performance as the defender of the proprietary interests indicated that
he was in agreement with them. As things turned out, the Crown
never revoked Penn's charter, but David Lloyd had done little
as the Attorney General of Pennsylvania to receive credit for
that fact.

David Lloyd's lack of concern for the fate of Penn's charter
resulted partly from the fact that he was himself becoming

more a colonist with interests of his own and less a proprietary
agent devoted to the interests of his employer. The New Mediterranean Sea Company, whose agent he was, failed, and although he represented clients as a defense attorney in civil
suits--he unsuccessfully defended a man in what is believed
to have been the first breach of promise suit in the legal history of Pennsylvania[27]--he was prohibited by the mores of
Pennsylvania Quakers from charging fees for such services.
On October 12, 1687, he accepted an appointment by the Council as Deputy Register General of Wills, and that office paid
him some compensation. [28] Such income, however, was meager, and Lloyd turned to land speculation as the surest way of
securing his material fortunes.

In 1687 Lloyd received a patent for a tract of land in Merion
Township, and, on October 1, 1688, he acquired a deed for
197 acres in the township of Chester. He developed the latter
tract into a plantation and, apparently with the intention of
raising farm products for trade, petitioned for and obtained
the permission of the Grand Jury of Chester to lay out a road
from the plantation to the public landing place on Chester
Creek. [29] Chester was a small shipping village of about 100
houses which was located on the Delaware River a few miles
southwest of Philadelphia. It had been founded by the Swedes,
the first European settlers on the Delaware, who had named it
Upland after a province in central Sweden, and its name had
been changed to Chester by Penn in 1682, probably at the suggestion of a former resident of the English city of that name.
Fertile farming country surrounded the village, and a few miles
away on Chester Creek the Chester Mills, erected in 1682 by
William Penn and other adventurers, ground corn and sawed
boards for the farmers of the county. [30] The agricultural setting
and the village atmosphere of Chester, reminiscent of Wales,
probably attracted Lloyd, as did the possibilities of making
money off the land.

An incident occurred in one of Lloyd's last appearances in
court during his first term as the Attorney General of Pennsylvania which suggests his lack of devotion to the defense of
Penn's interests. At the Bucks County Court of Quarter Sessions he entered a motion relating to the levying of fines and
forfeitures which the judges were hesitant to approve. Fines

and forfeitures were the property of the Proprietor and were collected by Penn's Commissioners of Property. The records of the court do not specify what Lloyd's motion was, but the judges thought "fitt to take time to deliberate upon it and to Speake with the Commissioners of propryety afore they return answer what Course must be taken for levying of the same. . . ."[31] The judges' language suggests that by 1688 Lloyd was taking a position on proprietary prerogatives which gave the judges pause.

By the end of 1688 David Lloyd's name no longer appeared in the court records as the Attorney General. The few meager facts to be gleaned from existing records indicate that sometime during the year Lloyd ceased to represent actively and to protect Penn's interests and tended to identify himself with the local interests of the colonists. It was not long before he turned against the Proprietor altogether.

# 4. The Lloyds Revolt

During the early months of 1688 David Lloyd expected that Penn either would return to Pennsylvania after nearly four year's absence or would place the government solely in the hands of Thomas Lloyd as his deputy. He had received a letter from Daniel Coxe informing him that Penn would be in the province sometime during the summer. Penn was enjoying the favors of his old friend James II, and Coxe had supposed that the colonists would profit from Penn's influence with the King and, presumably, with the Lords of Trade and Plantations who were responsible for the administration of the King's colonial policy. [1]

By late spring, however, Thomas Lloyd received a letter from Penn, informing him that the pressure of affairs at the King's court kept him in England. Penn declared his intention of making Thomas Lloyd his Deputy Governor of Pennsylvania and of commissioning two other persons "in the Character of Assistants either of whom & they [thy] self to be able to do as fully as I my self can do. " He added that he hoped to go to Pennsylvania to govern the province himself sometime during 1689. [2]

When Penn changed his mind during the summer of 1688 and commissioned as Deputy Governor Captain John Blackwell, a New England Puritan who had once served under Oliver Cromwell as an army officer, Treasurer at War, and Receiver General for Assessments, [3] David Lloyd reacted by drawing closer to his kinsman. Lloyd gave Blackwell's arrival in Pennsylvania

the same cold reception as did nearly all the colonists. Like
almost everybody else he remained away when Blackwell entered Philadelphia.

Thomas Lloyd was even more uncivil toward Blackwell than
most. Penn had hoped that Thomas Lloyd, the Board of Commissioners, and the Council would "receive this person [Black-
well] with kindness and let him se[e] it, & use his not being a
Friend to Friends advantage, " and that Thomas Lloyd would
cooperate with Blackwell to investigate antiproprietary senti-
ments in the colony "and if no way else, authoritatively to end
them, at least suppress them. "[4] Thomas Lloyd, however,
studiously ignored Blackwell's initial overtures of friendship
and even neglected to provide the new Deputy Governor with a
guide from New York to Philadelphia, although the latter had
requested one. [5] He refused, moreover, to honor Blackwell's
commission as Deputy Governor. As Blackwell later informed
Penn, Thomas Lloyd told him that he "was not Governor till
they [the Board of Commissioners] had surrendered" and said
that the Deputy Governor's commission was not "a sufficient
authority, till it were under the Great Seale. . . ."[6]

Thomas Lloyd was the Keeper of the Great Seal, having been
so commissioned by Penn in August, 1684, and he believed
that he had an "affixed Estate" to the office. The office gave
him considerable power in provincial affairs as did the office
of Master of Rolls, which he also held. No law, no ordinance,
no commission, no state paper of any kind had legal force unless it had properly affixed to it the great seal of the province
of Pennsylvania. As Master of the Rolls, Thomas Lloyd was
also keeper of the "Publique Records for the County of Philadelphia, & for the Entring of all Judgments of Courts, publique
Proceedings of Justice, Legal Cases & all other Instruments
w[hi]ch are by Law to be inrolled & Recorded. " He was, furthermore, responsible for the enrollment of all the laws of the
province, and the enrollment of the laws was a legal requirement to render them effective. [7]

Thomas Lloyd soon gave clear indication that he did not intend either to validate Blackwell's commission or to seal and
enroll any laws or ordinances which Blackwell might pass in
governing the province. His purpose was to use his offices as
Keeper of the Great Seal and as Master of the Rolls to obstruct

any attempt Blackwell might make to exercise the functions of Deputy Governor and thereby to render himself superior to Blackwell in the provincial government. Thomas Lloyd's hostility toward Blackwell arose partly from the objections of a Pennsylvania Quaker to being governed by a New England Puritan and partly, as has been suggested, [8] from his own frustrated ambition to become the Deputy Governor. David Lloyd's antagonistic attitude toward the Deputy Governor, however, is not quite as easily understood, because he was not a Quaker and had no such motive as had Thomas Lloyd.

The sources do not indicate that David Lloyd at any time clearly understood Penn's reasons for appointing Blackwell instead of Thomas Lloyd to the deputy governorship. They indicate that David Lloyd's interest in the political affairs of the English homeland had almost disappeared in the first two or three years of his life in Pennsylvania. He had corresponded with Penn's London offices during the autumn and winter of 1688 before Blackwell's arrival, but all that is known of the correspondence is that it concerned Penn's title to the Lower Counties. [9] His correspondence with Phineas Pemberton contained no mention of England. David Lloyd seemed unaware that Penn's commission to Blackwell had come at a time when popular antipathy in England to James II's second Declaration of Indulgence, his Catholicism, and his encroaching attitude toward the Church of England had swelled to revolutionary proportions after the birth of his son in June, and there is nothing to indicate that Lloyd saw the relationship between Penn's appointment of Blackwell and the impending abdication of the King.

During the summer of 1688 plans had been afoot to bring over William, the Protestant Prince of Orange whose wife was James's daughter Mary, to replace James on the throne. Penn's deep involvement in the politics of James's court had suddenly become perilous for a change in the monarchy could not but have a prejudicial effect on his fortunes and on his charter. Quakers were so closely associated with the Stuart monarchy in the mind of the English public because of the indulgences the Stuarts had granted them that a Quaker Deputy Governor, such as Thomas Lloyd, would only have aroused suspicion. Penn's advice to Thomas Lloyd and the Board of Commissioners to use Blackwell's "not being a Friend to

Friends Advantage, "[10] suggests that he had thought a Puritan
Deputy Governor more acceptable to a revolutionary government in England, should one come to power. If Thomas Lloyd
understood or appreciated this advice, he never showed it.
If David Lloyd read the letter and appreciated its contents,
he never showed it either.

Neither David Lloyd nor any other colonist in Pennsylvania
knew of the landing of William of Orange at Torbay until February 24, 1688/89, three months after the event, when the
Council was informed of the change in the monarchy by a man
who had just arrived from England. Only a month earlier the
Council had proclaimed "a day of Thanksgiving for the Birth of
the Prince," that is, the infant son of James II. Even after
the Council had been officially advised of the ascension of
William and Mary to the throne of England, it was reluctant
to proclaim the change in the monarchy, thereby revealing the
sympathy of its members for James II.[11]

Either oblivious of events in England or unappreciative of
what they meant in terms of the Proprietor's interests, David
Lloyd, several days after Pennsylvanians had learned of the
abdication of James II, was instrumental in provoking an open
battle between Thomas Lloyd and Blackwell for control of the
judiciary. David Lloyd opposed Blackwell as zealously as the
Quakers, and he had no intention of cooperating with him. As
principal clerk of the Supreme Provincial Court, David Lloyd
agreed with the Quaker justices of that court that they were
independent of the Deputy Governor and Council and, therefore, not subject to their orders--the very position which Nicholas More had taken in 1686. This conviction brought them
into inevitable conflict with Blackwell, whose duty was to defend the Proprietor's prerogative in all the branches of the
government.

The cause of the conflict was one Peter Ludgar, convicted
of robbery by the Sussex County Court of Quarter Sessions, who
appealed to the Supreme Provincial Court. The latter court
reversed the judgment against Ludgar, and the Sheriff of Sussex County, although confused by the Sussex County Court of
Quarter Session's reaffirmation of its original decision in the
case, released Ludgar from custody. The aggrieved Sussex
County colonist petitioned the Deputy Governor and Council for

the reimprisonment of Ludgar, and the latter subsequently ordered the Sheriff of Sussex County to confine Ludgar in the
county jail or workhouse, to whip him, and to subject him to
hard labor until the aggrieved party had been satisfied. The
Sheriff of Sussex County, however, failed to obey the order
of the Deputy Governor and Council, and Ludgar remained at
liberty. Ludgar then petitioned Blackwell and the Council for
a rehearing of his case, but Blackwell refused to consider the
petition until Ludgar was once more in confinement. Some of
the councilmen supported the Deputy Governor's position, but
others, particularly the Quakers, were offended by it. The
matter came to a head at a meeting of the Council on February
25. One of the Quaker councilmen, Samuel Richardson, angrily
asserted that he "did not owne the Gover[no]r to be Gover[no]r"
and insisted that "Wm Penn could not make a Gover[no]r."[12]
Richardson's outburst was an open attack on Blackwell's commission and on Penn's authority to appoint a deputy to govern
Pennsylvania in his stead. Blackwell responded immediately
by ejecting Richardson summarily from the Council, but the
incident warned him of the feeling that was running against
him among some members of the Council, and he endeavored
to restore harmony by agreeing to consider Ludgar's petition.
When he examined the Council's copies of the documents in the
case, however, he found them incomplete and contradictory.
The Council had two copies of the Supreme Provincial Court
decision, but they were imperfect and disagreed. It had no
clear proof that the Supreme Provincial Court had reversed
the lower court's judgment against Ludgar and no clear documentary statement of the reasons for its decision. Hence,
Blackwell and the Council requested that David Lloyd appear
before them with the original records of the Supreme Provincial Court's decision in the case.

David Lloyd, accordingly, appeared before the Deputy Governor and Council, but he refused to produce the records of
the Supreme Provincial Court. He spoke scornfully to Blackwell and said, among other things, "you may command the
Judges, and the Judges might order him. . . ."

Blackwell was deeply offended by David Lloyd's truculence
and ordered him to withdraw. Subsequently, Blackwell and the
councilmen who supported him adjudged David Lloyd in con-

tempt of the Deputy Governor and Council and discharged him
from his clerical offices in the courts, although they provided
that he could be reinstated if he repented to the satisfaction
of the Deputy Governor. [13]

David Lloyd did not repent. Instead he ranged himself openly
on the side of Thomas Lloyd against the Proprietor and his
deputy. On March 1 Thomas Lloyd appointed David Lloyd the
Deputy Master of the Rolls, Clerk of the Peace, and Clerk of
the County Courts of Philadelphia "to act therein according to
Law & uncontroled usage. . . ."[14] Thereby both Lloyds flung
down the gauntlet, and the struggle for control of the judiciary
was on. David Lloyd's acceptance of the clerical appointments
in the Philadelphia County courts constituted an important *coup*
in Thomas Lloyd's bid for power, because the clerk, not the
justices, prepared the judicial writs, decisions, and the other
documents of the courts. The clerk generally knew more about
the technical details of judicial procedure and about the law than
did the justices. Hence, by having the clerk appointed by himself and therefore responsible to him, Thomas Lloyd was able
to control the administration of justice in Philadelphia County.

Blackwell countered by appointing new justices to the Philadelphia County courts and affixed the Lesser Seals of the
Province to their commissions when Thomas Lloyd refused to
validate them with the Great Seal. Thomas Lloyd successfully
frustrated Blackwell's attempt to recognize the Supreme Provincial Court, but battle was joined again when Blackwell and
the Council appointed James Claypoole, who had three years
earlier recommended David Lloyd for the post, as clerk of the
courts of Philadelphia County, the position which David Lloyd
now held by Thomas Lloyd's appointment.

The Lloyds moved quickly to resist this new challenge to the
foothold they had gained in the judiciary. When Claypoole went
to David Lloyd and requested the records, papers, seal, and
other appurtenances of the clerk of courts, David Lloyd replied
that he had received instructions from Thomas Lloyd not to
deliver up the records to the man appointed by Blackwell.
Claypoole went away disappointed and reported the incident
to Blackwell and the Council.

Once again David Lloyd was called before the Deputy Governor and Council for an accounting, and Blackwell particularly

attempted to impress upon Lloyd the fact he and Thomas Lloyd had infringed upon the prerogatives of the Proprietor through his deputy. David Lloyd, on the other hand, showed Blackwell and the Council the commission which he had received from the Master of the Rolls, but under further questioning he acknowledged that Claypoole's request had been made by the authority of Deputy Governor Blackwell. For the first time David Lloyd wavered, and he promised to observe the order of the Deputy Governor and Council to deliver the records desired either to Claypoole or to Secretary William Markham, that day. Later in the day, however, he changed his mind partly and surrendered only a portion of the records and papers in his possession.[15]

Blackwell and his supporters in the Council were outraged by the conduct of David and Thomas Lloyd. The Council resolved that Thomas Lloyd was using his offices of Keeper of the Great Seal and Master of the Rolls to obstruct justice. Blackwell interpreted the commission that David Lloyd had received from the Master of the Rolls as an infringement upon the proprietary prerogative. He said that Thomas Lloyd was free to appoint a Deputy Master of the Rolls whenever he so desired, but that the commissioning of a clerk of court was a privilege reserved only to the Proprietor or his deputy. Griffith Jones, a member of the Council from New Castle, went even farther than Blackwell in his condemnation of the Lloyds. "It is the King's authority that is opposed," he said, "& looks to me as if it were a raysing a force to Rebell." It appeared to him, furthermore, that "the Keeper by these dealings is the Ruler, & not the Gov-[no]r & Councill."[16]

Griffith Jones's criticism was well taken, for David Lloyd had himself argued that the Proprietor governed in Pennsylvania by authority of the King, and any Deputy Governor of Pennsylvania acted, therefore, by the King's authority. Thomas Lloyd, moreover, was very clearly attempting, with David Lloyd's assistance, to govern Pennsylvania in direct opposition to Penn's commission to Blackwell. The Lloyd's rebellion, however, was more particularly directed against Penn than against the King. Penn's instructions to Blackwell threatened to deprive the colonists of the parliamentary privileges which they had acquired in their Assembly and of the mild administration of justice which had no parallel in the other colonies and in Europe.

According to a letter written by Blackwell at a later date,
Penn had enjoined the Deputy Governor to deny the right of the
Assembly "to do anything but say I or no: yea or nay; when
they come to pass bills for Laws. " He had instructed Blackwell further to prevent the Assembly from debating, amending,
or altering legislative bills, from retaining a clerk, and from
taking an information, since it was not a court of record.[17]
He thought that if the Assembly were allowed to "turn debators,
or Judges, or complainers" its partisans would "overthrow the
Charter quite in the very root of the constitution of it, for th[a]t
is to usurp the P[rovincial] councels part in the Charter and to
forfit the Charter itself."[18] He wrote Blackwell to "Let the
Government know that they are to follow the example of *Maryland* and the other provinces in reference to their submission to
authority in all cases of Government."[19] The example of proprietary Maryland meant the absolute submission of the colonists to executive prerogative. Penn, moreover, departed from
Quaker principles to some extent by indicating a desire that the
death penalty be imposed upon a woman in the Lower Counties
who had been charged with the crime of murder.[20] Capital
punishment was abhorrent to the Quaker conscience, and, although the provincial laws admitted the death penalty for murder and treason, the practice in Pennsylvania had been to
avoid capital punishment and to deal mercifully with persons
convicted of serious crimes.[21] To a certain extent the Lloyds
were protecting Quaker principles by contesting Blackwell's
administration of the courts, but they were also attempting to
dispossess the Proprietor and his deputy of one of their most
important prerogatives.

David Lloyd continued to work with Thomas Lloyd as the
Deputy Master of the Rolls, and Blackwell's efforts in April
and May to suppress the rebellion only seemed to make him
the more determined in his opposition to proprietary prerogative. The Supreme Provincial Court was rendered *hors de
combat* by the Lloyd-Blackwell conflict, and the Deputy Governor and Council instead functioned as the supreme appellate
court of the province. In April Blackwell prepared charges
against Thomas Lloyd for "high misdemeanors, Crimes, and
offenses" and excluded Samuel Richardson, who had earlier
questioned Penn's authority to commission a Deputy Governor,

from the Council. The freemen of Philadelphia County, distrustful of Blackwell, returned Thomas Lloyd and Richardson to the Council in the annual election held the same month, but Blackwell refused to accept their election or that of another Quaker, John Eckley. Blackwell asked the Council to organize a committee to prepare formal charges against Thomas Lloyd so that the rebellious Keeper of the Great Seal might be brought to trial. Moreover, he discovered that Joseph Growdon, a Quaker member of the Council, had a printed copy of the Frame of 1683, and the very fact that the Frame had been printed seemed to him a very serious misdemeanor. When questioned, Growdon refused to say who had printed the document or who had ordered it to be printed. Blackwell, who thoroughly disliked the Frame of 1683, told the Council that "the Proprietor had declared himself against the using of the printing presse,"[22] either forgetting or betraying his ignorance of the fact that Penn himself had had the Frame of 1683 and other documents printed in 1687 for the edification of the colonists.[23]

Blackwell's attacks on Thomas Lloyd and Joseph Growdon divided the Council. Robert Turner, Griffith Jones of New Castle, and Patrick Robinson sided with Blackwell. The Quakers, with the exception of Turner, were alienated by the Deputy Governor. In a letter to Penn they complained that Blackwell spoke of the Quakers as being "ffactious Mutinous, Seditious, turbulent & the like" and claimed the sole power to judge the qualifications of councilmen and assemblymen. Blackwell, they wrote, had questioned the propriety of the provincial laws and of the Frame of 1683 and had said that Penn had granted away prerogatives which only the King could grant. The Quaker councilmen feared that Blackwell's governorship would result in an exodus of Quakers from the province.[24]

Blackwell, realizing that the popular tide was against him, offered to surrender his commission if Penn would approve his return to Boston. But the Deputy Governor resolutely insisted that Thomas Lloyd and Samuel Richardson were "two highly criminal persons."[25]

The Lloyds remained undaunted by Blackwell's fury. They had prevented the Deputy Governor from reorganizing the Supreme Provincial Court and had obstructed his efforts to control the administration of justice in Philadelphia County. The next step was to prevent the Deputy Governor and Council from sitting in judgment as the supreme appellate court of the province, and that involved the parliamentary privileges of the Assembly and a conflict with Penn's instructions to Blackwell to curtail those privileges. Neither of the Lloyds was a member of the Assembly, but the Speaker of the Assembly was a man on whom they could rely to carry on the battle. John White, the Speaker, was a Quaker who, in addition to his duties in the Assembly, officiated as clerk of courts in New Castle County, one of the Lower Counties which was heavily populated with Anglicans, Presbyterians, and Lutherans. His leadership of the Assembly in resisting Blackwell's exercise of judiciary powers, however, soon resulted in his being drastically limited in his usefulness to the Lloyds.

The sequence of events which led to White's downfall and eventually to another clash between the Lloyds and Blackwell began when Blackwell and the Council, sitting as the supreme appellate court, attempted to adjudicate a three-year-old legal dispute between two New Castle farmers. Blackwell and the Council ruled in favor of the defendant in the action, and immediately Speaker White and the Assembly, holding that they were "the supreame Judges of this Govern[men]t, " requested that the Deputy Governor command a hearing before them of the decrees and action in the dispute. The Assembly, of course, was claiming a privilege far beyond any Penn had granted to it in the Frame of 1683, and Blackwell--rightly from the point of view of proprietary prerogative--ignored the Assembly's request as an impertinence. The Assembly nevertheless proved to have been right in bringing the verdict of the Deputy Governor and Council into question. Blackwell and the Council re-examined the case and reversed themselves in favor of the plaintiff. [26]

The litigation between the New Castle farmers, however, was not the issue at stake. The issue was the propriety of the Assembly's claim to supreme judiciary powers. This vexed Blackwell, and he recognized in John White another formidable opponent of proprietary prerogative whom he would have to bring to book. He soon had occasion to do so.

Between sessions of the Assembly, John White, as clerk of courts in New Castle County, somehow provoked the ire of the pro-Blackwell New Castle County judges, and the judges complained to Blackwell of White's alleged misdemeanors. Blackwell removed White from his clerical office and, as the Assembly convened in Philadelphia on May 10, had the Sheriff of New Castle arrest and imprison the harassed Quaker. [27] The Assembly was thereby deprived of its recognized leader at the very time that Blackwell was preparing to carry out Penn's instruction relating to that body.

With John White at least temporarily out of the picture, although the Assembly re-elected him its Speaker *in absentia*, David Lloyd entered the Assembly as its Clerk, so appointed by the Assembly on the first day of the new session. David Lloyd had not been elected to the Assembly and could not therefore become its Speaker; consequently he could not assume leadership. But as the Attorney General, as a proprietary agent who had turned against the Proprietor, and as a relative and lieutenant of the most powerful antiproprietary Quaker in Pennsylvania, David Lloyd could nevertheless exercise his influence on the assemblymen. His very action in accepting an office that Penn had specifically prohibited constituted an announcement that the Lloyds were moving to defend parliamentary privileges as well as the independence of Pennsylvania courts from proprietary control.

As the Clerk of the Assembly David Lloyd recorded Blackwell's advice to the Assembly that he intended to carry out Penn's instructions to cancel all provincial laws which the Assembly had enacted after August, 1684. [28] He also recorded the irate assemblymen's retort that they would "call the Violaters of the Liberties of Freemen of this Government to Account." [29] The Assembly was hopelessly divided, however, and, when enough assemblymen, anxious to prevent an open breach with Blackwell, withdrew to prevent a quorum from meeting, Lloyd remained with those assemblymen, mostly Quakers, who nevertheless continued in session to defend their parliamentary privileges.

David Lloyd continued to record the proceedings of the rump Assembly even though, because it lacked a quorum, its legality was open to question. He recorded the Assembly's resolution that the Assembly was the only proper court of justice to determine the fitness of any one of its members to sit as a representative of the people who had elected him and that White's continued detention in prison was a breach of parliamentary privilege. He prepared a writ of habeas corpus by order of the Assembly, instructing the Sheriff of New Castle County to appear before the Assembly with White and to show cause why White should be detained from attending the Assembly during its session. Lloyd also recorded the fact that the Sheriff refused to honor the writ. Either the Sheriff yielded to the pressure of public opinion, however, and released White anyway or White somehow broke prison, for the latter subsequently appeared at a meeting of the rump Assembly in Philadelphia.[30]

White's liberty and David Lloyd's activity as Clerk of the Assembly were sharply curtailed when Blackwell had the Sheriff of Philadelphia County place both men under arrest. Blackwell entered no formal charges against Lloyd and released him shortly after the arrest, but he retained White in custody. The rump Assembly accused three of the councilmen, Turner, Jones, and Markham, of having persuaded Blackwell to order the arrest of Lloyd and White. Those three councilmen, the assemblymen said, were the "chief Authors of the present Arbitrariness in Government and who are men unworthy, as we conceive, to be much consulted with, and unfit to be chief Magistrates. . . ." The assemblymen ordered that the Sheriff of Philadelphia County and the councilmen whom they considered responsible for the arrest of Lloyd and White be brought "before this House, to answer their contempt and Breach of Privilege."[31] Blackwell, however, ignored the rump Assembly's orders and representations, and his friends in the Council were not sufficiently awed by the Assembly to consider it a colonial High Court of Parliament. Lacking power even to confirm existing laws because a quorum was not present, the rump Assembly disbanded. So it was that David Lloyd's first term of service as a Clerk of the Assembly came to an end.

The Lloyds' resistance to Blackwell's attempts to carry out Penn's instructions appeared to have been weakened by the disbanding of the Assembly. Thomas Lloyd could still exercise his authority as Keeper of the Great Seal, and David Lloyd could continue to hamper the functions of the Philadelphia County courts by retaining possession of much of the county court clerk's office files and equipment, but they had lost the

only branch of the government through which they could effectively carry on the struggle against Blackwell. The significance
of this loss became evident when Blackwell and his friends in
the Council prepared and signed a declaration that all laws
which had been enacted before August, 1684, should remain in
force and that the Deputy Governor was authorized to issue
commissions for judges under the lesser seal.[32] The effect of
the declaration was to repeal the laws which had been enacted
after August, 1684, and to nullify the power which Thomas
Lloyd had exercised as Keeper of the Great Seal.

Thomas Lloyd responded by appealing directly to public
opinion. On June 4 he published a pamphlet at the office of
William Bradford, Philadelphia's only printer, and circulated
it among the colonists. The pamphlet, whose contents were to
be of lasting influence on David Lloyd's mind, denied the right
of the Deputy Governor to make laws without "the approbation
& Assent of the Freemen in provincial Council & Assembly"
and to pass any instrument with the lesser seal of the province.
It warned:

Should the ffree-men allow Such a Power to Declaration or Ordinances
be granted, they do herewith give up the Power of making Laws, creating Courts of Justice Raising of Monies and their severall other
Rights to the Will and Pleasure of the Governour, with a Select Numb$^r$
of his Counsellors contrary to the present provision, as secured by
Law and Charter unto them.[33]

It added that, although the Assembly had adjourned, it was
still legally in session, because Blackwell had neglected to
dismiss it. As long as the Assembly continued in session, it
said, the requirements of the Frame of 1683 that the laws be
confirmed or lapse for want of confirmation twenty days after
adjournment of the Assembly did not hold.[34]

The pamphlet had an immediate and decisive effect on public
opinion, and the scales shifted in the Lloyds' favor. Twenty
days after its publication Blackwell wrote to Penn, "I now only
wayt for the hower [hour] of my deliverance: for I see tis impossible to serve you in this place." He cursed Thomas Lloyd
as "a serpent of y[ou]r [Penn's] owne cherishing" and complained that he "thrusts his oare in every boat."[35]

Late in the summer of 1689 a Quaker visited Penn in England and successfully argued the case for the Lloyds' revolt

against the Proprietor and his deputy. He urged Penn to restore the old method of constituting the governorship in the
Council or in three Commissioners chosen by the Council and
to place Blackwell in some other proprietary office. Penn, who
was still unable to make his oft-postponed trip to Pennsylvania
because of complications which had arisen in his estate in Ireland, was not pleased with the Lloyds and was inclined to sym-
pathize with Blackwell. Yet Penn would not have Thomas Lloyd,
an old friend, "trod under, " and he yielded to his visitor's argument that if he could have one hour with Thomas Lloyd,
Lloyd would bring him over to his side. [36]

Penn subsequently chided Blackwell for indulging in quarreling and faction, commanded him to withdraw his intended prosecution of Thomas Lloyd, and permitted him to resign his
commission as Deputy Governor. Blackwell complained bitterly to Penn that he had been mistreated, but to no avail. On
January 1, 1689/90, the Puritan drank his bitter cup when he
formally surrendered his commission to the Council and
watched that body, now constituted with executive powers and
filled with his enemies, elect Thomas Lloyd its President. [37]
The Lloyds' revolt was a success.

David Lloyd owed much to the influence of his kinsman in
1689. Because of it he had taken an unequivocal position against
the Proprietor and his deputy. He had completely abandoned the
trust which Penn had placed in him as a proprietary agent and
legal representative. Thereafter David Lloyd drifted ever
farther away from Penn, and his name became increasingly
associated with the autonomous interests of the colonists.

# 5. "He Is the Proprietary's Attorney"

After 1689 David Lloyd placed himself squarely in opposition to the proprietary prerogative on nearly every issue. Conversely, he tended increasingly to represent the interests of the colonists which became more and more his own. His devotion to Thomas Lloyd had accounted, in part, for his break with Penn in 1689; his evident Whig convictions which caused him to reject an overweening executive prerogative also had something to do with it; and his expanding economic interests in the province undoubtedly conditioned his attitude toward any exercise of proprietary prerogative which might somehow imperil those interests. From 1689 on his growing economic interest in Pennsylvania paralleled his increasingly sympathetic association with the colonists in the pursuit of a common goal.

During and after 1689 David Lloyd increased his land holdings in Chester County. To the acreage which he had acquired in October, 1688, he added 103 acres with housing and improvements which he purchased for £100 from Anna, Andrew, and John Friend, descendants of an old Swedish settler, Neeles Laersen. On August 6, 1691, Lloyd received a deed to an unspecified amount of land in Chester from the executors of the estate of a deceased Chester Quaker. [1]

As David Lloyd extended his landed estate, he found himself spending an increasing amount of time in courts, either defending himself from suits brought against him or engaging in litigation against others--the usual state of affairs among

*41*

property-owning colonists of the time. During 1690 and 1691
he fought a running battle in the Chester County Court of Common Pleas against James Sandilandes, the powerful merchant
and landed proprietor of nearly the whole of Chester Township. On March 8, 1691/92, he and Patrick Robinson, retained as attorneys, successfully defended the executors of
the estate from which Lloyd had purchased land in Chester
from a litigious suit brought against them. [2]

In 1691 David Lloyd clashed with Penn's Commissioners
of Property on two fronts--the Town of Philadelphia and the
Welsh Tract. During the summer he became the Town Clerk,
the Clerk of the Board, and the Clerk of the Courts of the
Town of Philadelphia under a charter which Penn had granted
Philadelphia on May 20. As Deputy Master of Rolls, Lloyd
had personally recorded the charter, and the town government, consisting of a Mayor, Recorder, Clerk of the Town,
Board, and Courts, six aldermen, and six councilmen, was
organized by Quaker merchants and supporters of Thomas
Lloyd, who exercised considerable influence on affairs although he was not a town officer. [3]

David Lloyd was one of the town officers who directed his
efforts toward encouraging the growth of Philadelphia commerce by improving port facilities on the Delaware River
front. Philadelphia Quaker merchants had built up a thriving
trade with colonial, West Indies, and foreign ports, but there
were not enough wharves on the Philadelphia waterfront to
handle adequately the increasing amount of shipping. The public
landing place at Blue Anchor Tavern, suitable for the intercolonial trade, was too small for the larger ships from the
West Indies and Europe. A nearby cove, however, offered an
excellent opportunity for the development of a public harbor
sufficiently large to sustain such shipping. David Lloyd joined
thirty-one other Philadelphians in petitioning the Council to
erect a public wharf at that place, and the Council consented
to the petition. [4]

Penn's Commissioners of Property, however, had earlier
granted property rights on the harbor site to three private individuals who were building a house on the beach at the very
time that the Council was consenting to the petition for a public
harbor at the cove. The Council directed the three grantees

to halt construction of the house and promised them reimburse-
ment of the expenses which they had incurred in building the
unfinished structure. The latter nevertheless went ahead with
their plans and submitted their deed to David Lloyd, as Clerk
of Courts, to be recorded. Lloyd refused, however, and entered on the back of the deed, "Caveated because the Lott within
granted is supposed to be the cartable Landing Place of this
Town & so hath been accordingly ordered by the Governor and
Council; therefore this deed ought not to pass till further Inquiry be made therein."[5] Penn himself, in 1682, had reserved
the beach on which the lot was located as a "common free
landing for stones, logs, hay, lumber, and such other goods
as could not with like ease and safety be landed at any other
wharf and place."[6] David Lloyd's refusal to record the deed
was supported by Thomas Lloyd and the Mayor of Philadelphia
who forbade completion of work on the house at the Blue Anchor
Tavern beach.

The disappointed housebuilders complained to the Commissioners of Property in January, 1691/92, that they had suffered great losses because of the interference of Thomas Lloyd
and the Mayor of Philadelphia and because of David Lloyd's
refusal to record their deed. The Commissioners of Property
thereupon ruled that Thomas Lloyd and the Council, and David
Lloyd as Clerk of Courts, had, by their actions, infringed
"on the rights of the proprietary to dispose of all lots and
lands within this province, &c., by his commission to us.
. . ." They confirmed the patents which they had previously
granted the three purchasers of the lot.[7] The latter completed
building their house, and for a time a portion of the Blue Anchor Tavern landing place remained under private ownership.
For that reason plans to develop the cove and beach into a
public harbor were dropped--at least temporarily.

The fundamental issue in the Blue Anchor Tavern landing
place dispute was between community rights and private rights.
Did the community have the right to claim ownership of property
which it considered vital to its existence and well-being even
though private individuals claimed title to the property? John
Locke, in 1690, had rendered the opinion of the average Eng-
lishman of the time; he recognized the existence of communal
property, but he considered private rights superior to com-

munity rights when the property concerned was improved by private industry and unimproved by the community. [8] By this criterion, the private rights of the purchasers of the lot at Blue Anchor Tavern beach should certainly have been considered superior to the community rights of Philadelphia because the purchasers were improving the property in question just as the community was beginning to act. The community had made no previous improvements on the property. David Lloyd, however, was in agreement with other Philadelphia town officials who believed that, so far as the harbor site near Blue Anchor Tavern was concerned, the rights of the community were paramount. Their position, while it reflected the needs of a frontier community in America, was at variance with one of the dominant precepts in English economic thought--a precept with which the Commissioners of Property were faithfully in accord.

In supporting the community rights of Philadelphia against the private rights of the purchasers of the lot on the Blue Anchor Tavern beach, David Lloyd had again taken a stand on the side of the autonomous interests of the colonists against the proprietary prerogative as represented by the Commissioners of Property. In another incident which occurred during 1691 he found that Penn's Commissioners of Property tended to disregard the interests of the colonists and the promises originally made to the colony's first purchasers by Penn. This incident involved the Welsh Tract in which David Lloyd owned a parcel of land.

The Welsh Tract was an extensive area which Penn had granted to the Welsh as a barony with all baronial rights of self-government. The Welsh, however, had never availed themselves of their baronial privileges. They had established small farms in the Tract, and, because the Tract originally lay entirely in Philadelphia County, they had submitted themselves to the Philadelphia County government. Proprietary officers had also ignored the original purpose of the Tract and had thrown it open to settlement by other ethnic groups. Because the original survey of county lines had been inexact and inaccurate, in 1691 the Commissioners of Property relocated the Philadelphia-Chester county line so as to divide the Welsh Tract, separating the Welsh settlements of Radnor and Haverford from that of Merion. Consequently many Welshmen who had been paying taxes to Philadelphia County on their Tract property suddenly found that their property was in Chester County. David Lloyd's property in Merion Township was likewise affected. He and other Welsh Tract landowners had already paid or owed property taxes to Philadelphia County. Now they found that they were required to pay taxes to Chester County on the same property and for the same year.

David Lloyd took the matter to the Chester County Court of Common Pleas on behalf of the aggrieved Welsh Tract property owners. After presenting their case, he succeeded in securing an agreement that the Welshmen he represented would pay Chester County taxes and would be compensated for the taxes which they had already paid Philadelphia County. He also obtained a promise that the Welshmen's patents and deeds which stated that their property was located in Philadelphia County would be changed to designate location in Chester County. [9] The Welsh Tract incident was a relatively minor one, but it indicated the disparity which all too frequently existed between proprietary policy and the legitimate interests of the colonists-- a disparity which Lloyd would one day seek to remove by effecting sweeping reforms in the economic and political relations between the Proprietor and the colonists.

During 1691 David Lloyd, the Attorney General who was supposed to be defending proprietary prerogative, sided with the colonists not only in opposing Penn's Commissioners of Property, but also in effecting a change in the governmental structure of Pennsylvania and the Lower Counties without Penn's knowledge. Such a change had become necessary because the persistent quarreling between the Pennsylvania and Lower Counties members of the Assembly over the issue of military defense crippled the legislature. After the beginning of the War of the League of Augsburg, when the conflict between England and France spread to North America and resulted in the first Anglo-French intercolonial war, King William's War, Pennsylvania Quakers, true to the pacifism inherent in their faith, had successfully resisted Crown orders to prepare military defenses against potential French attacks from Canada. Relations between the Pennsylvanians and the Indians were excellent, and the powerful Five Nations in the strategic Mohawk

Valley, whose influence among Indian tribes extended as far
west as the Mississippi River, were pro-English. There were
several French-Indian sallies from Canada against the frontiers
of the English colonies, of which the colonists in Pennsylvania
and the Lower Counties heard rumors, but the Quakers thought
that there was little to fear. The non-Quaker colonists in the
Lower Counties, however, feared French naval power because
their long coast line facing Delaware Bay made them more
vulnerable to assaults from the sea than were the Pennsylvania
colonists farther inland. Hence, the Lower Counties were far
more ready and willing to prepare military defenses than was
Pennsylvania, and the bad feeling between the sections which
resulted from the Quaker refusal to appropriate tax money for
defensive purposes hampered legislative cooperation in the
Assembly.

David Lloyd, who officiated as Clerk of the Assembly, tried
to prevent the disruption of the legislature because of the sectional conflict. When, shortly after the opening of the 1691
session of the Assembly, the representatives from the Lower
Counties walked out of both the Assembly and Council, thereby leaving the Assembly without a quorum, Lloyd and three
Quaker assemblymen followed the disaffected representatives
all the way to New Castle in a vain effort to persuade them
to return to the Assembly. [10] Lloyd's failure to persuade the
Lower Counties representatives to return to the Assembly
left the Pennsylvania Quakers with no alternative but to make
a change in the form of the government.

Lloyd left no written evidence of his views on the political
crisis of 1691, but his concurrent and subsequent activities
strongly suggest that his opinions were similar to those expressed in a letter from the Assembly and Provincial Council
to Penn in May, 1691--a letter which he, as Clerk of the Assembly and Clerk of the Council, probably had a hand in writing. The authors of the letter clearly suspected that Penn was
in some way responsible for the disaffection of the Lower
Counties from the provincial legislature and that his purpose
was to make it impossible for the Quakers to govern. They
warned that the Proprietor could not lawfully deprive the colonists in Pennsylvania of their rights as freeborn Englishmen,
"which are not Cancelled by Comming hither." They thought

that Penn, especially after 1688, had been wielding greater prerogatives than the King. "Certainly the King our Sovereigne," they wrote, "Intends not that a Subject shall Exercise greater power over his people in a foreigne plantation, then he doth himself in Parliaments. . . ." They asked that Penn, if they could not have their English rights under Penn's Frame of 1683, let them "at Least Revert to the Good old English way of Government without any way of Alterations of English usages. . . ."[11] The letter presaged Lloyd's subsequent efforts to scuttle the Frame of Government which Penn had granted the colonists eight years earlier.

The Pennsylvania assemblymen then passed an act which provided that, in spite of the willful absence of representation from the Lower Counties, the Council and Assembly then in session were lawfully constituted and laws enacted by them were valid. David Lloyd, as Clerk of the Council, and the Pennsylvania members of the Council signed the act. One of the acts of Assembly thereby validated changed the form of the executive, so that Thomas Lloyd acted as Deputy Governor of Pennsylvania and William Markham became Deputy Governor of the Lower Counties.[12] Penn did not learn of the change in the government until September, and, although he rebuked the colonists for their discord and want of regard for him, he issued commissions which recognized Thomas Lloyd as Deputy Governor of Pennsylvania and Markham as Deputy Governor of the Lower Counties. Penn recognized the dual executive with great misgivings, however, and its duration was to be a brief one.[13]

David Lloyd had made his opposition to proprietary prerogative abundantly evident between 1689 and 1691, and Penn finally removed him from the office of Attorney General and replaced him with Patrick Robinson, the non-Quaker Irishman who had once been a partisan of Nicholas More and who had since become a loyal defender of proprietary interests.[14]

By 1691 David Lloyd had become closely identified with the Quakers who dominated the provincial and county governments of Pennsylvania, and his position on issues, including opposition to military defense in time of war, was at least similar to theirs. The exact date of Lloyd's conversion to Quakerism is unknown. According to the testimony of John Blackwell, he was not a Quaker in 1689.[15] In 1692, however, he appeared in

Quaker records as a member of the Quaker Yearly Meeting--
an indication that Quakers readily accepted him as one of their
leaders, for members of the Yearly Meeting were chosen representatives of the constituent Monthly Meetings.[16] From 1692
on Lloyd defended a *status quo* in which orthodox Quakers governed in such a manner as to protect the autonomous interests
of the colonists from the encroachments of proprietary and
Crown prerogatives.

David Lloyd became a Quaker at a time when schismatic tendencies were beginning to appear in the Society of Friends and
to challenge the political dominance of the Quakers in the province. Factional bitterness in the Society of Friends arose under
the influence of George Keith, a Scottish Quaker and close
friend of George Fox and William Penn who had taken charge
of the Friends' School in Philadelphia in 1689--an educational
venture which Penn had initiated that year. Keith had received
a master of arts degree at Marischal College, Aberdeen, Scotland, in his youth, and was more sophisticated than most Quakers in Pennsylvania, who were prejudiced against college
education. He was widely acquainted with religious thought in
Europe, and he became particularly infatuated with a doctrine
of the transmigration of souls which had been advanced by
Francis Mercurius, Baron of Helmons. Keith's theological
speculations, on which he lectured at Friends' School, led him
to the conclusion that the Quaker doctrine of the inner light was
in error--a conclusion which struck at the heart of the Quaker
religion. The Quakers contended that the inner light alone was
sufficient for salvation--a tenet which emphasized the spiritual
relationship between the individual and God without the mediation of a third party. The Quakers' belief obviated the necessity
of a church hierarchy and substituted for the ecclesiastical
policy of the churches the religious individualism of the Quaker meetings wherein any member could stand and preach if
the spirit so moved him. Those who demonstrated a closer
affinity to God than most and who therefore preached most
effectively became known as ministers, but there was no
officially ordained ministry in the Society of Friends. Keith
attacked the doctrine of the inner light because it excluded the mediation of Jesus Christ between God and man. He
concluded that no man could be saved by his own efforts alone

and that he must seek salvation in the knowledge of and belief in the outward Christ. [17]

David Lloyd concurred with the majority of Pennsylvania
Quakers who responded to Keith's attack on the doctrine of the
inner light by warning that to assume the indispensability of
faith in the outward Christ by all mankind "did not only exclude
from salvation whole nations, but also infants, and deaf and
dumb persons."[18] Lloyd attended the Yearly Meeting at Burlington, the Quaker capital of West New Jersey on the Delaware River approximately twenty miles upstream from Philadelphia, and participated in its discussion of Keith's heresy.
There he joined other members of the Yearly Meeting in dis-
owning Keith and in submitting epistles to the Monthly and
Quarterly Meetings in East and West New Jersey and Pennsylvania, exhorting Quakers to be faithful to the principles of
George Fox and to avoid a schism in the Society of Friends.
Lloyd also signed an epistle, along with other Quaker leaders,
which informed the London Yearly Meeting of the activities and
heresies of George Keith. [19]

Keith, who attracted a following among a minority of Quakers, attempted to set up a rival society which challenged the
political dominance of orthodox Quakers in Pennsylvania. He
questioned the propriety of Quakers' holding any position "in
the compelling part of worldly government" and circulated
printed pamphlets which, among other things, accused a Philadelphia County justice, an orthodox Quaker, of drunkenness,
land theft, gambling on a horse race, and disrespect for the
dead. [20] Orthodox Quakers responded by invoking Chapters
XXVIII, XXIX, and XXX of the Great Law which Penn, the
Council, and the Assembly had passed in 1682 and which prohibited slander, sedition, and abusive or malicious criticism
of magistrates or other persons holding public office. The
Grand Jury of Philadelphia County brought indictments against
Keith and two of his followers for violations of the Great Law,
and they were brought into the Philadelphia County Court of
Quarter Sessions for trial. Because the Attorney General, who
normally prosecuted criminal cases, was not a Quaker, the
Court permitted David Lloyd and John White to prosecute on
behalf of the provincial government. As the records show,
Lloyd conducted the entire prosecution alone. [21]

During the course of the trial Keith challenged Lloyd's right to prosecute inasmuch as he was not the King's Attorney.

"We have no King's Attorney, " Lloyd replied.

"I understand that Patrick Robinson is the King's Attorney, " asserted Keith.

"No, he is not. "

"But he is Attorney General. "

"He is neither King's Attorney nor Attorney General. "

"What is he then ?"

"He is the Proprietary's attorney, " answered Lloyd. [22]

The exchange was a revelation of how greatly David Lloyd had changed his mind since the day in 1687 when he had advised the Bucks County Court of Quarter Sessions that the Proprietor was the King's deputy and that therefore the Proprietor's Attorney General was also the King's Attorney.

Lloyd's prosecution of Keith and his followers proved successful, as it was bound to be in a court dominated by orthodox Quakers. The court subsequently fined the defendants £5 and denied them the right to appeal to the Pennsylvania Supreme Provincial Court or to the King-in-Council in England. [23] The sentence was a mild one, but it proved sufficient to dampen the enthusiasm of the Keithian following.

Even as sentence was passed, however, a new threat to Quaker government in Pennsylvania approached--a threat which was to project David Lloyd to leadership of Pennsylvania Quakers in opposing the prerogatives of the Crown. The Keithian trials, the schism in the Pennsylvania Society of Friends, the factional disputes between the province and the Lower Counties, and the refusal of Pennsylvania Quakers to provide for military defense created the impression among officials in the English government that "the publick peace and administration of justice [in Pennsylvania] is broken and violated. "[24] Penn himself was deeply in trouble with the Crown because of repeated, although untruthful, charges that he had plotted with Roman Catholics to restore James II to the throne of England. All through 1692 the King contemplated taking the government of Pennsylvania out of Penn's hands, and finally he commissioned Colonel Benjamin Fletcher, a regimental officer in the British army, to be the Royal Governor of Pennsylvania. Fletcher did not assume the governorship of Pennsylvania until April 20, 1693, [25] and until then the Quakers governed as they had in the past. But the Utopian experiment initiated by Penn in the Frame of 1682 and modified by him in the Frame of 1683 was already at an end, and David Lloyd had helped to destroy it.

# 6. Resisting the King's Governor

David Lloyd recognized that a King's Governor was a great-er threat to the autonomous interests of Pennsylvania than ever had been the proprietary prerogative. Penn, after all, had yielded when the colonists had been firm in their demands. An army officer bearing the King's commission could not be ex-pected to govern Quakers as leniently as had the Quaker Pro-prietor, even when one took into account Penn's commission to Captain Blackwell in 1688. Months before Fletcher's arrival in Philadelphia, Penn had warned the colonists "to insist upon your patent with wisdom & moderacon but steddy integrity" and to 'protest against any proceeding of the Governor of New York [Fletcher] upon his arbitrary Commicon.'"[1]

Fletcher's commission gave him all the powers of govern-ment which Penn had enjoyed, plus a veto power in legislation and sweeping military powers. Fletcher, who was also Gov-ernor of New York and West New Jersey, commanded the mil-itary forces of the middle colonies, and his commission author-ized him to levy, arm, muster, command, and employ the col-onists of Pennsylvania and the Lower Counties for military purposes. He could execute martial law in time of invasion, insurrection, or war, erect fortifications, and furnish arms and ammunition for military defense.[2] In effect his commission superseded much of Penn's charter, and Penn had cautioned Fletcher that the royal charter of 1680/81 remained never-theless in force, inasmuch as it had not been revoked as the result of *quo warranto* proceedings.[3] The royal charter was the very foundation of Pennsylvania self-government, and David Lloyd had no intention of letting the King's Governor deprive the colonists of it without a battle.

David Lloyd's battle, however, opened with a strategic retreat. He joined the exodus of Quakers from the Provincial Council when Fletcher arrived to take up the reins of government. At first Fletcher appeared eager to cooperate with the Quaker leaders. He offered Thomas Lloyd first place on the Council and asserted that Quaker officials could, if they wished, remain in the positions which they had formerly occupied. Thomas Lloyd, however, refused the offer, and orthodox Quakers, David Lloyd among them, refused to serve in the Royal Governor's administration. Fletcher soon replaced them with Anglicans and followers of George Keith. [4]

David Lloyd then ran for and was elected to a seat in the Assembly by the freemen of Chester County. [5] There he joined other Quakers who sought, as did Lloyd, to make the Assembly their citadel of resistance to the King's Governor. Quakers held 70 per cent of the seats filled in the first election under Fletcher's administration. [6] They had little faith in Fletcher's offer of conciliation and partnership and awaited the Royal Governor's first blow at the political institutions and laws they had built for themselves since 1682. They did not have long to wait. Fletcher struck his blow with unequivocating directness and decision. He told the Assembly of his firm conviction that his commission superseded and rendered void the royal charter of 1680/81, the Frame of 1683, and all acts of Assembly passed before the date of his commission.

Immediately antagonized, David Lloyd joined other Quaker assemblymen in remonstrating to the King's Governor that his commission superseded Penn's control of the provincial government only temporarily during the Proprietor's absence. Otherwise, the remonstrants asserted, the constitution and laws of the province remained in force. They requested that Fletcher confirm the royal charter of 1680/81 as the rights and liberties of the colonists of Pennsylvania. [7] This request, made either naïvely or with tongue in cheek, Fletcher ignored.

There was little that David Lloyd and his fellow assemblymen could do to save their constitution, that is, the royal charter of 1680/81 as interpreted and institutionalized by usage and acts of Assembly. Fletcher implemented his commission, as if it were the only constitution he needed, to reduce the representation in the Assembly from six to four from Philadelphia County and to three from each of the other counties. He made the Council an appointive, rather than elective, body and reduced the number of councilmen from eighteen to five. Because his duties as Captain General of New York, Pennsylvania and the Lower Counties, East and West New Jersey, and Connecticut were often likely to take him away from the province, he appointed William Markham his Lieutenant Governor of Pennsylvania and the Lower Counties. Fletcher's commission accorded Markham "full power and authorities to doe and execute whatsoever hee shall be by you [Fletcher] authorized and appointed to doe, in pursuance and according to the powers & authorities . . . granted unto you."[8] Much of Lloyd's dealings with Fletcher after 1693 had to be conducted through the agency of the Lieutenant Governor.

David Lloyd could not save the constitution, but he addressed himself to the task of salvaging as much as possible of the provincial laws which antedated Fletcher's commission. As a member of the Assembly's committee on laws, he considered ways and means of obviating possible objections to the provincial laws on the grounds that they were repugnant to English law. He and another assemblyman examined the laws in the office of Thomas Lloyd, Master of the Rolls, in which David Lloyd appears to have still been the deputy. There they found what David Lloyd must have known all along, that provincial laws which had been enacted after 1685 were not enrolled and remained unconfirmed by the King-in-Council. Few laws, in fact, had been confirmed at all, and only the titles of the unenrolled laws had been entered in a book, presumably for reference. David Lloyd and his companion reported their findings to the Assembly, but they did not explain why Thomas and David Lloyd had not acted earlier to enroll the laws of the province. [9]

David Lloyd and three other members of the Assembly subsequently attempted to persuade Fletcher to confirm the provincial laws which had been in force under the proprietary government. They brought Fletcher the book which contained the titles of the laws. The Royal Governor, however, refused to confirm the laws on the grounds that they had not been confirmed by the King-in-Council. During the argument which followed David Lloyd said that he had seen "some of those Laws, & doe know that they were delivered in to the privie Councill by Mr penn: & being no wayes disallowed, they must needs be of force."[10] Fletcher doubted Lloyd's story, as it was the first that he had heard of it. He pointed out also that none of the laws in question had been published under the Proprietor's great seal as required by the royal charter of 1680/81. Nevertheless, he agreed to a conference on the subject between the Council and ten members of the Assembly.[11]

At the conference which followed David Lloyd acted as the chief spokesman of the Assembly delegation, and Lieutenant Governor Markham led the delegation from the Council. At first Markham and the conciliar delegates pressed the arguments which Fletcher had advanced against confirmation of the provincial laws. Patrick Robinson, a councilman, argued that according to the charter the laws had to be sealed before they could be effective. "The Seale," he said, "is the soule and Life of the Laws...." David Lloyd and John White demurred. The seal, they insisted, was only a ceremony. They argued that "the sealing is not materiall to the making of a law, but the consent of the Governor, Council & assembly."[12] This interpretation of the seal was just the opposite of that which Thomas Lloyd had employed against Blackwell in 1689, but then the situation had changed, and like politicians of all faiths David Lloyd and John White tailored their arguments to fit the expediency of the moment.

David Lloyd then tried to shame Markham and the members of the Council, who were themselves colonists, for what he alleged was their want of local patriotism. "I am surprized," said Lloyd, "the members of Council, who have a joint interest with us in the province, and have acted by these Laws and satt in Courts of Judicature, should speak ag[ains]t their validitie. Our priviledges are yours." He summed up the Assembly's position when he asserted:

Who can be Judge whether these Laws be in force or not. None can be Judges but those that made them, since ther is no order from the king and Councill declarring them void; wee desire that they may be put in execu[ti]on. It wer hard that the want of the affixing a Seal, or

some such other Ceremonie, should destroy our Laws. And if wee
allow this att present wee must expect it for the future, That everie
new Governor, finding fault with some omission or other in the making
or publishing of our Laws, will declare them void, which is of evil
Consequence, and wee doe not know that ever wee shall have more
Laws. [13]

David Lloyd's argument made a favorable impression on the
councilmen. Patrick Robinson, speaking for the Council, asserted that the point at issue was the prerogative of the Crown
and that Fletcher was above all responsible to the Crown. Fletcher, he said, could not approve of any law which was repugnant
to the laws of England. He suggested, however, that the Assembly examine once more the roll of laws to make sure that it contained nothing repugnant to English law, and he was satisfied
that Fletcher would agree to the execution of the laws until
he had received further orders from the King and Queen. Later,
Fletcher reported to the Assembly that he had confirmed all
the laws except one, a law against stealing, subject to the
King's allowance. [14] David Lloyd and his fellow assemblymen
had won the first round of their conflict with royal prerogative.

The Assembly, however, was less fortunate in securing
Fletcher's approval of new legislation. Although King William's
War continued in full swing, Pennsylvania had made no contribution to the defense of the English colonies. David Lloyd and
his fellow assemblymen had no intention of acceding to Fletcher's earnest appeals for a war budget, not only because of the
Quaker testimony against war but because colonists of all
faiths opposed property and head taxes even for the support
of the government. [15] Fletcher retaliated by refusing to consider new legislation, including bills which the Assembly had
just submitted to him, until the desired appropriation had been
made and threatened that Pennsylvania, because of her failure to contribute to the general defense, "must expect to be
annexed to New Yorke or Maryland. "[16]

The Royal Governor and the Assembly having reached an
impasse, David Lloyd and several others took the leadership
in attempting to contrive a bargain with Fletcher. They reported a revenue bill, drafted by the Assembly, to the Govern-
or. Since the Assembly, however, had not put the bill to a

vote and since it did not bear the Speaker's signature, Fletcher refused even to look at the bill. One of the assemblymen begged the Governor to inform the Assembly of the dispo-
sition of the bills that had previously been submitted to him
and to excuse the Assembly's failure to enact the revenue bill.

David Lloyd was more outspoken. "To be plain with the
Governor," he said, "here is the Monie bill, and the house
will not pass it until they know what is become of the other
bills that are sent up."

Fletcher exploded, "I came not here to make bargains nor
expose the king's honour. I will never grant anie such for
all the monie in your Countrie."

The assemblymen threw still another unsigned bill on the
table and departed in ill humor. [17]

Subsequently David Lloyd and several assemblymen who had
attached themselves to him prepared a document in which they
asserted what they believed to be the Assembly's rights and
privileges, and they wanted it to be entered into the minute
book of the Assembly. [18] Lloyd was quite clearly spoiling for
battle.

The majority of the assemblymen, however, did not care
to follow David Lloyd in an all out conflict with the royal prerogative. They sought rather to achieve the passage of new
legislation by working out a compromise with Fletcher and
were unwilling to enter as a permanent record a paper which
might have further antagonized the Royal Governor. On the
day following David Lloyd's unhappy encounter with Fletcher,
the Assembly submitted to the Governor and Council a bill
levying a tax of one penny per pound on all personal property
and real estate and a tax of six shillings per capita on all freemen who possessed not more than £100 and were therefore not
subject to the penny per pound tax. The bill specified that the
revenue derived from these taxes was to be employed for the
support of the government. With this bill was attached a roll
of 203 laws and a petition of right which the Assembly wanted
Fletcher to put into execution in the province. Although Fletcher wished that the tax bill had been expressly for the defense
of Their Majesties' plantations rather than for the support of
the government, he was only too glad to obtain such a bill
passed by the Assembly and signed by the Speaker. He ac-

cepted it, passed most of the proposed laws after several of
them had been amended, and ordered that the new laws be executed by all civil officers in the province and the Lower Counties until the King's pleasure should be further known.[19] The
compromise was a success.

David Lloyd and a few assemblymen, however, were not
satisfied. They insisted that Fletcher grant the Assembly the
additional privilege of debating legislative amendments proposed by the Governor and Council and warned "that the Assent of such of us as were for sending up the Bill for the Supply
[the appropriation bill] this Morning, was merely in Consideration of the Governor's speedy Departure; but that it should not
be drawn into Example or Precedent for the future.[20] Fletcher,
however, paid little attention to the demands and warnings of
a small minority.

Neither David Lloyd and other Pennsylvania colonists, on
the one hand, nor Fletcher, on the other, were happy about
the state of political affairs in the province. The Quakers dis-
trusted Fletcher, but many of them did not want to return to
Penn's Frame of 1683 unless it were radically altered. Fletcher, on his side, despised the Quakers whose pacifism made
it difficult to secure the cooperation of Pennsylvania in advanc-
ing the English war effort against the French. He preferred the
company of the New York Anglican merchants, who chafed at
the growing commercial competition from Philadelphia and the
Connecticut and New Jersey ports and who complained that alleged violation of the navigation acts by Pennsylvania, Connecticut, and the Jerseys was injurious to the economy of New
York. Fletcher and his New York friends thought that the best
way to overcome both the commercial rivalry of the neighboring colonies and the obstructionism of the Quaker pacifists in
the Pennsylvania Assembly was to secure the annexation of
Connecticut, the Jerseys, and Pennsylvania to New York. In
June they instructed their representative in London to memori-
alize the Lords of Trade to carry out the proposed annexation.[21]

At about the same time David Lloyd, his friends Phineas
Pemberton and John White, John Bristow, the President or
eldest Judge of the Chester County Court, and other Quakers
drafted "Some Proposals what may be done for the ffuture good
of the Province in respect of the Governm[ent]."[22] This paper

designated Lloyd, White, Pemberton, and Bristow as emissaries who were to go to England for the purpose of negotiating
an agreement with Penn. If they succeeded in "perfectly" adjusting "the method of Governm[en]t with him [Penn] thereby
to prevent all future disputes between the people and him" then
they were to assist Penn in an effort to restore the proprietary government. Should these negotiations fall through, then
the emissaries were to get Penn's assistance "in procureing
the Governm[en]t to be committed to a person who may reside
among us and be grateful to us. . . ." An alternative was to
obtain the removal of the seat of the province to a place sufficiently far from the sea and threat of invasion "that the Civill
Governm[en]t may in manner of a corporation be committed
to magistrates of their own choosing. . . ." In that case the
Pennsylvanians would be willing to be placed under the military
command of the Royal Governor of Maryland and "yearly to
rayse a Supply ffor the King and Queens occasions. . . ." If
all else failed, then Lloyd, White, Pemberton, and Bristow
were to ask the Crown to annex Pennsylvania to Maryland rather than to New York.[23] Lloyd and his friends appeared to have
felt that Lionel Copley, the weak and inefficient Royal Governor of Maryland, would be easier to deal with than was Fletcher.

For some reason Lloyd, Pemberton, White, and Bristow
never went to England, and no attempt was made to carry out
the proposals. Fletcher, however, learned of the Quaker plans
to send Lloyd and his friends to London, and he complained to
the Secretary of State at Whitehall of Quaker obstructionism
in Pennsylvania. "Some Quakers who have acted in the Gov[ern-
men]t by M^r Pen's Comission and are very fond of Lording it
over theire bretheren," he wrote, "are now sending theire
Delligates to Court in hope to gett M^r Pen restor'd or themselves impower'd to Act, or at last if these faile they desire
to bee under the Govern[men]t of Mary Land. . . ." These
were Quakers, he added, who had "declined to Act under theire
Majesties Comission."[24] He complained that Thomas Lloyd
was using his office as Keeper of the Great Seal to obstruct
the Royal Governor's administration, as he had Blackwell's,
by refusing to affix the great seal of Pennsylvania to Fletcher's
commission and to the commissions which the Royal Governor

had given to the judges, sheriffs, and other officers of his appointment. Fletcher was rather scornful of David Lloyd but wrote that David Lloyd and other "less people" had "all as much in theire [power] lay endeavired to baffell my endeaviors in the Prov[in]ce for theire Maj[es]ties service."[25]

The Crown never adopted Fletcher's annexation proposal, but David Lloyd, Quaker members of the Assembly, and Quakers generally were subjected to persistent attacks by Anglicans, Presbyterians, and followers of George Keith. George Keith himself published an antislavery tract, *An Exhortation & Caution to Friends concerning Buying or Keeping of Negroes*, which strongly insinuated that Quakers were hypocritically following the un-Christian practice of buying, selling, and owning slaves.[26] Enemies accused David Lloyd of having illegally added a sentence of life imprisonment to a jury's verdict of guilty when he was Clerk of the Philadelphia County Court of Quarter Sessions in 1691. At that time the jury had found one Charles Butler guilty of misprision of treason for having disseminated counterfeit money. Misprision of treason, in Pennsylvania law, was punishable by death, but it was not clear that the judges of the Philadelphia County Court of Quarter Sessions had passed any specific sentence on Butler. Lloyd, as Clerk of the Court, had filed a sentence of life imprisonment and total forfeiture of the goods, chattels, and profits of the land owned by Butler during his lifetime. When Butler petitioned the Governor and Council against Lloyd on August 1, 1693, the Council decided that the petitioner had been victimized by legal technicalities and recommended that Fletcher grant him a pardon. The Council questioned Lloyd about the severity of the sentence but made no decision as to its legality.[27]

The assault on David Lloyd's integrity did not hurt him politically any more than did the attacks on Quakers generally affect the Quaker hold on the Assembly. In the election of April, 1694, a majority of Quaker representatives was returned to the Assembly by the freemen of the province. David Lloyd was re-elected by the freemen of Chester County, and on April 10 the members of the Assembly for the first time chose him to be their Speaker.[28] During 1694 he succeeded his kinsman, Thomas Lloyd, who died sometime that year, as the political leader of Pennsylvania Quakers.

As Speaker of the Assembly, David Lloyd continued the Assembly's drive, begun the previous year, to secure the Royal Governor's confirmation of all provincial laws enacted under the proprietary government. Fletcher had confirmed most of the laws included in the Assembly's petition of right in 1693, but he had objected to the mildness of Pennsylvania's criminal code and had refused to sanction laws which did not prescribe the death penalty for such crimes as stealing. Lloyd placed himself at the head of the Assembly committee on laws which, in a conference with the Provincial Council, secured the insertion of the laws about robbing and stealing and of a law about runaway servants, which had been omitted in 1693, [29] in the roll of laws.

On April 11 Lloyd brought the latter laws to Lieutenant Governor Markham, Fletcher being absent from the province, and insisted particularly that the law about stealing be included in the roll of laws sanctioned by the Royal Governor. Lloyd said that the laws had been omitted from the petition of right by the Clerk of the Council and pointed out that, because of the absence of such a law, "people might be exposed to a triall for their Life for every small & trifling theft." Markham explained that Fletcher had not continued the law about stealing, because he had considered it "repugnant to the Laws of England." Lloyd replied that an attempt had been made at the conference to reconcile that law to the prevailing law on the same subject in England. [30] Clearly, however, the Quaker assemblymen, loyal to the principles of George Fox, could not have made a part of that law the death penalty required by English law for crimes involving property. Fletcher, just as clearly, wanted the death penalty for stealing, and the Quakers were not willing to grant any punishment for such crimes more severe than forfeiture and whipping. Markham, reluctant to debate legislative matters with Lloyd, said that he had written to Fletcher about the matter and that Fletcher, in his letter of reply, had "put the Judges & Justices in a way which wold effectualie take off anie danger that the people might be in for want of the s[ai]d Law." He did not explain in more precise terms what this meant but added that, inasmuch as the Assembly was soon to be adjourned, "He intended not to meddle with Legislation." [31]

Markham's announced intention of adjourning the Assembly
conflicted with Lloyd's desire to keep the Assembly in session.
Markham, of course, was carrying out Fletcher's verbal instructions to adjourn the Assembly to May 1 rather than to
have it make laws in the Royal Governor's absence. Evidently
Fletcher did not trust Markham, who was himself a colonist,
to deal with the Quaker-dominated Assembly. Lloyd objected
to the date of adjournment specified in Fletcher's instructions,
stating that the Quaker Yearly Meeting was to begin on April
27. Since the Quaker assemblymen wished to attend the Meeting, Lloyd requested that, if there must be an adjournment, it
be extended to May 20 so that the Assembly would have time
to conclude its business. Markham thereupon withdrew with
his Council to discuss the matter, as did Lloyd and the Assembly.

While Markham and the Council were changing the date of
adjournment from May 1 to May 22, Lloyd appointed a committee of four, among them Phineas Pemberton and Samuel
Carpenter, to prepare a remonstrance to the Lieutenant Governor. The remonstrance, which Lloyd presented to the Lieutenant Governor upon the Assembly's return to the Council
room, stated that the Assembly had convened by virtue of
writs signed by Markham, "which gave us no other expectation but that wee might proceed in Legislation & redressing
the grievances of the people whom wee represent." The Assembly considered the order to adjourn inconsistent with Markham's writs because the business before the Assembly had
not been concluded. Moreover, the remonstrance stated that
the order to adjourn was repugnant to the privileges of the
legislative authority and to the powers granted to the Lieutenant Governor in Fletcher's commission.[32] Lloyd's conduct
in having this remonstrance prepared and in handing it to Markham before Markham had a chance to say a word was ill-con-
sidered. If Lloyd had been more patient, Markham would have
announced the Council's action in changing the date of adjournment, and trouble would have been avoided. But such conciliation would not have suited Lloyd's purposes. Lloyd was after
nothing less than an encroachment on the royal prerogative
and a resulting enlargement of the Assembly's parliamentary

privileges. In playing this kind of game Lloyd did not hesitate
to use rough tactics.

Markham read the remonstrance, but he appeared anxious
to avoid an argument. He said nothing about the Council's
change of the date of adjournment but asked Lloyd to postpone the matters discussed in the remonstrance to the next
session of the Assembly that they might be considered by Governor Fletcher in person. Lloyd, however, said that he had
no instructions from the Assembly to reopen the subject at a
later date. He spoke briefly on the parliamentary privilege
of the Assembly to adjourn itself. Then, according to the minutes of the Assembly, the Governor, Council, and Assembly
mutually agreed to adjourn. The Assembly subsequently returned to its meeting place, and Lloyd, with the consent of
the assemblymen, formally adjourned the Assembly. The
minutes of the Council stated, however, that Markham ordered the Assembly adjourned. [33] The minutes of adjournment recorded in the journals of the two bodies revealed the
stubborn refusal of either Lloyd or Governor Fletcher to yield
on this significant issue. But they revealed, also, that in this
act of obstinacy Lloyd had established a precedent which was
subsequently to become the standard practice of the Assembly.

The adjournment prevented Lloyd from making an issue of
Quaker grievances against the Royal Governor's administration.
This was one of the reasons for his objection to an early adjournment. Nevertheless, just before the Assembly adjourned
he handed Markham a written list of grievances, part of which
concerned judicial practices by court officers who had been
commissioned by Governor Fletcher. Undoubtedly the written
list of grievances was far less effective than a verbal conflict
between the Assembly and the Royal Governor might have
been. A verbal conflict would have gone far to mold public
opinion and possibly to force the Royal Governor's hand. The
written list, however, could be shelved and forgotten, and
the evidence indicates that Fletcher made little effort to obviate the grievances of the Quaker-dominated Assembly.

Meanwhile the exigencies of war continued to plague the
peace-loving Quakers of Pennsylvania, and ominous military
developments on the New York frontier posed a tricky prob-

lem for David Lloyd as the Speaker of a Quaker-filled Assembly. The English based their defense of that frontier on
friendly relations with the powerful Five Nations, or Iroquois
as the French called them, who dominated strategic Mohawk
Valley and ruled other Indian tribes far to the west. Count
Frontenac, the Governor of Canada, was attempting, however, to make alliances with the Five Nations and other Indian
tribes located in the English colonies, apparently for the purpose of preparing a military offensive against the English. His
designs were known in England, and in the spring of 1694 Governor Fletcher received a letter from Queen Mary commanding
him to obtain from the Pennsylvania Assembly sufficient funds
to feed and clothe the Five Nations. Such a gesture of liberality
to the Indians, the Queen thought, would effectively prevent
their defection to the French.[34] When the Assembly reconvened late in May, Fletcher presented it with the request made
in the Queen's letter and expressed the hope that, although
the Quakers would neither carry arms nor raise money for
military purposes, the Assembly would not refuse "to feed
the Hungrie and Cloath the Naked."[35] Lloyd and his fellow
Quakers, however, were not deceived by this apparently humanitarian gesture and recognized it as a military expediency
designed to further the English war effort.

Lloyd saw in the Queen's request, though, an opportunity to
solve part of the financial problem which he had acquired as
one of the two administrators of the Thomas Lloyd estate. The
estate was heavily indebted and badly in need of ready cash. A
bill, passed by the Assembly, empowered widows and executors of estates to sell land for the payment of debts,[36] but it
would have taken time to raise money by the sale of land, and
the estate's creditors wanted to be paid. Thomas Lloyd had
never succeeded in obtaining his back salary as a former Deputy Governor of the province, and David Lloyd employed the occasion of the Queen's request to secure an appropriation of
£200 from the Assembly for the Thomas Lloyd estate in recognition of the late Quaker leader's services in the provincial
government. The Assembly added to that appropriation another
£200 for Markham's past services as Deputy Governor of the
Lower Counties and stipulated that the balance of the revenue
collected from a property tax of one penny per pound and a

six shilling per capita tax was to be expended on food and clothing for the Indians. To make sure that the tax revenue would
be expended in the manner provided by the bill, David Lloyd
and the Assembly added a provision that the Assembly should
appoint its own treasurer to collect the taxes and to account
to the Assembly for all collections and expenditures, thereby
ignoring the Pennsylvania Receiver General who held office
under the King's commission. [37]

On a day when Fletcher was absent from Philadelphia Lloyd
had the appropriation bill presented to Lieutenant Governor
Markham, who, as a prospective beneficiary of the bill, might
have been expected to give it his approval. Lloyd was soon
disappointed, however, for Markham objected that the bill did
not comply with the Queen's letter. He refused to pass a bill
which levied taxes on Her Majesty's subjects for his own or
any other private person's or estate's benefit. He said that
the proper procedure was to appropriate money for the security
of the frontiers and for the assistance of New York, "and then
to pray their Ma[jes]ties would be pleased to allow out of that
sum what you intend" for the Thomas Lloyd estate and Markham. [38]

Lloyd thereupon dropped his scheme to obtain an appropriation for the Thomas Lloyd estate, but he resolved not to give
Fletcher and Markham the appropriation bill they wanted. Instead he wrote a letter to the Queen, approved by the Assembly,
which stated that "Wee find upon perusall of the minute of Assembly held here about 12 Mo[nths] agoe, that the rate, or
tax, then granted to the King and Queen, was in Complyance
to the aforesaid Letter [from Queen Mary in 1694], so farr as
the religious persuasion of the most part of the Assemblie
could admitt. . . ."[39] Lloyd added that the revenue collected
from the tax of 1693 amounted to £760. [40] He said that the Assembly had agreed to appropriate suitable funds out of the
provincial treasury for food and clothing for the Indians, allowing a "Competent Considera[ti]on" to the Lieutenant Governor for his past year's services. "Therfor," Lloyd concluded, "wee desire that wee may be accordinglie Represented
to the Indians & not reckoned among those that refuse to Comply
either with the Queen's Letter or thy Just Commands, which
otherwise may prove of ill consequence to us."[41]

Lloyd, however, succeeded only in angering the Governor. When Fletcher returned to Philadelphia, he called the Assembly before him and berated it for its failure to prepare a satisfactory appropriation bill for the security of Their Majesties' plantations in America. "You have now satt nineteen dayes without the Least Considera[ti]on of their Ma[jes]ties Service in the Securitie of the province, " he said. "You have applied the first part of yor time in the searching for grievances, which will all appear to be the effects of yor owne weaknes in not redressing you by the due course of the Laws, there not being one of the foure you took such pains to hunt for but must reflect upon yor proprietor or yorselves. "[42] The Governor specifically objected that such appropriation offers as Lloyd and the Assembly had made would fall far short of satisfying the Queen's request for food and clothing for the Five Nations. [43]

Lloyd and his fellow Quakers had no intention of giving Fletcher the appropriation he desired, and Fletcher made no effort to compel them. He approved most of the legislation passed by the Assembly, but rejected bills which Lloyd had secured from the Assembly in an obvious attempt to further self-government in the province, particularly one which would have regulated the fees and salaries of court officers--a prerogative reserved to the Governor and Council by Fletcher's commission because regulation of court fees and salaries was tantamount to control of the courts. The Governor then dissolved the Assembly, but Lloyd, stubbornly refusing to yield to Fletcher a prerogative over the adjournment and dissolution of the Assembly, led the Assembly back to its meeting place at the widow Whitpain's and dissolved it himself after taking a vote of the assemblymen. [44]

Thus, Lloyd successfully led the Quakers in an obdurate refusal to yield their religious principles in spite of the exigencies of wartime and the Queen's instructions to the Governor. Moreover, he had acquired for the Assembly parliamentary privileges which Penn had denied it--the right to initiate legislation and to sit on its own adjournments--although the latter privilege was not recognized by the Governor. On the other hand, Lloyd had failed to secure the passage of laws which would have given the Assembly control of the courts.

Nevertheless, the ultimate effect of his leadership in 1694 was to discourage the Crown from making any further effort to govern Pennsylvania directly by its own commission. By August, 1694, the tide of war was in England's favor, Penn had been cleared of all suspicion of disloyalty to the Crown, and his petition to the Lords of Trade and Plantations for the restoration of proprietary government in Pennsylvania was granted after he had promised to govern the province personally and to provide for the military security of the province and Lower Counties. [45]

Lloyd's leadership of the Quakers in the Assembly came to an end after the restoration of the proprietary government, and he left the Assembly altogether. Lloyd, who had contributed to the wreckage of proprietary government in Pennsylvania in 1692, had led a resistance to the King's Governor which forever poisoned the minds of responsible Crown officials to any thought of attempting to govern Pennsylvania directly again. Penn was indebted to Lloyd for the restoration of proprietary government. But, as subsequent events were to show, Lloyd remained just as determined to encroach upon proprietary prerogative as he had been to encroach upon the Crown's.

# 7. The Frame of 1696

David Lloyd, in his leadership of the Assembly Quakers during 1694, had not alienated Crown officers, other than, perhaps, Governor Fletcher, and he regained the good will of the Proprietor and his deputies. Sometime after the restoration of the proprietary government Penn again commissioned Lloyd the Attorney General of the province. On March 12, 1694/95, Lloyd appeared as King's Attorney in the Chester County Court of Quarter Sessions, and a month and a half later he represented the Crown in a case involving the alleged violation of the Navigation Acts.[1] William Markham also thought well of Lloyd in spite of their conflicts over the Queen's request for a war appropriation the year before. Markham, who, at the Queen's command, was Penn's Deputy Governor of Pennsylvania and the Lower Counties with unlimited powers, nominated Lloyd to the Provincial Council on April 7, 1695, in recognition of Lloyd's "Loyalty to Our most gracious KING WILLIAM and ffidelity to Our Proprietor. . . ."[2] Thirteen days later Lloyd was elected by the freemen of Chester County to a three-year term on the Council--the Frame of 1683 being once more in force--and he first sat as a member of the Council on April 23.[3]

Even before Lloyd was elected to the Council, however, he sat in a Council meeting in an ex officio capacity at the request of Deputy Governor Markham.[4] The problems which had plagued the royal government and the proprietary government before 1694 remained unsolved. The war against France continued, and, although the trend of war was now in England's favor, the Crown still hoped to obtain military aid from the stubborn Quakers of Pennsylvania. The Queen, in restoring the government of Pennsylvania and the Lower Counties to Penn, had placed the Quaker Proprietor under the military command of Governor Fletcher of New York and had instructed Penn to provide a quota of not more than eighty men or the equivalent in money for the common defense of the colonies. Her request was a moderate one, and Fletcher now demanded that Pennsylvania send the quota to New York by August 1. Fletcher's demand was the principal business discussed at the Council meeting which Lloyd attended on April 15. [5]

Lloyd and other leading colonists, however, were more immediately concerned about the unresolved constitutional problem than they were about the English war effort. Many colonists were unhappy about Penn's continuation of the Frame of 1683 and wanted a new frame of government. Lloyd was one of them, and so was Samuel Carpenter, whom Penn had appointed to act as one of two assistants to Deputy Governor Markham because Markham's ill health sometimes disabled him from executing the duties of his office. The other assistant, Dr. John Goodson, however, supported the continuation of the Frame of 1683. [6] Colonists in both Pennsylvania and the Lower Counties tended to divide into factions over the issue, one faction following Carpenter, the other Goodson.

Markham himself appeared to favor those who wanted a change in the constitution. On May 28 he appointed a committee of six councilmen to consider a new frame of government. Among them were Samuel Carpenter, representing Philadelphia County, and Lloyd, representing Chester. Goodson was not a member of the committee. [7]

Lloyd and his fellow committeemen soon became aware of the fact that the constitutional issue and the English war effort were closely related in Markham's mind. They might have a new frame of government only if they complied with the Queen's request for a military contingent or its equivalent in money. Yet, Lloyd and the other Quakers on the committee were averse to violating their religious scruples against war. They avoided an open clash with the Deputy Governor by asserting that no decision could be reached without the consent of the Assembly and that the Assembly could not be called because harvesting was then in progress. Thus Lloyd and other Quakers in the Council stalled until the Assembly convened on September 9.

Lloyd and other members of the Carpenter faction could not, however, very well pass up the opportunity Markham had given them to encroach upon the Proprietor's prerogative by creating their own frame of government, even if it meant compromising with their religious principles. In mid-September Lloyd and eleven other councilmen discussed the problem with a committee from the Assembly. The outcome of the conference was a recommendation to Markham that money be appropriated for the support of the government and for no other purpose, and that a new frame of government be enacted by the Assembly as an act of settlement.

Markham was agreeable to the recommendation, and he appointed Lloyd and several other councilmen to present the recommendations to the Assembly as proposed legislation. A few days later the Assembly submitted to the Deputy Governor and Council two legislative bills--one appropriating £250 for the support of the government, £300 to Markham for services as Deputy Governor, and the balance of revenue collected from property and per capita taxes to defray the existing debts of the provincial government; the other an act of settlement containing a new frame of government.

The two bills were so worded, however, that the enactment of one depended on the enactment of the other. Observing this fact, Markham objected that he wanted the appropriation bill enacted first and the act of settlement withheld for further debate. Moreover, he wanted his salary as Deputy Governor excluded from the appropriation bill. He was unimpressed by the protest of one of the councilmen that it was the English way to redress grievances before taxing the people. Convinced that the Quakers did not intend to provide a satisfactory appropriation in response to the Queen's request, the Deputy Governor dissolved the Council and Assembly. [8]

Sometime during the winter of 1695/96 Lloyd and several other Quaker leaders, including Carpenter and Goodson, received a letter from Penn warning that their refusal would be used against them by their enemies. People in England, he

said, could not understand why, although they were required
to pay towards the prosecution of the war in North America,
Pennsylvania colonists found it difficult to contribute their
share of the colonial defense.[9] Penn's warning was valid. Enemies were already stirring up trouble for the Pennsylvanians.
Governor Fletcher of New York had already written to the
Lords of Trade and Plantations, complaining that the Pennsylvania colonists "have as little regard for the interest of their
proprietor M[r] Penn as they have for His Maj[es]tys service
and are endeavoring to erect a new modell of Government of
their own invention and by their own Authority."[10] The English
government was fully cognizant of what was going on in Pennsylvania. Markham, however, did not see Penn's letter, and
for some reason Penn did not address a similar warning to
his Deputy Governor. Goodson, strangely enough, withheld
Penn's letter from Markham, and the Deputy Governor knew
nothing of it until October, 1696, when Arthur Cook, one of
the recipients of the missive, showed it to him.[11]

In spite of Penn's warning, Lloyd and other councilmen were
determined to effect a change in the constitution, and, after the
Assembly convened on October 26, they informed Markham
that a constitutional settlement would have to be achieved as
a prerequisite to the conclusion of other business. Markham
felt that he was powerless to give the province a new frame
of government without Penn's approval, but he nevertheless
appointed Lloyd and three other councilmen to confer with
members of the Assembly in a joint committee. The views of
Lloyd and other adherents of the Carpenter faction prevailed
in the joint committee. After a brief deliberation the joint
committee decided to base its answer to the Queen's request
on a provision

That the Governor at the Request of the Assembly, will be pleased
to pass an Act with a Salvo to the Proprietary and People; and that
he will also issue out his Writs for choosing of a full Number of Representatives on the tenth Day of the First Month next, to serve in
Provincial Council and Assembly according to Charter [i. e., the new
frame], until the Proprietary's Pleasure be known therein; and, that
if the Proprietary shall disapprove the same, that then this Act shall
be void, and no ways prejudicial to him nor the People, in relation
to the Validity or Invalidity of the said Charter.[12]

This provision constituted a declaration of the colonists' right
to make their own constitution independently as a stopgap
measure pending the Proprietor's approval. The Assembly
approved the joint committee's report unanimously.

The joint committee report changed Markham's mind. Taking
the initiative, he presented to the Assembly some heads of a
frame of government which he claimed were of his own authorship and which included "some emendations & altera[ti]ons"
of the Frame of 1683. On November 7 the Deputy Governor and
Assembly enacted a bill including the new Frame and a revenue
measure providing a sum of money for the assistance of New
York.[13]

David Lloyd's specific contributions to the writing of the
Frame of 1696 cannot now be determined. He was at least one
of those who were chiefly responsible for the Frame, and the
Frame's contents suggested the framework of Pennsylvania
government of which Lloyd was to become the chief exponent a
few years later. The Frame of 1696 certainly reflected Lloyd's
political thought at the time, and he defended it in the factional
battles that followed its enactment.

The Frame of 1696 contained the parliamentary privileges
which the Assembly had claimed during Fletcher's administration. It recognized the privilege of the Assembly to initiate
legislation, to sit on its own adjournments, to redress grievances, and to impeach criminals. Moreover, it granted members of the Assembly an increase in salary from three to four
shillings per day of attendance plus travel pay. Both the Council
and Assembly remained elective bodies, but the Council's
legislative powers were somewhat reduced as the Assembly's
were increased. The Governor and Council could still propose legislative bills, and the Council could meet with the Assembly in joint session to discuss legislation. The Frame
specified, however, that 'proposed and prepared bills, or such
of them as the Governor with the advice of the Council shall in
open Assembly declare his assent unto, shall be the laws of
this province and territories thereof."[14] It made the Council
chiefly an advisory body to the Governor with primarily ad-
ministrative powers, including the erection of courts, and it
also empowered the Governor and Council to sit as a court in
judgment upon impeachments brought by the Assembly.[15] The

Frame contained one clause which Lloyd did not altogether ap-
prove--that requiring merchants and shippers to swear prescribed oaths in compliance with trade and navigation acts.
The clause was obviously a sop to the Crown at a time when
the English government was tightening its controls of overseas
trade and shipping, especially in the colonies, and Lloyd, as
he later testified, never accepted it as applying to Pennsylvania. [16]

The Frame of 1696 entered life in adversity, and it was
never a healthy infant. Its legality remained in doubt as long
as it did not have the sanction of the Proprietor. Goodson and
his followers refused to accept it, and they continued to believe that the Frame of 1683 had been automatically revived
by the restoration of the proprietary government and that it
remained in force. They refused to pay the taxes levied by the
Assembly to provide financial assistance to New York, and in
Philadelphia County they elected representatives to the Assembly and Council under the Frame of 1683 in opposition to
representatives elected under the new Frame. Markham rejected the Goodsonian representatives, and they never took
their seats in either branch of the provincial government. The
Goodsonians protested that the Frame of 1683 had not been
legally altered, but Markham ignored them. [17] Goodson's followers then appealed directly to Penn not to give his assent
to the new Frame and complained that the Council and Assembly were already levying taxes without waiting for Penn's
ratification of the Frame of 1696. They alleged further that
the Council was not of popular choice and that the Assembly
did not take the people into its confidence. [18]

David Lloyd, Carpenter, and others, on the other hand,
wrote to Penn warning against the endeavors of the Goodsonians
to "put us into Confusion by pretending to be for the Charter
[Frame of 1683] in opposition to the . . . Settlem[en]t made
Last Sessions to continue untill thy Pleasure be known." They
asked Penn not to be hasty in expressing dislike of the new
Frame lest he bring the province into confusion and give a
handle to their enemies. [19] Penn himself said nothing about the
constitutional issue until he was able to cross the Atlantic to
govern Pennsylvania in person.

Lloyd saw the Carpenterian victory clinched in May, 1697,

when Markham and the newly elected Assembly passed an act which confirmed the legal status of the Frame of 1696 and of all laws enacted by the Assembly during October and November, 1696.[20] The passage of this act constituted ratification of the Frame and laws by the colonists rather than by the Proprietor, but it effectively frustrated Goodson and his followers, and they made no further attempt until 1700 to oppose the administration of the new Frame.

Thus, Lloyd had been one of the leaders of the Carpenterian faction who succeeded in achieving a constitutional revision which guaranteed a larger measure of self-government than the colonists had been granted under previous frames.

# 8. "A Great Box . . . and a Little Babie"

On March 31, 1697, as the factious quarrel over the Frame
of 1696 was nearing an end, David Lloyd married a second
time. Sarah, his first wife, had died sometime after the birth
of their only son Tommy, several years earlier, [1] and Lloyd
had subsequently been attracted to the youthful daughter of
Joseph Growdon, a Cornish Quaker and landowner. Hence,
on the last day of March forty-one-year-old David Lloyd and
seventeen-year-old Grace Growdon were married in a Quaker
wedding at the Growdon mansion, "Trevose," on the high,
rolling land adjoining the Neshaminy River in Bucks County. [2]

The marriage was a happy one for Lloyd, although the
bride was twenty-four years his junior. She was reputed to be a
pious girl of excellent character, intelligence, and common
sense. [3] Moreover, the Growdons were a substantial, well-to-
do family which had good connections with Quaker leaders in
England. A first purchaser, Joseph Growdon had taken his
wife and children from Cornwall to Pennsylvania in 1682. Three
years later, after purchasing 10,000 acres of land, most of
it in Bucks County, he had built his home, "Trevose," named
after his father's estate in Cornwall. He had served in many
positions in the provincial government, and was one of the five
or six most prominent Quakers in Pennsylvania. [4] Marrying
into the Growdon family gave Lloyd an improved social position
in the Quaker community, which was to strengthen him in his
political resistance to Crown and proprietary prerogatives
in the years to come.

Even as David Lloyd and his young bride were accepting the compliments of their wedding guests, the Welsh Quaker was in trouble with Crown officers. Only three days earlier Edward Randolph, the Surveyor General of Customs, had asked him, as the King's Attorney in Pennsylvania, to arrest one John Deplovy, and he had refused. His refusal was difficult for a Crown officer to understand, for the point at issue was Crown prerogative. Randolph accused Deplovy of having illegally carried tobacco directly to Scotland instead of clearing his cargo at a port in England first, as required by the trade and navigation laws. From Randolph's point of view the arrest of such a violator, who had struck a blow at the very heart of the English economy, the mercantile system, could hardly have been refused by a King's Attorney loyal to the Crown and devoted to the economic interests of the homeland. Yet Lloyd had refused, and Deputy Governor Markham himself supported Lloyd's refusal by denying Randolph's request that he appoint someone else to act as King's Attorney in Lloyd's place. Randolph was perplexed, bitter, and vindictive. [5]

David Lloyd had evinced no objection to the enforcement of the Crown's trade and navigation laws in the colonies until after Parliament had passed a new Navigation Act in 1696. On the whole, enforcement of navigation laws by colonial governors had been lax, and violations had been frequent in colonial trade. When Crown officers had brought charges against colonial ships for violating the navigation acts, trials had been conducted in the common law courts in the colonies, where judge and jury had frequently been biased in favor of the defendants. Lloyd had represented the Crown in such a case in 1695, and the court had found in favor of the defendant. [6]

After the passage of the Navigation Act of 1696, however, David Lloyd had refused to represent the Crown any longer in maritime cases. He had, according to Randolph, protested that, as Attorney General of Pennsylvania, "he served for the Province only, and thereupon refused to put several forfeited Bonds in Suit." [7] Randolph had then complained about Lloyd to the Board of Trade, which had been created by the Navigation Act of 1696 as the successor to the Lords of Trade and Plantations. The Board of Trade had forwarded Randolph's complaint to the Lords Justices, declaring Lloyd unfit to hold the

office of Attorney General, and had recommended his removal.
The Lords Justices, however, had failed to act on the Board of
Trade's recommendation, chiefly because they had no real legal
jurisdiction over attorneys general in proprietary colonies.
Even as the Lords Justices had been deciding his fate, Lloyd
had, on November 10, 1696, defended a vessel against Crown
prosecutors at a court in West New Jersey.[8] Hence, Lloyd's
refusal to arrest Deplovy for violation of the navigation laws
gave Randolph further reason to inform the Board of Trade
of Lloyd's alleged disloyalty.[9]

Randolph's insinuation that Lloyd was disloyal to the Crown
was not entirely true. Lloyd opposed royal prerogative, as he
did proprietary prerogative, only when it interfered with what
he considered to be the legitimate local interests of the colonists. The Navigation Act of 1696, although generally it was
not to become effective until 1698, contained provisions already in operation which Lloyd sincerely believed to be gross
encroachments on the rights and liberties of freeborn Englishmen in Pennsylvania. One of those provisions to which Lloyd
particularly objected required that merchants and shipowners
in Pennsylvania and the Lower Counties swear oaths of loyalty
to the Crown and of obedience to the laws of trade and navigation. To swear any kind of oath whatever constituted a serious
violation of Quaker religious principles. Neither Lloyd nor
any other Quaker could conscientiously obey any law which
required swearing oaths. Lloyd represented the Quaker shipowners in explaining their position to Randolph, and he told
the Surveyor General of Customs that the Quakers would rather
lose their ships than swear an oath. When Randolph reminded
Lloyd that a clause in the Frame of 1696 required the swearing
of oaths in compliance with trade and navigation laws, Lloyd
replied that the clause "was never intended to be observed in
Pensilvania," and he accused Randolph of attempting to use the
oath requirement "as a snare to entrap them."[10] Randolph
angrily reported the conversation to the Board of Trade and
asserted that Pennsylvania colonists regarded themselves as
independent of the Crown and did not acknowledge William III
as their sovereign lord and King.[11] The latter assertion struck
uncomfortably close to the truth, and the Assembly, which
had theretofore evinced little enthusiasm for the change in the

English monarchy, declared, in May, 1697, its loyalty to
William III. [12] The Assembly's declaration of loyalty, however, was, as things turned out, hardly enough to allay the
suspicions of the Crown officers.

During the same month that the Assembly proclaimed its,
and the province's, loyalty to William III, David Lloyd's reluctance to prosecute maritime cases was bringing on a critical
situation in the relations between the province and the Crown.
His refusal even to prosecute men accused of piracy gave a
handle to Crown officers and their colonial supporters who
were only too happy to be thereby presented with an excuse
for condemning all Quakers because of the alleged wrongdoing
of one. Piracy, as Lloyd well knew, had become a menacing
problem to English merchant shipping, largely as an after-
math of the War of the League of Augsburg. During the war
numerous privateers, armed vessels owned and manned by
private persons, had been retained by the English and French
governments to prey on each other's shipping. When hostilities
concluded early in 1697, many of these privateers turned to
piracy. Indeed, some had been engaged in piracy even during
the war. [13] After William III had proclaimed that certain designated pirates should be brought to trial, David Lloyd, as Attorney General of Pennsylvania, arrested and imprisoned three
of them whom he found in the province. Lloyd doubted, however, that the pirates could be brought to trial because their
crimes had been committed at sea and there was no court of
competent jurisdiction in Pennsylvania. [14]

Lloyd's refusal to have the accused arraigned before the
Philadelphia County Court of Quarter Sessions for piracy constituted an act of disobedience to the King's proclamation. The
Attorney General's position was supported by some of the colonists, but it had somehow to be explained to the Proprietor
whose charter might once again be in danger of forfeiture because of it. Consequently, on May 25 Lloyd and several Quaker
leaders wrote to Penn explaining that, inasmuch as the alleged
pirates' crimes had been committed on the high seas, "wee
are . . . most of us of opinion that the Govern[o]r cannot Grant
a Speciall Commission for their Tryall w[i]thout Incroaching
on the Jurisdiction of the Court of Admiralty." [15] Lloyd, as the
letter indicated, believed that only the High Court of Admiralty

had jurisdiction over the crime of piracy and that the alleged pirates, therefore, could not be tried in the common law courts of Pennsylvania.

The letter to Penn was still in mid-ocean when the situation created by Lloyd's refusal to prosecute the accused men rapidly deteriorated. In June the alleged pirates somehow escaped from their prison in Philadelphia. Captain Robert Snead, a recent immigrant from Jamaica and a Justice of the Peace in the Lower Counties, subsequently reported to Governor Francis Nicholson of Maryland, who was Vice-Admiral for Maryland, Pennsylvania, and West New Jersey and an implacable enemy of the Quakers, that the alleged pirates were at liberty and were going about the country at will. Snead implied that the Quakers had surreptitiously liberated the prisoners, but Lloyd wrote to Phineas Pemberton that "the privateers who broke prison are gone"--an indication that, if anyone had helped the prisoners to escape, Lloyd, at least, knew nothing of it. Francis Jones, a shipowner in New Castle, later informed Penn that the alleged pirates had broken out of prison with the assistance of friends and that only one had been recaptured. [16]

Other colonists than Quakers and other colonies than Pennsylvania, however, were lax in prosecuting violators of the trade and navigation laws. By May, 1698, the Crown took positive action to ensure that such violators would be brought to justice. Although the Navigation Act of 1696 contained several offhand allusions to "vice-courts of admiralty" without specifying how such courts were to be constituted, what their powers were, or how their business was to be conducted, the High Court of Admiralty undertook the establishment of these courts in the colonies from Massachusetts Bay to Barbados as its sole prerogative and set up its own rules. In the courts of vice-admiralty the common law did not prevail and trials were held without jury. A court of vice-admiralty had not yet been established in Pennsylvania, but the High Court of Admiralty was already taking steps to organize one.

With the appearance of courts of vice-admiralty in the colonies, Lloyd and the Quaker merchants of Philadelphia thought an act of Assembly incorporating the substance of the Navigation Act of 1696 had become necessary. They believed, as they subsequently informed Penn, that such a law would serve to inform the colonists of the provisions of the Navigation Act and "to remove those Jealousies that o[u]r Enemies had raised by repr[e]senting us to the world as a people whose ffortuens are wholly advanced by Illegal Trade. "[17] Deputy Governor Markham agreed with them, and he asked the Council and Assembly to make laws which would serve to incorporate the Navigation Act of 1696 and other trade and navigation laws into provincial law. Lloyd and several other members of the Council conferred with representatives of the Assembly in a joint committee, and after eight days of deliberation they reported a legislative bill "for preventing frauds and regulating abuses in trade, " which soon after became law. [18]

Lloyd and the legislators with whom he collaborated in writing the Pennsylvania Act of Trade had, however, interpreted the Navigation Act of 1696 in a manner which was not likely to be accepted by officers of the Crown. Their concern, indicated by the contents of the act, was not so much to provide an effective answer to the critics of the Quaker merchants, as Lloyd and the Quaker merchants subsequently wrote to Penn, as it was to insure that all maritime cases except piracy would be tried by jury in Pennsylvania courts of common law. A passage in the Navigation Act of 1696 specified that violators of the English navigation and trade acts would forfeit one third of their ships and goods to the Crown, one third to the Governor of the colony in which the action took place, and one third to the informer who was to "sue for the same by Bill Plaints or Information in any of His Majesties Courts of Record att Westminster or in any Court in His Majesties Plantations where such offense shall bee committed. "[19] The Pennsylvania Act of Trade stipulated that actions against violators of the English trade and navigation laws "shall be according to the course of the Common Law, known practice of the Courts of record within this government by twelve Lawful men of the neighborhood, where the offence is Committed. "[20] The Navigation Act of 1696, however, did not specify trial by jury, except for a negative statement that upon any actions brought in the colonies against ships or goods for illegal importation or exportation "there shall not bee any Jury but of such onely as are Natives of England or Ireland or are borne in His Majesties said Plantations. "[21] Nor did the Act specify courts of com-

mon law. It merely stated "any Court in His Majesties Plantations where such offense shall bee committed"--a passage
which easily lent itself to conflicting interpretations.

Crown officers and enemies of the Quaker leaders roundly
attacked the Pennsylvania Act of Trade, particularly because
of its provision for jury trials in common law courts in cases
involving alleged violation of English trade and navigation laws.
John Moore, an agent of the Board of Trade who resided in
Philadelphia, thought the Pennsylvania Act was repugnant to
the Navigation Act of 1696. [22] The High Court of Admiralty,
which interpreted the Navigation Act of 1696 to mean that
in the colonies cases involving violation of the English navigation laws should be heard in courts of vice-admiralty, appointed Robert Quary, a Philadelphia Anglican merchant, to
act as Judge of Vice-Admiralty in a court that he was to establish in Philadelphia.

Aware that they were walking a tightrope from which they
might at any moment plunge to political self-destruction, Lloyd
and two prominent Philadelphia Quaker merchants wrote to
Penn, a month and a half after the passage of the Pennsylvania
Act of Trade, defending their interpretation of the Navigation
Act of 1696. They wrote that the Navigation Act implied that
alleged violations of the English trade and navigation laws by
Pennsylvania colonists should be tried by jury in Pennsylvania
courts of common law. They denied that the Court of Vice-Admiralty, when established in Pennsylvania, could have jurisdiction over such maritime cases when alleged violations occurred
in the inland waters of the province. They believed that Penn's
charter took precedence over the Navigation Act of 1696 in
matters pertaining to port development and navigation in the
inland waters of Pennsylvania. [23] A clause in Penn's charter
gave the Proprietor and his deputies sole jurisdiction over
the inland waters, and the Pennsylvania Act of Trade contained
a provision that authorized the Governor and Council to declare the geographical limits of ports and to appoint collectors
of customs to reside at the ports. Lloyd and the Quaker merchants believed, however, that only the Court of Vice-Admiralty would have jurisdiction over crimes committed on the high
seas. They chafed at Quary's delay in erecting the court so
that men accused of piracy could be promptly arraigned and

prosecuted. At the same time they doubted the propriety of
Quary's commission to be its judge. Quary, they informed
Penn, was one of the leading merchants in the province and an
agent for the Pennsylvania Company, a private monopoly owned
by wealthy adventurers in England who were exploiting Pennsylvania commerce and fur trade. Lloyd and his friends believed that Quary's position in the Pennsylvania Company rendered him "in a great measure if not altogether incapable of
being Judge specially to Try Seizures of Ships & goods." They
were certain that Quary would be prejudicial to all merchants
and traders in Pennsylvania, except to himself and the Company he served. [24]

Quary himself had his doubts about establishing a Court of
Vice-Admiralty in Pennsylvania--for reasons other than those
stated by Lloyd and the Quaker merchants, of course. In a
letter dated July 9, 1698, five days after Lloyd and the Quaker
merchants had written to Penn, Quary complained to Governor
Nicholson of Maryland that the Pennsylvania Act of Trade effectively destroyed his commission as Judge of Vice-Admiralty
because it disabled him, so he thought, from erecting a Court
of Vice-Admiralty in Pennsylvania. [25] Quary, as he later informed the Board of Trade, had at first been reluctant to accept his commission, because he believed the colonists of
Pennsylvania "to be a perverse, obstinate and turbulent people who will submit to no laws but their own, and have a notion
that no Acts of Parliament are of force among them except such
as particularly mention them." [26] He had nevertheless accepted
his commission, although in July he hesitated to publish it, because he felt frustrated by the High Court of Admiralty's in-
judicious choice of court officers to serve with him. The High
Court of Admiralty had given commissions to Edward Chilton
as Advocate and to Robert Webb as Marshal. Chilton, however,
was in England and did not wish to go to America. Webb, who
lived some eighty miles from Philadelphia, a considerable distance in those days, was incapacitated by a leg ailment. Quary
wanted John Moore to replace Chilton as Advocate, but Moore
wanted assurances that he would receive his fees and salary--
assurances which Quary was not free to give him. [27] Quary finally established his Court of Vice-Admiralty in Philadelphia

later in the summer of 1698, and Moore reluctantly accepted appointment as Advocate.

Crown officers continued their attacks on the Pennsylvania Act of Trade throughout the summer of 1698. Governor Nicholson wrote to the Board of Trade that the Pennsylvania act set a bad example which proprietary colonies might follow to the detriment of the royal provinces. Randolph, also in a letter to the Board of Trade, angrily assailed the Pennsylvania act as a "shamm Law" which "utterly destroyed the design & Intent" of the Navigation Act of 1696. [28]

Lloyd, meanwhile, kept a discreet silence. He had said what he had to say in the Council-Assembly committee which had written the Pennsylvania Act of Trade and in the letter to Penn. As Quary went about the business of establishing the Court of Vice-Admiralty in Philadelphia, Lloyd gave him no reason to believe that he was anything but eager to have such a court erected. When Quary, who was frequently out of the province on business trips to neighboring colonies, asked Lloyd to act as his Deputy Judge of Vice-Admiralty, Lloyd readily accepted. [29] Quary, who thus proved himself no more judicious than the High Court of Admiralty in his choice of court officers, soon learned what a great mistake he had made.

Lloyd's reason for accepting appointment as Deputy Judge of Vice-Admiralty is not clear, but his appointment coincided with the development of a maritime case in which he was very interested. About four months earlier the Collector of Customs at New Castle had seized the sloop *Jacob,* owned by John Adams, a Philadelphia merchant, for alleged violation of the English trade and navigation laws. The sloop had been bound from New York to Philadelphia with a cargo of several kinds of English manufactured goods, five bolts of canvas, and five barrels of East India goods. The Collector of the Customs had charged that the *Jacob*'s captain had been unable to produce the legally required certificate of clearance and had given the sloop and its cargo into the custody of Webb, the Marshal of the Court of Vice-Admiralty, whose leg had healed sufficiently to enable him to perform the duties of his office. Adams had subsequently obtained a certificate of clearance for the *Jacob* from New York and had presented it to Quary, but Quary had

refused to recognize the certificate and had asserted that
Adams could recover the *Jacob*'s cargo only by suit at law. In
September Adams petitioned Deputy Governor Markham for a
replevin of the cargo, but Quary was absent from the province,
Lloyd was acting as the Deputy Judge of Vice-Admiralty, and
Markham was unwilling to take any action until Quary had re-
turned to Philadelphia.

John Adams then took the matter to the Philadelphia County
Court of Quarter Sessions, and Anthony Morris, one of the
judges and a Philadelphia Quaker merchant, consulted Lloyd
as to the action he should take. Lloyd advised him to take the
*Jacob*'s cargo from the custody of Marshal Webb and to return it to Adams. Morris thereupon granted Adams a writ of
replevin, and Marshal Webb was summoned before the Philadelphia County Court of Quarter Sessions to give reason why
the cargo should not be restored to its rightful owner.

Lloyd, even though he was still the Deputy Judge of Vice-
Admiralty, appeared as Adams' attorney in the hearing which
followed. Marshal Webb, speaking in his own defense, produced the royal commission under the broad seal of the High
Court of Admiralty and Quary's warrant for the seizure of the
*Jacob*'s cargo. On the frontispiece of the commission were
stamped the effigies of the King and Queen of England. Lloyd,
as Quary later described the scene, took the commission and
held it up so that everybody in the courtroom could see it, and
said, "What is this? Do you think to scare us w[i]t[h] a great
box (meaning the seal in a tin box) and a little Babie (meaning
the picture or effigies aforesaid); 'tis true, said hee, fine pic-
tures please children; but we are not to be frightened att such
a rate. . . ."[30] A titter ran through the crowded courtroom.
Lloyd's raillery amused the colonists who were almost to a
man in sympathy with Adams. Instead of reproving the laugh-
ing spectators, the judges, according to Quary, joined in the
merriment. When quiet was finally restored, the court ruled
in favor of the plaintiff. Subsequently, the Philadelphia County
Sheriff took the cargo from Webb and returned it to Adams.

When Quary returned to Philadelphia and learned what had
happened, he was furious. He had been completely deceived
by Lloyd, and considered his speech at the Philadelphia County
Court of Quarter Sessions "insolent & disloyal."[31] He wrote

to the Board of Trade of the incident and appealed to the Deputy Governor and Council against the action that had been taken by the Philadelphia County Court of Quarter Sessions. Markham and the majority of the Council resolved that the issue of the writ of replevin had not been an act of government but rejected Quary's application for the restoration of the *Jacob's* cargo to the custody of the Marshal of the Court of Vice-Admiralty. [32]

Lloyd and the judges of Philadelphia County now challenged the legality of the Court of Vice-Admiralty, which Quary had erected. The judges, acting under Lloyd's advice, told the Deputy Governor and Council that they "did not know of any Court of Admiralty erected, nor p[er]sons Qualified as wee know of to this day, to hold such Court."[33] Lloyd argued, as defense attorney at a session of the Court of Vice-Admiralty, that the court did not exist by virtue of any commission from the King.[34] At a meeting of the Council, Lloyd declared, as Quary subsequently reported to Penn, that "whoever were Instrumental or aniewise aiding in erecting & encouraging a Court of admiraltie in this province, were greater enemies to the Liberties & priviledges of the people than those th[a]t established & promoted ship monie in king Charles the first's time."[35]

Lloyd's defense of the autonomous rights of Pennsylvania, the real issue in the *Jacob* case, carried on into 1699, but, in his fulminations against Crown prerogative in the regulation of shipping in Pennsylvania's inland waters, he overextended himself. Because of Quary's detailed, although one-sided, reports Lloyd's conduct was under the scrutiny of the Board of Trade. The Board of Trade already had in its files much derogatory information about Lloyd, including a report that Lloyd, as Attorney General of Pennsylvania and the Lower Counties, had threatened to indict armed militiamen in the Lower Counties for inciting a riot when they had attempted to train as an artillery unit. In August, 1699, four members of the Board of Trade, including the philosopher John Locke, recommended to the Lords Justices of England "That it is not fit that . . . David Lloyd sho[ul]d be continued in any publick Imployment whatsoever in the . . . Province."[36] The King-in-Council, upon the Board of Trade's advice, repealed the Pennsylvania Act of Trade, because of its clauses providing for the common-

law trial by jury of all violations of English trade and navigation laws and excusing Quakers from swearing oaths required
by the Navigation Act of 1696, and instructed Penn to remove
Deputy Governor Markham, Judge Anthony Morris, and Attorney General Lloyd from their offices. The Board of Trade,
upon transmitting the King-in-Council's instructions, further
ordered Penn to remove Lloyd from all other offices he held
beside that of Attorney General and to give due obedience to
the Court of Vice-Admiralty. [37]

Hence, Lloyd's defense of the *Jacob* at a session of the Court
of Vice-Admiralty at New Castle on November 10-12 was an
anticlimax. The decisions had been made at Whitehall, and his
arguments were enfeebled by them. Nothing that he could say or
do was likely to impress Judge Quary now. Lloyd insisted on
a jury trial as was provided, he claimed, by the Navigation Act
of 1696 and by the Pennsylvania Act of Trade. Quary, however,
ruled against a jury trial and issued a decree for the condemnation of the sloop and its cargo. Lloyd then claimed that the
vessel was a castaway and should therefore be forfeited to the
Proprietor in accordance with the charter which Charles II
had granted to him in 1680/81. Quary overruled this claim
and judged the sloop lawful prize. [38] This appears to have been
the last time that Lloyd ever attempted to challenge the jurisdiction of the Court of Vice-Admiralty in cases involving alleged violations of the English navigation acts in Pennsylvania
waters.

Lloyd, however, continued to hold his public office even
after Penn arrived during the winter of 1699. Penn was as
much opposed as Lloyd to the extension of the Court of Vice-
Admiralty's jurisdiction to alleged violations of the English
navigation laws in Pennsylvania waters. Hence, he was reluctant to remove Lloyd from all positions of public trust.
After the King, in February, 1699/1700, ordered Penn to ap-
prehend pirates in Pennsylvania and the Lower Counties--pi-
rates from St. Mary's and the Red Sea--and to forward them,
witnesses, and other evidence to England for trial, Penn appointed Lloyd to be chairman of a Council committee for the
preparation of a legislative bill against piracy. The result was
an act which so pleased the Crown that Penn subsequently received a commission to try piracy cases in Pennsylvania. [39]

Quary, however, would not permit Lloyd to avoid punishment so easily. The Judge of Vice-Admiralty was pleased that
Penn had removed Markham and Judge Morris from the government of Pennsylvania, [40] but he would not have Lloyd, whom
he considered an even greater wrongdoer, go scot-free. In
May, 1700, he presented a memorial in writing to Governor
Penn and the Council, accusing Lloyd of disloyalty to the
Crown. Lloyd asked the Governor and Council for an opportunity to reply to this serious charge, but his request was turned
down because he was not yet on trial. The next day, May 15,
the Council voted to suspend Lloyd from his Council membership until a trial had been held. [41] Penn subsequently removed
Lloyd from the offices of Attorney General and Clerk of Philadelphia County Courts and announced his intention of prosecuting Lloyd at the next session of the Philadelphia County
Court of Quarter Sessions. [42] As things turned out, Lloyd was
never brought to trial, but he never again received a commission from Penn for any public office in Pennsylvania.

Lloyd, because of Quary's formal charge that he was disloyal to the Crown, was a marked man. Even those who had
laughed when Lloyd had ridiculed the Judge of Vice-Admiralty's commission at the Philadelphia County Court of Quarter
Sessions in 1698 shrank from him now. Anthony Morris, in
full retreat from his earlier position in the *Jacob* case, told
Penn that he had signed the writ of replevin on the advice of
"th[e]m th[a]t knew the Laws," that is, Lloyd. Confessing himself in error, Morris apologized to Penn for his part in the
affair. [43] Isaac Norris, the young Quaker merchant recently arrived from Jamaica, who had married the late Thomas Lloyd's
daughter, wrote to his brother-in-law that he feared his connections with David Lloyd in the *Jacob* affair would ruin him. [44]
Philadelphia Quaker merchants obtained the records of Lloyd's
administration of his several public offices and held meetings to discuss what they should do about him. Penn feared
that Lloyd might cause him to lose his charter. When Lloyd
offered to plead his cause at Westminster Hall, Penn argued
that this procedure would never succeed except possibly to
give the Crown an occasion to place Pennsylvania once more
under a royal governor. [45] Thomas Lloyd's widow, Patience,
quarreled with David Lloyd over his deteriorated relations

with the Crown and the Proprietor, but, when other Quakers attacked him, she took his side and together they quarreled with his critics. [46]

Lloyd's disgrace was mitigated by a feeling among several of the leading Quakers that he was, after all, "the most active and assiduous councillor" against the Crown officers who advocated the return of royal government to Pennsylvania. The majority of the freemen of Chester County continued to support Lloyd. Lloyd, however, never again had the confidence of Penn and the wealthier and more conservative Quaker merchants. [47]

# 9. The Reforms of 1701

In the autumn of 1700 David Lloyd and his family lived in a brick house on Second Street, near what is now Moravian Street, opposite the fortresslike mansion, the "Slate-Roof-House," which Samuel Carpenter had recently constructed and in which William Penn, his second wife Hannah Callowhill, their newborn son John "the American," and their daughter Letitia had lived during the previous winter. Penn and his family had removed to their freshly remodeled home at Pennsbury in Bucks County, but Penn's erudite, somewhat unbending, young Irish secretary, James Logan, remained at the Slate-Roof-House and Lloyd saw much of him. Lloyd's first impressions of Logan are unrecorded, but Logan wrote to Penn's oldest son in England that he thought Lloyd "a man very stiff in all his undertakings, of a sound judgment, and a good lawyer, but extremely pertinacious and somewhat revengeful."[1]

Philadelphia had grown considerably between the time Lloyd had first set foot on Pennsylvania soil in 1686 and the autumn of 1700. More than a thousand inhabited houses now filled the town. Most of them were three-story, red-brick buildings, and they evinced a tendency to follow the architectural style of London more than had the houses in the earlier years of the colony.[2] The population had swelled, not only from European immigration, but also from population movements in the mainland colonies. During King William's War, Quaker pacifism had proved attractive to many colonists who had moved to Pennsylvania rather than endure the rigors and exactions of military

*89*

life on the frontier. Many such colonists had come from New York,[3] Anglicans, chiefly artisans and shopkeepers, outnumbered Quakers, and they had their own church, Christ Church, a brick structure erected in 1695, which had galleries holding more than five hundred persons.[4] Quaker merchants and landed aristocrats nevertheless still dominated the political and economic life of Philadelphia, and their new meetinghouse at Market and Second streets was used by the Assembly as its meeting place.[5]

Although Lloyd was out of favor with the Quaker merchants of Philadelphia, his life had become interwoven with theirs in recent years. He was the coexecutor, with two Philadelphia Quaker merchants, of the estate of Richard Hoskins, a Philadelphia Quaker merchant who had died in London earlier in the year, and was responsible for the education of Hoskins' son and four daughters.[6] Isaac Norris worried about his association with Lloyd, but the two were coexecutors of the Thomas Lloyd estate, and their efforts to settle the estate kept them working together. Thomas Lloyd had died penniless and heavily in debt, although his estate included great tracts of land in Pennsylvania, the Lower Counties, and West New Jersey. He had never received any compensation for his years of service in the government of the province. Lloyd's past efforts to obtain an appropriation from the provincial government for the Thomas Lloyd estate had failed, but he and Norris had discharged a small part of the estate's indebtedness with the proceeds from the sale of five hundred acres of the estate to a West New Jersey colonist.[7]

Lloyd, although he lived in Philadelphia, continued to base his material wealth on land speculation. In addition to his earlier land acquisitions he now owned a subscription to a large tract of land in the western backwoods on Susquehanna River at or near the mouth of Conestoga Creek, where he and other land speculators, encouraged by Penn, hoped to establish a settlement and to erect a new city. Lloyd also planned to build a new town in Chester County on the land which he had purchased from the Friend family in 1688. To this tract he had added land acquired from the church wardens of the Swedish congregation, and in 1699 he had laid out plans for a market place and streets. His petition to the Council for permission

to carry out the plans was still pending because of opposition
by Jasper Yeates, a councilman and prominent Anglican, who
objected that the Swedish church wardens had had no right to
sell church land to Lloyd. [8]

Like most landowning colonists, including Quaker merchants,
Lloyd was deeply concerned about the confusion which existed
in the administration of the Proprietor's land policy--a fact
which he had communicated to Penn two years earlier. [9] After
the death of Thomas Holme, Pennsylvania's first Surveyor
General, in 1695, the records of the Pennsylvania Land Office had fallen into incapable hands. Inaccurate surveys had
been made; neighbors had quarreled over the location of property lines; and long delays had occurred in the granting of land
patents to purchasers by Penn's Commissioners of Property.
Books in the Surveyor General's office had lain open and im-
properly kept, subject to erroneous entries and alterations. [10]
Penn's commissioning of Edward Pennington as Surveyor General in 1698 had not been viewed with general satisfaction.
"Oh! the great Confusion, " Lloyd and Quaker merchants had
written to Penn, "that is like to be through the . . . remiss-
ness of the Survey [o]r General with respect to the old Settlers
patents that were called in & resurveys granted to others who
are now like to be ousted of their possessions." Lloyd had
wanted Penn to appoint new Commissioners of Property and
a new Surveyor General, and he had hoped that Penn's return to Pennsylvania would result in the correction of existing
discrepancies in the administration of the Land Office. [11]

Now that Penn was back in the colony old grievances could
be aired with a reasonable expectation that a satisfactory solution could be reached. With the economy in a depressed condition the air was full of grievances. Grain, especially wheat,
which was raised in most of the counties, flour, and bread
had, until 1699, been the chief articles of export, especially
to the West Indies, but scarcity of coin in the West Indies had
resulted in a diminishing demand for Pennsylvania foodstuffs
in that quarter. In 1700, consequently, the agricultural counties of Pennsylvania were in a recession. Trade had turned to
tobacco, but tobacco was grown chiefly in Kent and New Castle
counties, and only the planters in the Lower Counties and the
Philadelphia merchants profited. Even so, insufficient ship-

ping and harbor facilities in Philadelphia resulted in the piling
up of large quantities of tobacco on Delaware River wharves,
and tobacco planters grumbled that the law against piracy deprived them of a lucrative trade through unlawful channels.
Pennsylvania and the Lower Counties had from the beginning
depended on their export trade for the importation of coin, and
with trade declining money was becoming increasingly scarce.[12]

An obvious solution to the congestion on the Delaware River
waterfront was the expansion of existing harbor facilities. David and Thomas Lloyd and other leading Philadelphians had
regarded the cove and beach near Blue Anchor Tavern as a
logical site for a public harbor, but Penn's Commissioners
of Property had frustrated their efforts to develop its potentialities for the public use. The purchasers of the lot on the
beach had long ago finished building their house, and retained
possession of the property. Lloyd and many Philadelphians,
however, still hoped to realize their dream of converting the
beach into a thriving and commercially profitable public harbor. They could do nothing with the Commissioners of Property, of course, but they might still persuade Penn. In October, 1700, Lloyd and several Philadelphia merchants appeared
before Penn and the Council and handed the Proprietor--or
Governor, for he now officiated in that post--a petition signed
by thirty-two Philadelphians including themselves. Lloyd,
speaking for his townsmen, "pleaded that the Landing place in
Debate had been publick from the first settling of the Town &
therefore no private p[er]son ought to take up or appropriate
any thing of the publick to their own private use." He admitted that the public landing place had never been surveyed,
but asserted "that the Town had always claimed it, that they
were Surprized at the Grant [of the lot to private purchasers],
and as soon as p[er]ceived it was likely to be taken away they
by publick Authority opposed it, and still claim it as their
due. . . ."[13] The purchasers of the lot, on the other hand,
contended that the alleged grant of the beach near the Blue
Anchor Tavern to the town of Philadelphia as a public harbor
could not be proved, whereas they had documentary proof of
their grant. The Council subsequently resolved that the disputed lot should be considered public property and that the pur-

chasers should be compensated by the town for their losses.[14] Penn, however, delayed making any final decision.

Penn, in fact, made few decisions during the autumn of 1700 that at all satisfied Lloyd. Even the Assembly, whose Speaker was now Lloyd's father-in-law Joseph Growdon, fell far short of the aggressive Welshman's expectations. Growdon asked Lloyd and John Moore, with whom Lloyd had become quite friendly, to assist the Assembly in preparing legislation--a parliamentary privilege which Penn at long last recognized as belonging to the Assembly. Lloyd and Moore agreed, Penn acquiesced, and in November, 1700, Lloyd and Moore went down to New Castle where the Assembly was in session.[15] Whatever influence Lloyd was able to exert there through his father-in-law and his capacity as legislative adviser did not result in legislation entirely satisfactory to him. The law confirming the property rights of the colonists, the chief legislative enactment of the session and a measure of particular interest to Lloyd, only partly satisfied him. The property law allowed the Proprietor, within two years after its publication, "to resurvey or cause to be resurveyed any person's land within this province or territories [the Lower Counties], allowing four acres in the hundred over or under the difference of surveys, there be more land in the number of acres than the said tract so surveyed was laid out for." It also allowed six acres per hundred of surplus land to freeholders who suffered losses in property owing to the construction through their lands of roads and highways. All surplus lands, it provided further, "shall be to the proprietary, and the possessor thereof shall have the refusal of it from the proprietary at reasonable rates."[16] It contained no guarantees, however, that its provisions would be carried out, and it did not provide for a more satisfactory administration of the Land Office.

Lloyd particularly objected to the price which Penn exacted for the concessions he made in agreeing to the passage of the property law. Penn was heavily in debt and was prepared to make some concessions to the colonists in exchange for money. He had started his Pennsylvania venture on the wrong foot financially. From the very beginning he had indebted himself to Philip Ford, a wealthy London merchant and steward of

Penn's Irish estates. Unable to pay his debt to Ford, Penn, in 1697, had finally consented to give Ford a mortgage on Pennsylvania, after Ford had promised that the mortgage would always be regarded as a "dormant Security" and would never be used to prejudice Penn or his heirs in their pro- prietary rights. Ford had also promised that he would never press Penn for the money but would receive payments in any manner Penn wished to make them, and Penn had agreed that payments would be made from his revenue derived from land sales, rents, and other perquisites accruing to him in Penn- sylvania. The ink had hardly dried on the mortgage papers, however, before Ford had expressed his desire to sell Penn- sylvania. At Penn's urgent request Ford had indulgently given him preference to buy back the proprietary. By a deed, dated April 10, 1697, Ford had agreed to convey the proprietary to Penn on condition that Penn would pay him £12, 714 5s. sterling within three years after the date of the deed, and Penn had paid £157 as a down payment.[17] Penn's revenue from Penn- sylvania, however, had been meager; the colonists had per- sistently refused to pay their quitrents; and Penn had been unable to meet the terms of the mortgage and deed. The three years granted him by Ford had already passed, and Penn's property rights in Pennsylvania were at stake. Ford had granted him a time extension to make good the terms of the deed, and Isaac Norris, who was in Penn's confidence, had suggested to Ford that Penn might raise the money in Pennsylvania, "if he and the People hit it in other matters, " but he had added the warning that "we are poor."[18] In order to secure Penn's approval of the law confirming the property rights of the colo- nists, therefore, the Assembly passed a companion law which appropriated £2, 000 for the Proprietor out of revenue to be collected in property and head taxes.[19]

Lloyd opposed the proprietary tax law from the beginning. Years later he explained his opposition on the grounds that he doubted the authority of the Assembly to make laws as long as it held its sessions in the Lower Counties, where Penn's proprietary title was in doubt.[20] He had, however, assisted the Assembly in preparing legislation at New Castle--an in- dication that he was not as disturbed about Penn's title to the Lower Counties in 1700 as he was in later years. The fact is that the proprietary tax was not at all popular in Pennsylvania. Isaac Norris observed that "malcontents are not well pleased, and some, I hear, endeavour to withstand paying."[21] At a time of depressed economic conditions and of a scarcity of money, the colonists were not happy that their Assembly had taxed them heavily in order to take out of circulation a large sum of money which Penn was more than likely to send to England. Moreover, Penn and the colonists were, as usual, in sharp disagreement over the constitution of the provincial government. Penn did not approve of the Frame of 1696 and wanted to restore the Frame of 1683. The Assembly, however, sought a frame in which its parliamentary privileges would be expanded--a frame which Penn would not grant. Finally the Assembly agreed that Penn should govern according to his charter and the Act of Union until an agreement on a new frame had been reached. Lloyd, who also wanted a new frame, appears not to have believed that the Act of Union, which the Governor, Council, and Assembly had passed in 1682 to unite the Lower Counties to Pennsylvania under a single government, remained in force--at least so he wrote in later years.[22] At any rate, Penn's reluctance to grant a frame which the colonists desired was another reason for the colonists' unwillingness to pay the proprietary tax.

There is little evidence of social intercourse or correspondence between Lloyd and Penn during the fall and winter of 1700. Penn, who was either at New Castle where the Council was in almost continuous session the second half of October and all of November, or at New York where he conferred with other colonial governors, or at Pennsbury, kept in touch with Lloyd's activities through prominent colonists and through his secretary Logan. Lloyd, on the other hand, remained in Philadelphia and made little or no effort to contact his onetime employer. Not until after the tragic death of Lloyd's son does any communication between Lloyd and Penn appear.

Lloyd's little boy Tommy died suddenly in June, 1701. Lloyd and his wife, both away from Philadelphia at the time, left the boy in the care of a kinswoman who evinced a rather extreme conception of how children should be punished. Tommy committed some childish prank which aroused the anger of his caretaker, and the woman locked him up in a closet to teach him better manners. Subsequently, for some reason or other, the woman forgot the child, and, when she finally remembered to release him from his dark prison, he was fatally ill from shock. He died during the morning of June 2 and was buried in the Quaker burial ground on Arch Street. Tommy's death was a blow to both David and Grace Lloyd. Penn, who had been blessed with a son and a grandson within the space of a year, and the Philadelphia Quaker merchants were sympathetic toward the bereaved parents. [23] Penn during the remainder of the summer evinced a more conciliatory attitude toward Lloyd than he had at any time after he had received Quary's memorial against the former Attorney General..

From July to September Lloyd and Penn communicated both directly and through James Logan, who continued to make his home at the Slate-Roof-House in Philadelphia. The messages between Penn and Logan, which mentioned Lloyd, were brief and cryptic and alluded to motions and plans which were not clearly explained, but Lloyd appeared to have been attempting to convince the Proprietor that a constitutional settlement involving the political secession of the Lower Counties from Pennsylvania and a greater measure of legislative autonomy for the province would be to his advantage. In July Penn instructed Logan to hear Lloyd's advice, "and see if a medium can be found." [24] About a month later Lloyd approached Penn with a suggestion which the latter seemed almost of a mind to accept. "David Lloyd," the Proprietor wrote to Logan, "makes a probable motion to me, which hear and consider." [25] Upon further consideration, however, Penn realized that Lloyd's proposals were not entirely consistent with proprietary interests. Still he hoped for a compromise. Early in September he wrote to Logan, "Ply David Lloyd discreetly; dispose him to a proprietary plan, and the privileges requisite for the people's and Friends' security." [26] Lloyd, however, had decided against making any further efforts to settle with Penn personally. He told friends of his unsuccessful negotiations with the Proprietor and made public his views that the Proprietor's prerogatives in the government of Pennsylvania were more limited than Penn cared to admit. "They tell me," Penn wrote to Logan, "what David Lloyd has declared as to my powers in proprietary matters, by which I perceive it is

public. " He instructed his secretary to inform Lloyd, in the
company of Samuel Carpenter and others, of the Proprietor's
views. It was "now or never, " he wrote. He further ordered
Logan that, while Lloyd was pressing his own plans, he should
expedite the Proprietor's affairs "with all possible vigilance
and expedition. "[27]

Lloyd, even though he held no public office, was actually in
a stronger position than Penn. He had a crafty politician's
ability to mobilize public opinion in his favor, and in 1701 he
was riding a wave of antiproprietary sentiment. Colonists were
angry that Penn had persuaded the Assembly to enact a tax
measure at a time when money was scarce. There was grum-
bling that Penn had asked too high a price for land that was
poor and unyielding. Some colonists resented the fact that
Penn, in his eagerness to sell land in the early years of the
province, had made promises which he had not always kept.
Even leading Quakers in England were antagonized by Penn's
failure to keep a promise which he had made to George Fox
in 1681--a promise to give Fox 1, 250 acres of wild Pennsylvania land and a lot and 16 acres in Philadelphia. Fox's
will, drawn up in 1686 but unproved in Doctors' Commons,
bequeathed the deceased Quaker leader's Pennsylvania lands
to his sons-in-law and stipulated that the Philadelphia acreage
should be the site of a Quaker meetinghouse, burial ground,
school, and botanical garden. One of the sons-in-law, Thomas
Lower, who was a friend of the Growdon family, employed
Lloyd to represent the Fox estate in Pennsylvania, but Lloyd
was unsuccessful in his efforts to persuade Penn and the Land
Office to confirm Fox's will. Feeling against Penn ran so high
that most freemen stayed home rather than vote on election
day, a fact which the Proprietor observed was "an ill precedent for elections. "[28]

Lloyd's position was stronger than Penn's also because Penn
was in danger of losing his charter and his doubtful title to
the Lower Counties. Penn was not only unable to pay off the
mortgage Ford held against Pennsylvania, but owed the Crown
£6, 000 in quitrents for the Lower Counties, due from the reign
of James II. The Lords of Treasury had reminded Penn that
continued failure to satisfy the debt might result in his loss of
those counties to the Crown.[29] Furthermore, a powerful anti-

proprietary faction in the English Parliament was attempting
to enact a bill which would convert all proprietary colonies
into royal provinces. Therefore, Penn was faced with the necessity of returning immediately to England to protect his
charter. [30]

By September, 1701, Lloyd had mobilized public opinion to
the point where he could take advantage of Penn's plight to effect constitutional and land reforms at the expense of proprietary prerogatives. On September 18 he and three artisans and
small merchants of Philadelphia delivered a lengthy petition,
containing sixty-eight signatures, to the Assembly and conferred with an Assembly committee at the home of Anthony
Morris. [31]

The petition was a revelation of what Lloyd was after. Generally speaking, he wanted a proprietary grant confirming the
property rights of the colonists and making concessions in land
distribution, a guarantee of municipal interests and improvements in Philadelphia, and a new frame of government. More
specifically, he wanted measures which would most greatly
limit Penn's prerogative in the political, economic, and judicial affairs of the province. He was trying to secure the autonomous interests of Pennsylvania by proprietary grant. To
that end he had mobilized public opinion at a time when Penn
was at a serious disadvantage. One of the requests in the petition was that Penn grant the colonists "Such an Instrument as
may Absolutely secure & Defend us in our Estates & Propertyes
from himselfe his heirs & assignes forever or any claimeing
from under him them or any of them as also to Clear all Indyan
Purchases."[32] In other words, Lloyd and the colonists who
thought as he did wanted the Proprietor to guarantee that the
colonists would be forever protected in their property rights
from himself, his heirs, and his successors, and their intention was probably as much to secure the colonists' property
rights against the possible loss of Penn's charter to the Crown
or to a private creditor as it was to secure them against Penn
and his family. With such a guarantee the colonists would always be able to say, "What has been granted to us we shall
never relinquish."

The contents of the petition showed that Lloyd wanted land
reform above all. He wanted assurances that long delays in

the granting and confirmation of land patents, common in the past, would be avoided in the future and that surveyors' secretaries and other officers in the government who took and exacted fees other than those allowed by provincial law would in the future be punished. Furthermore, he wanted Penn to appoint Commissioners of Property who were "p[e]rsons of Integrity & Considerable known Estates," and to guarantee the enforcement of the property law of 1700. The petition stipulated that "the Tenn Acres in the Hundred may be Allowed According to the Proprietors Engagements."[33]

Only three days before Lloyd and his friends brought the petition to the Assembly, Penn had displayed a tendency to interpret the property law of 1700 in his own favor. He had settled a dispute between two freeholders over the ownership of some overplus land lying between their properties by taking up the disputed tract himself and by offering to sell so much of it as the disputants could pay cash for. Lloyd and his friends considered Penn's action in the dispute a violation of the spirit and intention of the property law, which was to safeguard the interests of the colonists rather than those of the Proprietor. To be sure, the law permitted Penn to take up unclaimed surplus land and to sell it as he wished, and he was probably within his rights in this case. Nevertheless, his handling of the dispute put him in a bad light with the colonists.

Penn, furthermore, had, earlier in the year, erected a special court of inquiry before which he had summoned many colonists to show the titles of the lands which they claimed to own. Colonists resented the erection of the court and its investigatory procedures, and Lloyd and his friends asserted that the court was "Contrary to their [the colonists'] Rights & Privilidges as free born English Subjects And not Warranted by any Law Custom or Usage of this Province as we know of." They asked the Assembly "to Represent the Same as a great Agrievance & Endeavour th[a]t no Such thing be allowed for the future." Certain that Penn had been misled by bad advisers, they requested that the Assembly see to it "that Such person or persons as Advised him to Erect the Court receive such reprehension or other prosecution for such their Ill Advice as you shall think fitt." Moreover, they wanted the Assembly to investigate and determine "by what Authority per-

sons have been sent for by warrants & mandates, Signed
Alleadged by the Gov[e]rnors order to his great Dishonor &
the Infringement of the Subjects Liberty. . . ." Such persons, they said, should "be Examined & receive such Re-
proofe for the same as may deter him or them from such practices for the future."[34] Above all, they wanted a definite assurance from Penn "That no p[e]rson or p[e]rsons shall or
may at any time hereafter be Lyable to Answer any Complaint
matter or thing whatsoever relateing to Property before the
Gov[e]rnor or his Councill or in any other place but in the
Ordinary Courts of Justice."[35]

Lloyd and his friends also desired guarantees of municipal
improvements and rights in Philadelphia. They requested that
Penn confirm the public ownership of the landing places at
Blue Anchor Tavern and Penny Pot House and assure the townsmen that leases would in the future be granted to make enclo-
sures on the town common. The petitioners asked further that
the streets of Philadelphia be regulated and bounded and that
the ends of streets which extended to the banks of the Delaware
and Schuylkill rivers be unlimited so that they might be further
extended into the Delaware River--a necessary prerequisite
to the development of port facilities. They reminded the Assembly also of Penn's long-forgotten and unkept promises that
Philadelphia lots should be rent-free and that county justices
might grant licenses to drinking houses, as was the custom in
England.

The petition contained no details as to the frame of government its signers wanted, but Lloyd and his friends discussed
the proposed new frame with the Assembly committee and
particularly insisted that the mode of government described
in the Frame of 1683 be abandoned. They also persuaded the
Assembly committee that the property law of 1700 should be
inserted in a proprietary grant and that freeholders should
"have Privilidge to purchase of their Quitt Rents as fformerly
Promised as in his [Penn's] Booke Call'd Brieff Account Date
1682."[36] Lloyd and his friends were determined to make all
Penn's forgotten promises valid.

Subsequently, the Assembly committee reported to the Assembly the petition and the additional requests which Lloyd
and the three artisans and merchants had made, and the As-

sembly recommended them to the Proprietor. Penn was greatly
offended by the demands which were thus made upon him. He
told the Assembly that "he would never suffer an Assembly to
intermeddle with his Property, least it should be drawn into
a Precedent, if it should please God, a Gov[erno]r should preside here distinct from the Propr[ieta]ry."[37] Three days before Lloyd and his friends had submitted the Philadelphia petition to the Assembly committee, Penn had told the Assembly,
"Think, therefore, since all men are mortal, of some suitable
expedient and Provision for your safety, as well in your Privileges as Property, and you will find me ready to Comply with
whatsoever may render us happy, by a nearer Union to our Interest."[38] He had meant that the colonists should consider their
privileges, especially their freedom of religious worship, before their property rights. Yet the Philadelphia petition consisted chiefly of demands upon Penn's prerogatives in matters
concerning property.

Lloyd succeeded only partly in forcing his wishes upon Penn
through the medium of a popular petition to the Assembly. The
Proprietor agreed to give the colonists a charter securing
their property rights and preventing delays in the grant of land
patents, but he privately intended that he alone should be its
author. He promised, however, that he would insert the property law of 1700, after if had been amended by the Assembly,
into the charter of property. Furthermore, he confirmed the
public ownership of the landing places at Blue Anchor Tavern
and Penny Pot House and expressed willingness to accept an
act of Assembly establishing fees and perquisites of justices
and other court officers. He refused, however, to part with
his quitrents, to grant away his prerogative in the adjudication of property disputes, or to permit county justices to grant
licenses independently of his prerogative. He asserted, moreover, that he would allow ten acres per hundred of surplus
land only for ends proposed by law. The Assembly remonstrated against Penn's refusal to part with his quitrents, but
the Proprietor was adamant, asserting that he would need the
quitrents if he should ever lose a public support.[39]

With his father-in-law Growdon once again the Speaker
of the Assembly, Lloyd assisted the Assembly in the preparation of legislative bills. The Philadelphia petition had only

The first page of the charter of property, 1701

partly covered the projects that were in his mind. Land reform was his foremost interest, but he also envisaged sweeping judiciary reforms and constitutional revision. The "Act
for Establishing Courts of Judicature in this Province and
Counties Annexed" was his chief legislative contribution in
1701.

Lloyd had been criticized for having burdened the judiciary
act of 1701 with too much detail, [40] but one of the most glaring
deficiencies of the earlier judiciary acts had been the absence
of such detail, and the consequence had been considerable ju-
ristic confusion. The appellate jurisdiction, for example, had
shuttled back and forth in uncertain fashion between a Supreme
Provincial Court, which had only occasionally been in session,
and the Governor and Council. Few cases had ever been addressed to the court of last resort, the King-in-Council. Lloyd,
for the first time in the judicial history of Pennsylvania, clearly defined original and appellate jurisdictions in Pennsylvania
and the Lower Counties and described in detail the functions
of each court in the judiciary system.

In writing the judiciary act of 1701, Lloyd divided the courts
of the province and Lower Counties into two jurisdictions, the
original and appellate. He assigned most original jurisdictions
to the county courts and all appellate jurisdictions within the
geographical limits of Penn's proprietary to the Governor and
Supreme Provincial Court, with the King-in-Council as the
court of last resort. He reserved to the Supreme Provincial
Court the original jurisdiction in criminal cases involving
treason, murder, manslaughter, rape, sodomy, buggery,
burglary, and arson.

Lloyd gave the county courts greater equity jurisdiction
than they had previously enjoyed. In the first years of Pennsylvania, Penn and his Council had exercised chancery powers,
but the trend after the middle 1680's had been increasingly toward the administration of equity by the county courts. [41] The
judiciary act of 1693 had given the county courts equity jurisdiction over cases which involved less than £10. [42] The act
written by Lloyd in 1701 eliminated that restriction and authorized the county justices "to hear and decree, all such matters
and causes of equity as shall come before them" and "to force
obedience to their Decree in Equity, by Imprisonment, or Se-

questration of Lands, as the case may require."[43] Hence,
Lloyd conceived the administration of equity as the exclusive
original jurisdiction of the county courts.

Lloyd, recalling the dispute between the Philadelphia County
Court of Quarter Sessions and the Court of Vice-Admiralty in
1698, endeavored to describe those maritime cases which he
believed were properly within the jurisdiction of the county
courts. Provincial and Crown authorities still did not agree
as to the extent and limitation of the Vice-Admiralty Court
jurisdiction within the geographical limits of Penn's proprietary. Penn, eight months earlier, had contended, in a letter
to the Lords of Admiralty, that the jurisdiction of the Vice-
Admiralty Court was limited to trade and piracy and did not
extend to actions of merchants and others suing for provisions
furnished to, or work done for, seagoing vessels.[44] Lloyd went
even farther, however, when he entered a clause in the judiciary act of 1701 which authorized county justices to adjudicate
all maritime cases within their jurisdictions which were "by
the laws and usage of the Kingdom of England, not within the
Cognizance and proper jurisdiction of the Admiralty." Moreover, he specified that the trial of causes between merchants
and seamen should be by a jury of their peers, that is, by
"twelve Indif'erent Merchants, Masters of Vessells, or Ship
carpenters, as the case may require," or by twelve other "law-
full men of the neighborhood."[45]

Lloyd described five kinds of county courts in the judiciary
act of 1701: general sessions, quarter sessions, common pleas,
biennial orphans' courts, and justices of the peace. He detailed
the times of the year in which each court should be in session
and the duties and functions of each court, and he inserted a
clause allowing the county justices to create special courts
whenever the need for them should arise.

Although Lloyd wrote the judiciary act of 1701 so as to permit each court, county and provincial, to make its own rules,
he added certain limitations upon the courts' rule-making powers. One limitation prohibited the courts from exacting greater
fees than were allowed by the law of the province. The courts,
however, could set fees which were not otherwise provided for
by an act of Assembly. Another limitation prevented the courts
from making rules which debarred persons from holding public

office within the jurisdiction of the courts merely because they could not for conscience's sake swear oaths. Lloyd also added a clause instructing county justices to observe as nearly as possible "the methods and practice of the Kings court of common pleas in England, having regard to the Regular process and proceedings of the former county courts, always keeping to Brevity, plainess and verity, in all Declarations and pleas, and avoiding all Fictions and Colour in pleadings."[46] At this point he evinced a dislike of such fictions as ejectment which had been developed in English legal practice as a substitute for real actions because it required few writs and because the form was always the same. Fictitious allegations, however, often led to injustices and to prolonged and costly litigation. Sir Edward Coke, the great defender of the common law in the late sixteenth and early seventeenth centuries, had opposed the fiction of ejectment,[47] and many colonists, like David Lloyd, preferred real actions. Nevertheless, many colonial justices, who were not sufficiently versed in the law to know the many kinds of writs required in real actions, preferred fictions because of the simplicity of procedure in fictitious actions. Lloyd attempted to circumvent this difficulty by including in the judiciary act of 1701 a detailed description of the forms of writs used in real actions.[48]

Lloyd, furthermore, wrote into the judiciary act of 1701 a clear description of the process of appeal from the county courts. The aggrieved party was to appeal first to the Governor whom the act empowered to grant all remedial writs. The writ granted was then to be heard before the provincial court-- any two provincial justices constituting a quorum--which would then render judgment. If the provincial court rendered judgment against the appellant, the appellant could then appeal to the King-in-Council, and there was no limit of money value in cases appealable to this court of last resort. If the appeal to the King-in-Council should fail, then the appellant would have to comply with the sentence or judgment originally imposed against him by the court in which the original action was instituted.[49]

Lloyd also took pains to account for the shortage of clerical help and attorneys trained in England. The inadequacy of existing clerical help and attorneys resulted frequently in techni-

cal and mechanical errors in the preparation of writs and
other legal papers--errors which all too often led to injustices
because of legalistic technicalities. Such injustices were not
limited to the colonies; the common law process in England
was often cluttered up with legalistic technicalities because
of errors committed in local courts. [50] Lloyd, who, like most
English colonists everywhere, was impatient with legal technicalities, hoped to eliminate such discrepancies in Pennsylvania
legal process by clearly defining the limitations of writs of
error. [51] The conscious selectivity and reforming tendencies
of such a trained lawyer as Lloyd in his adaptation of the English common law to colonial jurisprudence have generally been
overlooked by historians. Historians of Anglo-American law
have too uncritically accepted the opinion of a New Hampshire
judge that "the ignorance of the first colonists of the Common
Law" resulted in the loss of "a great mass of antiquated and
useless rubbish" and in the gain of "a course of practice of
admirable simplicity. "[52] Certainly this judgment did not hold
true for colonial Pennsylvania during the formative period of
her law and jurisprudence.

Lloyd entered a clause in the judiciary act of 1701 authorizing the Governor to grant writs of error, but he stipulated that
the Governor could grant such writs only when errors were
in law, not when errors were clerical mistakes, technical de-
fects in pleas, process, or pleading, or want of form in any
writ, return, bill, plaint, declaration, pleadings, verdict, or
proceedings. [53] This stipulation supplemented and extended the
clause in the "Laws Agreed upon in England, " passed by Penn
and the first purchasers in 1682, which required "That all
pleadings, processes, and records in courts, shall be short,
and in English, and in an ordinary and plain character, that
they may be understood, and justice speedily administered. "[54]

Lloyd entered another clause in the judiciary act of 1701
authorizing the Governor to grant writs of habeas corpus and
all other remedial writs without unnecessary delay. All of
these writs were to be heard and adjudicated by the Supreme
Provincial Court. [55] Hence, Lloyd's intention was that the Governor's function in the appellate jurisdiction should be limited
to the issue of remedial writs and to the transmittal of appeals
to the Supreme Provincial Court. Thereby he denied the Gover-

nor powers of adjudication in appeals from the county courts. He did not mention the Provincial Council anywhere in the judiciary act of 1701.

Lloyd described the Supreme Provincial Court as consisting of five justices, appointed by the Proprietor, who were to hold two sessions a year at Philadelphia and whose jurisdiction was to extend over the entire province and Lower Counties. He was aware, however, of the hardships endured by the poorer colonists who had been required to travel long distances to Philadelphia in order to appeal decisions rendered by the county courts, and he desired to bring justice as cheaply as possible to the very doorstep of every colonist. Therefore he made the Supreme Provincial Court a circuit court which was to hold sessions annually every spring and fall in every county. [56]

Although Lloyd recognized the prerogatives of the Proprietor in the erection of courts and the appointment of justices, his judiciary act of 1701 constituted a considerable abridgment of the Proprietor's powers in judicial matters. He deprived Penn of the authority to adjudicate appeals from the county courts, either by himself or through his Deputy Governor. Lloyd's carefully detailed description of the dates of session, the jurisdiction, the duties, and the functions of each court indicated that he desired the judiciary to be administered by the Act of Assembly rather than by proprietary instructions, executive writs, or the arbitrary demands of a Deputy Governor. He concluded the judiciary act of 1701 with a clause repealing all former judiciary laws. [57]

After Lloyd had completed the judiciary act of 1701 and the Assembly had passed it, his services in the preparation of legislative bills were over. The Assembly rewarded him by giving him an order upon the Provincial Treasurer for £50. [58] Lloyd's activities as a popular leader and unofficial lawmaker, however, had earned for him the opprobrium of the Proprietor's friends, including the Provincial Treasurer, Samuel Carpenter, whose partisan Lloyd had been five years earlier. Carpenter refused to honor the Assembly's order until Lloyd had made a formal application to the Governor and Council for his salary as an employee of the Assembly. Either Lloyd made no such application, or he was turned down. At any rate, the Assembly construed the incident as an affront to its authority,

and it ordered Carpenter to appear before it and to account for
his refusal to comply with the Assembly's order for the payment of Lloyd. The Assembly then served a note upon Carpenter for £50 payable to Lloyd. Carpenter said that if Lloyd
brought him the note in person he would pay it. Lloyd did not.
So the bickering went, back and forth, but Carpenter never released the desired money from the provincial treasury. Finally,
the Assembly had to rely on its own resources, and it paid
Lloyd twenty pieces of eight, Spanish coin being more readily
available to the colonists than English pounds sterling. [59]

Penn, pressed for time and hastily concluding his business
in the province before leaving for England, formally approved
passage of the judiciary act of 1701 on October 28, even though
by so doing he signed away important prerogatives in the provincial judiciary system. But throughout the month of October
he evinced great reluctance to grant away any other of his prerogatives, as requested in the petition which Lloyd and his
Philadelphia friends had submitted to the Assembly several
weeks earlier. He bickered with the Assembly all month before finally yielding to the pressure of circumstances and to
Lloyd's insistence, and he signed and sealed the Frame of 1701
on the same day that he approved passage of the judiciary act
of 1701. [60]

There is no agreement among historians as to the authorship of the Frame of 1701, [61] and there is no evidence that Lloyd
participated in its preparation, aside from persuading Penn to
abandon the political experiment which he had initiated in 1682.
The Harringtonian devices that had characterized the Frames
of 1682 and 1683--the bicameral legislature featuring a powerful Council, the ballot, indirect election, and rotation--were
omitted in the Frame of 1701. Moreover, the new Frame constituted an important advance over the Frame of 1696, which
Lloyd had supported before Penn's return to Pennsylvania, in
that it gave the Assembly even greater powers than it had enjoyed after 1696. It constituted the Assembly as a unicameral
legislature and gave formal recognition to the parliamentary
privileges which it had claimed for itself in the past--the choice
of its own Speaker, Clerk, and other officers, self-adjourn-
ment, appointment of committees, preparation of legislative
bills, impeachment of criminals, judgment of the qualifications

and elections of its own members, and the redress of grievances. [62] The powers given to the Assembly by the Frame of
1701 were the realization of Lloyd's wishes during and after
Pennsylvania's experience with royal government.

More important to Lloyd was Penn's extreme reluctance to
grant away any of his proprietary rights in so far as they concerned his land, quitrents, and administration of the Land Office. Penn insisted that he alone should prepare the charter of
property, which Lloyd and other Philadelphians had requested
in their petition to the Assembly. But he would not let the Assembly see the document and objected that the Assembly was
amending the property law of 1701 without his personal direction. He and the Assembly were entirely unable to agree on
the amount of surplus land he should grant to the colonists.
Penn was willing to grant no more than was allowed by the
property law of 1700; the Assembly wanted to amend the law
so that every freeholder in the province would have a 10 per
cent share of land declared surplus after surveys. [63] By the
time Penn went down to New Castle to await embarkation on
a ship bound for England, it appeared that no settlement was
to be made between himself and the colonists as to the desired
land reforms. Lloyd then resolved to take matters into his
own hands.

On October 29, Lloyd, Isaac Norris, and other Philadelphians followed Penn and his family to New Castle, determined to obtain from the Proprietor not only the charter of
property but other grants and economic benefits, while they
still had the opportunity. Lloyd had already written a draft of
the proposed charter of property, and he brought it to New
Castle with him. He did not approach Penn directly, however.
Instead, he sent friends with the charter of property, and they
urged Penn to sign it. Harassed and hurried, Penn did not have
time to read the document carefully, but he signed it with reservations. He appended to the document an agreement in his
own handwriting in which he explained that he lacked time "to
digest and thoroughly consider the Charter of Property in all
the branches of it, especially in point of courts, and powers
therein expressed." [64]

Lloyd's purpose in writing his proposed charter of property
was to settle "whatever related to the Proprietor's Lands &

his Proprietary Powers, & divers powers of Government in
the manner of a Corporation."[65] Only a portion of the document remains, and the only reference to the "divers powers
of Government" is a clause which states that the Proprietor,
his heirs, lieutenants, or commissioners "w[i]th the Consent
of the General Court herein after mentioned Shall . . . divide
the residue of the s[ai]d Countrey [Pennsylvania] into more
countys as Occasion Shall from time to time require."[66] There
is no other mention of the "General Court" in the remnant, and
one can only surmise that what Lloyd had in mind was the erection of a corporate colony similar to Rhode Island but under
the aegis of the proprietary charter. The passage just quoted
strongly implies that Pennsylvania's undeveloped western lands
were to be politically organized by the joint action of the Proprietor and his deputies, on the one hand, and the colonists
through a "General Court," on the other--the Proprietor being
precluded from making any decision as to his own proprietary
lands without the consent of the "General Court." If this is what
Lloyd had in mind--and the evidence, although scanty, indicates
something of the sort--then the idea was indeed a revolutionary
one.

The existing remnant of Lloyd's draft of a charter of property
consists almost entirely of a redefinition of property rights
within the context of the proprietary colony. Lloyd accepted
Penn's charter of 1680/81 as the basis of the colonists' property rights and as the authority for the geographical extent of
the province. Moreover, he accepted the traditional feudal
relationship between the King, the Proprietor, and the colonists. The Proprietor held of the King, and was, therefore,
beholden to him. The colonists held of the Proprietor, and
were, therefore, beholden to him. The King, however, was
the supreme monarch, and both the Proprietor and colonists
were, in the last analysis, subject to his will. Lloyd accepted
these feudal relationships, as modified by the seventeenth-century conception of the monarch, but his proposed charter of
property indicated that he wished to deprive the Proprietor
of some feudal prerogatives which proved inconvenient to the
colonists and to establish in their stead more modern concepts
of property.

One of the feudal prerogatives, which Lloyd's draft of a charter of property denied the Proprietor, was the right of escheat in cases of felony and death intestate. As things were, property belonging to a person convicted of a felony or to a person who died without having made a legal provision for the posthumous disposal of his estate automatically became the possession of the Proprietor by right of escheat. Lloyd substituted for the right of escheat the modern concept of fee simple. He stipulated that lands owned by persons without heirs or assigns should revert to the person or persons who had originally sold or otherwise deeded the lands to the deceased. For example, X sells one hundred acres of land to Y. Y subsequently dies intestate. Customarily the Proprietor would claim possession of the land by right of escheat. Lloyd, however, would have had the land revert to X, who might be the Proprietor or any other landowner in the province. Moreover, Lloyd provided that lands belonging to persons convicted of felony should go, not to the Proprietor by right of escheat, as was the custom, but to the relatives of the convicted felon, as if no felony had been committed. [67] These clauses in Lloyd's proposed charter of property supplemented a clause in the Frame of 1701, which provided that the estate of a freeholder who died by casualty, accident, or suicide should revert to the family of the deceased rather than to the Proprietor by right of escheat--an indication of Lloyd's influence in the making of the Frame. [68] All of these clauses constituted an establishment of the idea that property belongs to its owner, heirs, and assigns forever, as well as a deprivation of the Proprietor's right of escheat.

Much of Lloyd's draft of a charter of property consisted of confirmations of certain classes of land titles and protections against certain Land Office practices which he believed to be unjust. In writing this portion of the document Lloyd no doubt had in mind his own doubtful title to the church lands in Chester, which he had purchased from the Swedish church wardens in 1693, and to the land he had obtained from the Friends in 1689. [69] But he also had in mind the titles of old settlers to lands which they had taken up or had occupied before Penn had received his charter in 1680/81. He wrote into the proposed charter a confirmation of all land titles that had been obtained by purchase, gift, grant, or assurance by any person or persons from any religious meeting or congregation, town, or

county, and titles to lands that might in the future be sold
or otherwise might be disposed of to any person or group. Also,
he entered a confirmation of all property rights which antedated Penn's charter. He realized, however, that the latter
confirmation, if unqualified, would conflict with acquisitions
made by others after 1681. Therefore, he added that property
rights antedating Penn's charter should be confirmed only if
the instruments of grant, sale, or conveyance had been properly validated with the great seal of the province.

Lloyd also wrote a clause that deprived the Proprietor,
his agents, and commissioners of the right to vacate any grant,
patent, or conveyance of any lands, tenements, or heredita-
ments because some legal form or technicality had been omitted
in the transaction. Freeholders, as he saw it, should not have
to suffer for the want of skilled and efficient law clerks and
attorneys to prepare and complete properly the forms used in
land transactions. Another clause, written by Lloyd, implied
that the Land Office had permitted certain privileged landowners to take up more lands than were described in their
original patents. The clause prohibited the allowance to such
privileged landowners of surplus lands provided for by the
property law of 1700, as it had been amended by the Assembly.

Lloyd, in another part of his draft, prescribed certain liberties and prohibitions on the part of the colonists in the uses of
proprietary lands. He envisioned a public domain that would
be used to advance the public interest. He desired the free public use of harbors, ports, bays, waters, rivers, isles, and in-
lets, and he wished the Proprietor to give the colonists the
public right to establish ferries and to erect bridges for the
public use. Whatever was requisite to the public interest should
be kept out of private hands. He meant this rule to apply only
to proprietary lands, however, not to lands owned by individual
colonists. He provided for the free private use of all water-
ways, landings, woods, meadows, wild life, quarries, and
minerals which were located on lands owned or rented by the
colonists. There was a place in Lloyd's socioeconomic views
for both public enterprise and private initiative coexisting to
their mutual advantage, but his stipulation was that whatever
was used in the public interest would have to be at the Proprietor's, not the colonists', expense.

Lloyd added several prohibitions to the protections and liberties which he desired the Proprietor to grant the colonists. A clause in his draft of a charter of property denied the confirmation of land titles to any person or persons for a greater quantity of land than was allowed by proprietary grant or sale and by the amended property law of 1700. One effect of this clause would have been to prevent squatting on proprietary lands which Penn had not yet sold or otherwise disposed of, but whether there was a tendency on the part of immigrants at this early date to settle on western lands without purchasing or obtaining a proprietary grant to them is not clear.[70] At any rate, it was clear that Lloyd wanted a well-regulated land administration in which every acre of land would be accounted for by legal title, deed, grant, or other conveyance.

Lloyd, in preparing his draft of a charter of property, wrote only of the proprietary lands in Pennsylvania. Penn objected to Lloyd's exclusion of the Lower Counties and promised that he would grant them a charter of property, "if they require it from me."[71] He did not mention his own draft of a charter of property, which he had refused to show the Assembly earlier in the month, and indications were that he had changed his mind about granting any such charter at all. He agreed, however, to suspend for six months a final decision on the proposed charter of property, written by Lloyd. Then he would either sign it or reject it, depending on whether "affairs at home require us to change measures for the general good." He nevertheless confirmed as much of the charter as related to land titles, but he declined all portions of it which tended to deprive him of his proprietary prerogatives, evidently because he thought them dangerous to the entire colony as well as to himself.[72] He was not prepared to accept Lloyd's plan for the administration of proprietary lands. He had already endeavored to safeguard his proprietary rights by giving his secretary James Logan full powers, by his commission, to administer the proprietary land policy, the Land Office, and the Surveyor General's office. According to the commission, Logan could investigate all land titles and claims in the province and Lower Counties, grant resurveys, draw up land patents and grants, collect quitrents, and sue for the recovery of rents owed the Proprietor by colonists who refused to pay them.[73]

Penn signed all of his principal grants to the colonists in
1701 during the last three days he was on American soil. He
granted a charter that incorporated Philadelphia as a city,
gave extensive judicial and economic powers to the mayor and
aldermen within the city and county of Philadelphia, allowed
the popular election of the Philadelphia County Sheriff, and
permitted inhabitants of the city to purchase freeman status
from the city corporation. He also granted a charter to the
townsmen of Chester, raising their town to borough status.[74]
Moreover, Lloyd and other colonists took full advantage of
Penn's haste to obtain from the harassed Proprietor other
grants that had more to do with their own private business
interests than with political and land reforms.

On October 31 Lloyd and several of his business associates
in the Susquehanna Land Company persuaded Penn to sign a
list of concessions for the development of the company's tract
on the Susquehanna River near Conestoga Creek. These concessions authorized the company to lay out townships of not
more than six thousand acres each and individual farms of not
more than five hundred acres each. The entire tract was to
be organized as a county, and after fifty families had settled
thereon they were to be authorized to elect two persons to represent them in the Assembly. When the population should grow
to one hundred families, the county was to be represented by
four members of the Assembly. County courts were to hold
their sessions in the chief town of the tract, and the Proprietor
was to grant a charter for the town's government. The concessions gave each purchaser all mines found in his land, but
reserved two-fifths of valuable minerals extracted therefrom
to the Proprietor, clear of reservations due to the Crown. All
lands were guaranteed freed from Indian claims by the Proprietor, and purchasers were authorized to make roads and bridges
to their tracts from the older settlements. Lands adjoining
roads and highways leading to the Susquehanna tract were to be
settled by persons who would erect and maintain inns and stages
for the accommodation of travelers to and from the tract. Purchasers were to set up a committee to survey, allot, bound,
and regulate the lands, towns, and lots in the tract, to lay out,
mark, and clear the roads, to make bridges, and to do whatever else should be necessary to carry out their purposes.[75]

As these concessions indicate, Lloyd and his associates envisioned an ambitious program of land speculation on the Susquehanna and intended to control the political organization of
the tract as it became populated.

Lloyd and Isaac Norris attempted to obtain from Penn a
settlement with the Thomas Lloyd estate. Complaining that
Thomas Lloyd's estate "was greatly Impaired and his Debts
are still unsatisfied," because the deceased had not received
a compensation for his services in the provincial government,
they urged Penn to give them "an ord[e]r to Receive So much
out of the tax or Impost mony as may pay what may be judged
Reasonable for us to have. . . ." How much that would be was
to be decided by friends chosen by themselves and Penn. The
two executors of the Thomas Lloyd estate also asked Penn to
grant them 1,000 acres on Indian River in Sussex County to
make up for an equal amount of land which had been taken from
them by the Marylanders in the unsettled border dispute between Penn and Lord Baltimore. The Proprietor agreed to
give Lloyd and Norris 1,000 acres in some place other than
Indian River, but he refused to grant away any part of his im-
posts and tax revenue, saying, "What I have not received I
cannot pay. I am above all the mony for Lands I have Sould
twenty thousand pounds sterling out of purs upon Pensilvania. . . ."[76]

While Lloyd and other colonists were trying to get concessions in land and political privileges from Penn, Penn himself was hoping to get sufficient revenue from the £2,000 proprietary tax law, for which collection machinery was being
set up, and from other sources to pay off his debts to the Crown
and to Philip Ford. The Proprietor had asked the Quakers to
raise a private subscription of £1,000 for him in meetings,
and he had instructed his Commissioners of Property to sell
as much land as possible, "while land is high and valuable.
. . ."[77] After he was at sea, on November 3, he sent instructions to Logan to "get in quitrents; sell lands according to my
instructions to my commissioners; look carefully after all
fines, forfeitures, escheats, deodands, and strays, that shall
belong to me as proprietor and chief governor," indicating
thereby that he did not intend to give up such feudal prerogatives as the right of escheat in spite of his promises. He wanted

the province and Lower Counties to be resurveyed "in the most frugal manner, " and he hoped that the Assembly would assume responsibility for paying the Deputy Governor's and Attorney General's salaries. He wanted economy and increased revenue as means of getting himself out of debt. [78]

Lloyd was not happy that Penn had left the colony without signing and affixing the Great Seal of Pennsylvania to his draft of a charter of property. He had more at stake in land reform than in any other reform won by the colonists during the last four days in October. He resolutely opposed paying the proprietary tax which was about to be collected, and he was not alone in his opposition. Trade with the West Indies was dead, and money was scarcer than ever. For that reason alone colonists resented Penn's demands upon them for money. According to Logan, even one of the proprietor's old friends "refused to subscribe one farthing" to the money being collected at Quaker meetings for Penn. [79] Moreover, Logan reported that Lloyd campaigned against payment of the proprietary tax by spreading false reports in Chester County that Penn had not affixed the Great Seal of Pennsylvania to the Frame of 1701 and other grants and had "made a sham of the whole. "[80] Lloyd, eight years later, denied Logan's allegations when they were revived but admitted that many colonists had opposed the proprietary tax because they had not been able to "get allowances upon resurveys, as the law directed, nor confirmations of their legal and equitable claims to their lands and estates, being the consideration for which that tax was granted. "[81]

Penn did not take a copy of Lloyd's draft of a charter of property to England with him, but he had ample time on board ship to reflect upon the experience of his last four months in Pennsylvania. He was bitter. "God forgive those wretched people that have misused me so, " he wrote to Logan in January, 1701/2. [82] He asked Logan to send him a copy of the proposed charter of property and instructed his newly appointed Deputy Governor, Andrew Hamilton, a Scotsman who was also the Governor of East and West New Jersey, to do nothing about the proposed charter of property until further notice. After Penn had received and read the document, he made his final decision. He sent Logan his total rejection of the proposed grant which Lloyd had tried to force upon him. [83]

From Lloyd's point of view, Penn's rejection of the land reforms contemplated in the proposed charter of property rendered incomplete the reforms of 1701. The constitution had been revised, a new judiciary law was on the books, Philadelphia had a new charter, and the Assembly had more parliamentary privileges than ever before. But Lloyd had failed in his greatest endeavor--to obtain from Penn a grant to the colonists of much of his proprietary rights over Pennsylvania lands.

# 10. Lloyd's Wealth and Popularity Grow

By 1702 Lloyd was already one of the most important land-owners and speculators in Pennsylvania. Besides his extensive land holdings in Chester County, on the Susquehanna River, and in Merion Township, acquired before 1700, he had pur-chased, or had otherwise obtained title to, 1,800 acres of un-surveyed land in the Welsh Tract, and property in the city of Philadelphia. He rented out a Philadelphia house to William Bradford, printer for the Society of Friends, at £6 sterling per annum and owned, besides his own home, a lot on Fifth and Walnut Streets. In May, 1702, he purchased 1,000 acres of land in Bucks County, and he later had his title transferred to an equal amount of land in Chester County. In September he obtained a deed for four lots in Philadelphia and subse-quently sold those lots and the lot on Fifth and Walnut to a mer-chant for £83 6s. 8d. Lloyd also acquired from his father-in-law Growdon a deed for 666 acres of land in Sussex County.[1]

Land values were increasing rapidly because of the demand from incoming settlers, and Lloyd and other landowners ex-pected to profit from them. Lloyd, Logan, Penn, and the Phila-delphia merchants anticipated considerable returns on their Susquehanna investment, and Lloyd had taken particular care to obtain concessions from Penn which would further the devel-opment of the project and enhance its value. They needed more money, however, to carry out their plans, and subscriptions were hard to get. Colonists and immigrants evinced little en-thusiasm for subscribing to a colonizing project so far to the

west, and Lloyd and other company officials were too pressed
by their other affairs to push sales.[2]

Most of Lloyd's land was in Chester County, for which he
had a decided preference, and there he could expect to make
more than a comfortable living by speculating in land. Economic conditions, however, were not good. Trade continued to be
dull, and money, aside from that brought in by immigrants
and attracted from neighboring colonies by the high valuation
the Pennsylvania Assembly placed on coin, was as scarce as
it had been for several years past. There was no market for
wheat in the West Indies, and prices had fallen so low in that
area that goods purchased in Pennsylvania sold at a loss in
Barbados, Jamaica, and other West Indian ports. All trade
in Pennsylvania was "by discount and transfer of debts," and
the Proprietor's tenants paid their rents in wheat. Logan reported to Penn that he could not find one out of ten colonists
who was able to pay his debts.[3]

Lloyd, in spite of the economic depression, continued to
increase both his landed wealth and his influence in provincial
affairs. He was friendly to all and popular, but not in the eyes
of Logan, Penn, and Judge Quary. Logan wrote to Penn, "D.
Lloyd carries smooth, but is the same at heart. He aimed a
home blow at the charter, which would have satiated him with
revenge if it can be done; for it appears to me to be levelled
for thy ruin."[4] Penn wrote to Logan, "A[nthony] M[orris] and
David Lloyd. --Let these ungrateful men see that I suffer for
them . . . they may meet with their match after a while that
have so basely treated me--unworthy spirits!"[5] Judge Quary
was in England making a personal report to the Board of Trade
that "David Lloyd's ridiculing the King's Commission for holding a Court of Admiralty had been proved. . . ."[6]

Such expressions of animosity affected Lloyd very little.
Even while Quary was reporting to the Board of Trade, Lloyd
was in the good graces of John Moore, the King's Advocate
and Deputy Judge of Vice-Admiralty in Pennsylvania. Moore
appointed Lloyd his Deputy King's Advocate, and the City Corporation of Philadelphia appointed both men advocates for the
city. Both Lloyd and Moore were in agreement on important
issues, particularly the constitution of the Pennsylvania judiciary system as Lloyd had described it in the judiciary act

of 1701. Moreover, Moore's correspondence with Judge Quary, the Board of Trade, and other Crown officials during 1702 contained no significant complaints about the government of Pennsylvania--a fact attributable to Moore's close relations with Lloyd that year. [7]

Lloyd owed much of his popularity in 1702 to the widespread antiproprietary sentiment in Pennsylvania caused by the economic depression and the proprietary tax which the Assembly had imposed in 1700 to raise £2,000 for Penn. Many were unwilling to pay the tax, but even colonists who were not opposed to it were, with few exceptions, unable to do so. The Philadelphia merchants, friends of the Proprietor, paid their taxes in money, and some less wealthy colonists paid by distress, that is, they relinquished personal property in lieu of cash. The freemen of Bucks and Chester Counties, however, refused entirely to pay the proprietary tax. One Philadelphian, Joshua Carpenter, the brewer and Anglican brother of the Quaker Provincial Treasurer, hid his plate, pewter, and other valuables, "drinking out of nothing but earthenware," to avoid having to pay his tax by distress, and only the timely intervention of David Lloyd saved him from arrest and imprisonment. [8]

Philadelphians were hard-pressed also because of the smallpox epidemic which ravaged the city during the spring of 1702. Lloyd, who had been stricken during an epidemic of malignant fever three years earlier, endured this new plague unscathed, but his old friend Phineas Pemberton lost his life to it. Growdon contracted the dreaded disease, too, although he survived it, and he turned over his business affairs to Lloyd temporarily. The epidemic was so severe that Logan believed it a contributory factor in the economic depression. [9] Their troubles mounting daily, most colonists were none too happy about the Proprietor's demands upon them for money.

Antiproprietary sentiment was manifest in the City Corporation of Philadelphia. Penn had appointed the mayor, recorder, city clerk, aldermen, and common councilmen before returning to England, but most of the city officials tended to follow the leadership of David Lloyd. Joshua Carpenter, who openly resisted paying the proprietary tax, was an alderman, and the mayor, Edward Shippen, a wealthy Quaker merchant who was usually loyal to Penn, conducted his office in a manner inimical

to proprietary interests. Logan, disappointed by the turn of
events, wrote to Penn that the city charter "which should bind
the people to thee, sets them so much for themselves, that
there is too little regard paid thee, and scarce any to thy interest."[10] Virtually the only members of the corporation on
whom the Proprietor could rely were the recorder, Thomas
Story, a Quaker missionary from England, and the city clerk,
Robert Assheton, a recently arrived trained English lawyer.[11]

Logan's letters to Penn, the chief source for the events of
1702, strongly indicated that Lloyd and his closest associates
were using the Philadelphia city charter as a means of driving
out proprietary influence in the Philadelphia County courts.
The Philadelphia County justices were loyal friends of the
Proprietor, and had issued a warrant for levying the proprietary tax by distress--a warrant bitterly opposed by most Philadelphians, including Joshua Carpenter and Lloyd. Lloyd and
Moore, as advocates for the city, advised the corporation that
the city charter gave the aldermen the right "to act as justices
in the Court of Common Pleas, for both city and county. . . ."[12]
The Philadelphia city charter empowered the mayor, recorder,
and aldermen to act as justices of the peace and of the Philadelphia County courts, specifically naming the courts of quarter sessions, oyer and terminer, and gaol delivery.[13] Although
it did not mention the Philadelphia County Court of Common
Pleas, the inference could be drawn that such had been the
Proprietor's intention. The county justices had asked the city
officials to join them in signing the warrant for levying the
proprietary tax by distress, and one alderman had responded.
The city charter, however, did not state that city officials
should serve as county justices to the exclusion of county justices specifically commissioned as such by Penn. Lloyd was
claiming a right for the aldermen which Penn had not specifically granted them, and by so doing he was attempting to extend further the reforms which he had played a leading role
in obtaining the year before. Deputy Governor Andrew Hamilton, Logan, and "some considerable lawyers" resolutely opposed Lloyd's attempt to make the city corporation supreme
in the county courts. Logan reported to Penn that Lloyd and
Moore "daily blow them up to such mettle, I really know not
what to make of the face of things among us,"[14] and he ac-

cused them of "endeavoring to stop the courts, and procrasti-
nate acts of justice."[15]

Logan believed that Lloyd and Moore were attempting to
give the Crown occasion to take over the government of Pennsylvania by creating disturbances such as those "when the
King took it into his hands before."[16] There was little enthusiasm for proprietary government on the part of either the
antiproprietary colonists or the Proprietor's friends in 1702.
The colonists generally believed that the War of the Spanish
Succession, which began in May, would "oblige the Parliament
to carry on that act annexing the colonies to the Crown, for
their better security and defence. . . ." Friends of the Proprietor, as Logan observed, were "weary and careless on
government," and desired only that Penn "make good terms"
with the Crown for himself and the colonists.[17] Lloyd did not
express any particular preference for either a proprietary
or royal government, but, as had been his wont after 1689,
he indicated that his chief interest was in promoting the autonomous interests of Pennsylvanians.

Lloyd was in favor of electing and organizing a new Assembly
on October 1, 1702, in accordance with the Frame of 1701, so
that he might promote legislation based on his rejected draft of
a charter of property. Penn, however, was opposed to the organization of an Assembly until the Crown had confirmed existing Pennsylvania laws and the new Deputy Governor, Andrew
Hamilton, and he so informed Logan.[18] Nevertheless, the freemen of the province met at their voting places on October 1
and elected four assemblymen from each county and two from
the City Corporation of Philadelphia, as was stipulated in the
Frame of 1701. Nicholas Waln, a Quaker who had formerly
been proproprietary in politics, nominated Lloyd to represent
the city and county of Philadelphia in the Assembly, and Lloyd
received more votes than any other Philadelphia County candidate. The three other representatives of Philadelphia County
elected to serve with Lloyd were the city aldermen, Anthony
Morris and Griffith Jones, and a Philadelphia County justice
of the peace, Samuel Richardson. All four were Quakers, and
Logan complained that they were "the stiffest men" the freemen of Philadelphia County could have chosen.[19]

The day after the election Deputy Governor Hamilton and

his Council, which Penn had appointed and organized by ordinance to represent his interests, met, discussed the election, and concluded that a session of the Assembly was to be avoided. Logan, who had earlier been admitted to participation in Council meetings, "got down stairs and was present" and agreed with the Deputy Governor and Council that the newly elected Assembly should not convene, declaring that "all our study should be only to preserve peace and good order, and prevent occasions of complaint."[20] Lloyd, Morris, Jones, and Richardson immediately retaliated by writing a public notice warning that failure to hold a session of the Assembly would constitute a forfeiture of the colonists'privileges under the Frame of 1701. Lloyd presented the notice to the Philadelphia County Sheriff, who subsequently published it.[21]

The situation was complicated, however, by the refusal of the Lower Counties to accept the Frame of 1701. During 1701 the Lower Counties had expressed a desire to separate from the province and to have a legislature of their own, and Penn had agreed that they could do so, provided that the separation was carried out "upon amicable terms and a good understanding."[22] The Frame of 1701 contained a provision for the eventual legislative separation of the Lower Counties from the Province.[23] The provincial councilmen, who had considerable economic interests at stake in the Lower Counties, feared separation, and their fears were increased by the failure of the Lower Counties to hold an election for representatives in the Assembly on October 1. When the provincial assemblymen met in Philadelphia on October 14, as provided by the Frame of 1701, no representatives from the Lower Counties appeared, and the fourteen members present did not constitute a quorum.[24] Because of the Lower Counties' desire for legislative separation, Lloyd's legislative plans were jeopardized.

# 11. The Lower Counties

Lloyd wanted to effect the legislative separation of the Lower Counties as speedily as possible, so that the provincial Assembly could direct its attention to legislative business. The other provincial assemblymen were in full accord with him. A clause in the Frame of 1701 provided that, in the event the province and the Lower Counties agreed to separate legislatively, the number of provincial assemblymen would be doubled and a separate Assembly would be established in the Lower Counties. Accordingly, Lloyd and other provincial assemblymen recommended that the Deputy Governor and Council increase the representation from each Pennsylvania county by four and recognize the legislative separation of the Lower Counties from the province.[1]

Deputy Governor Hamilton, Logan, and the entire Council absolutely opposed legislative separation. Most of the councilmen were merchants who depended largely on the tobacco trade, and most of the merchantable tobacco was grown in the Lower Counties. Logan collected much of Penn's quitrents in the Lower Counties in the form of tobacco. Because of the strained relations between Pennsylvania and the Lower Counties, the traffic between the Lower Counties and Philadelphia had dwindled to a trickle, and Logan had found it almost impossible to do business with the tobacco planters. Yet, as Deputy Governor Hamilton told the assemblymen, Lower Counties tobacco remained Pennsylvania's "Principal Returns in Trade to England. . . ." He feared that, if the Lower Counties separated legislatively from Pennsylvania, "Traffick would be so Clogg'd & Incumbered that it would be wholly lost to us. . . ."[2] Logan, moreover, feared that legislative separation would play into Judge Quary's hands and would result in the loss of the Lower Counties to the Crown.[3]

The Deputy Governor and his Council, nevertheless, asked the assemblymen to remain in Philadelphia until after they had sent writs of election to the Lower Counties. If the Lower Counties elected assemblymen accordingly, then a full Assembly could be convened. Lloyd stubbornly opposed such a procedure, but the rest of the assemblymen agreed to a month's adjournment to give the Lower Counties time to elect their representatives.[4]

Lloyd continued his opposition, even after the Lower Counties had elected their assemblymen and the latter had appeared in Philadelphia. When the assemblymen from the Lower Counties met Deputy Governor Hamilton, the Council, and the Pennsylvania assemblymen on November 16, Lloyd insisted that the meeting was a convention, not a legislative Assembly. Councilman Thomas Story judged that they could nevertheless act as an Assembly, and the Deputy Governor asked the assemblymen from the Lower Counties and from Pennsylvania on what basis they were willing to come to business as a legislature. Lloyd wrote a reply, signed by ten other provincial assemblymen, including his father-in-law Growdon, that the representatives of the province were "both willing and desirous to proceed in order to act in Assembly, according to the Directions of the Charter [i.e., the Frame of 1701], being the foot on which we conceive ourselves called and convened."[5] The representatives of the Lower Counties refused, however, to cooperate with assemblymen who were elected in accordance with a Frame which they did not recognize. They were, however, "cheerful and willing, when warrantably convened, to proceed in Assembly, to answer her Majesty's Commands, and such other Matters of Importance as shall then be laid before them. . . ."[6] Neither reply pleased the Deputy Governor, who asked once more if the representatives from Pennsylvania and the Lower Counties would act together in legislation.[7]

Both Lloyd and the Deputy Governor had changed their minds about holding an Assembly. Lloyd no longer cared to have an

Assembly convene and seemed willing to postpone his legislative plans for a time. Hamilton, on the other hand, now had a definite need for an Assembly. The War of the Spanish Succession had spread to America, and the French and English were again in conflict on their colonial frontiers. Lord Cornbury, the Governor of New York, was calling for intercolonial cooperation in constructing fortifications at Albany in anticipation of a French-Indian offensive in that quarter. Hamilton had a letter from Lord Cornbury requesting £350 from Pennsylvania, payable by March, 1703.[8] Just as Lloyd had obstructed the appropriation of money for military purposes during King William's War, so he now endeavored to frustrate Hamilton's desire to hold an Assembly in order that Lord Cornbury's request might be satisfied.

Lloyd stubbornly opposed any further consideration of Hamilton's request for legislative cooperation between the Lower Counties and Pennsylvania. Growdon was in agreement with Lloyd, but other Pennsylvania assemblymen appeared willing to compromise. The Lower Counties were decidedly opposed to joining Pennsylvania in convening an Assembly, and Logan supposed that Lloyd and Growdon were "of a party" with the representatives of the Lower Counties. Because of the opposition of Lloyd, Growdon, and the Lower Counties, Hamilton saw no profit in continuing what was clearly a hopeless stalemate, and he dismissed the assemblymen.

Before Lloyd and the other provincial assemblymen dispersed to their several homes, however, they submitted an address to the Deputy Governor, requesting that he recognize the legislative separation of the two sections by doubling the representation from the Pennsylvania counties in accordance with the Frame of 1701, adding an additional member for each of Bucks and Chester counties so that there would be no doubt of a quorum. Lloyd signed this address, but he and his father-in-law abstained from affixing their signatures to an appended memorandum which expressed the intention of Pennsylvania assemblymen to proceed to legislation immediately. Hamilton never agreed to that request.[9]

Lloyd thoroughly disapproved of Hamilton. Hamilton not only prevented the separation of the Lower Counties from Pennsylvania but publicly declared his intention of organizing a militia in the province as soon as his commission had been confirmed by the Queen-in-Council. [10] His want of royal confirmation was his weakness as a Deputy Governor, and Lloyd exploited it in the county courts, where he pointed out that Hamilton was unqualified to act as Deputy Governor because he lacked royal approval as required by the statute of the seventh and eighth of William III. Hamilton, Lloyd said, was only a "Conservator of the Peace."[11]

Surprised and hurt by Lloyd's attack on his authority as Deputy Governor and conscious of the weakness of his own position, Hamilton removed with his wife and family to Amboy in East New Jersey, and Pennsylvania saw no more of him. Penn finally succeeded in obtaining the Queen's approval of Hamilton's commission, but Hamilton died unexpectedly of a fever on April 16, 1703, while still in Amboy. The powers of the Deputy Governor then passed into the hands of the Provincial Council.

The Council was as adamantly opposed to the legislative separation of the Lower Counties from the province as Hamilton had been, not only because of its members' own private interests but also because of the importance of the Lower Counties to Penn's financial affairs. Penn was greatly in arrears to the Crown for the rent of the Lower Counties. His estates in Ireland and England were encumbered, and he had no means of balancing his accounts. Consequently, during the summer of 1703 Penn submitted an offer to the Auditor General of the Plantations to surrender the governments of Pennsylvania and the Lower Counties to the Crown in exchange for a sum of money and satisfaction of his indebtedness for the Lower Counties. [12]

Legislative separation might well jeopardize Penn's title to the Lower Counties and might thereby frustrate his effort to sell the government to the Crown. Nevertheless, Lloyd and his friends decided to take matters into their own hands in achieving legislative separation. On October 1, 1703, they successfully led a movement to implement the article of the Frame of 1701 which allowed the Pennsylvania counties to double their representation in the Assembly if the Lower Counties refused to be represented in the same legislature with the province. Each of the three provincial counties elected eight representatives, four more than in 1701, and with two representatives of the City Corporation of Philadelphia Pennsylvania had a total of twenty-six assemblymen. Meanwhile, the Lower Counties submitted no election returns, and their exclusion from the Assembly was therefore complete.[13] Hence, the election was conducted in such a manner as to present the legislative separation of the sections to the Council as a *fait accompli.*

Philadelphia County once more elected Lloyd to the Assembly and chose other assemblymen who were in full agreement with Lloyd, not only as to the legislative separation of the sections but as to the enactment of Lloyd's draft of a charter of property as provincial law. Lloyd's colleagues of 1702, Griffith Jones, Anthony Morris, and Samuel Richardson, were also re-elected, and they were joined by a city alderman, Joseph Wilcox, a Philadelphia ropemaker, Isaac Norris, Lloyd's coexecutor of the Thomas Lloyd estate, and two others. James Logan, unhappy about the election returns, reported to Penn: "As for David Lloyd, I find he must be in; therefore resolve, as honorably as possible, to fall in with him, it being, as things stand, of absolute necessity."[14]

The antiproprietary victory became even clearer when, on October 5, the aldermen and common council of Philadelphia elected Anthony Morris to the office of mayor and when, ten days later, the Assembly chose Lloyd to take the chair as its Speaker. Logan conceded that, in view of existing circumstances, the elevation of Lloyd to the Speakership "very well befitted for the public good, whatever he might cover underneath."[15]

Lloyd knew from Thomas Lower of Penn's intention to sell the government of Pennsylvania and the Lower Counties to the Crown, but Lower had mistakenly informed him that Penn intended also to sell the Crown his rights to the land. Lower's advice to Lloyd was to settle and secure existing property rights in Pennsylvania, "before any new claimer comes to answer."[16] What Lower did not know, and therefore did not tell Lloyd, was that Penn was attempting to sell the government of the colony to the Crown while retaining his proprietary rights in the land. Penn's proposals to the Crown were that all proprietary rights in the land be confirmed to him and his heirs, that the Crown grant him and his heirs a permanent patent for the Lower Counties, that the form of the provincial government remain unchanged, and "that the laws and constitution thereof be confirmed by the Queen, except such a few as I shall object against." Penn also wanted £30,000, one half-penny per pound on all Pennsylvania and Lower Counties tobacco, and the privilege of nominating the Governor and Vice-Admiral of Pennsylvania. [17]

Lloyd, acting upon Lower's semiaccurate information, moved at once to make the law of the province the articles of his rejected draft of a charter of property. Five days after he became Speaker he sent a committee of assemblymen to procure the draft from the Council. The Council obtained from Logan, the custodian of such important state papers, the draft and Penn's letter rejecting it, but it would not permit Lloyd to have the original documents. Instead it made up copies which were submitted to the emissaries from the Assembly. At the same time it resolved to prorogue the Assembly, which it did not believe was legally convened because it contained no representation from the Lower Counties. [18]

Lloyd, however, anticipated the Council's intention of proroguing the Assembly, and, under his direction, the Assembly resolved to adjourn to May 1, 1704. This move embarrassed the Council. It did not want the Assembly to continue in session when Lloyd and his followers had so clearly revealed their intentions of separating the sections legislatively and of enacting the draft of a charter of property. At the same time, it was unwilling to acknowledge the right of the Assembly to do anything without its authority. The President of the Council asked the Assembly by what right it presumed to adjourn for so long a time, almost six and one-half months. The Assembly thought that the Frame of 1701 gave it the right to sit on its own adjournments during the whole year. The Council denied this. The Assembly could adjourn from morning to afternoon, or from one day to the next, but adjournment from October to May, said the Council, was contrary to the language of the Frame of 1701. The Frame allowed the assemblymen the right "to sit upon their own Adjournments, " but it did not specify that this right could be extended during an entire year; at the same time it did not say that the right could not be so extended.

The Assembly assumed that it could be. The Council based its denial on the fact that no precedent for such a right could be found in English practice or in the practice of any other government. This argument did not appeal to Lloyd and his followers in the Assembly who were setting their own precedents. Further debate seemed futile. Even while Logan was attempting to arrange a meeting of the whole Assembly with the Council, the Assembly disbanded and its members went to their several homes until May 1. Confronted with another *fait accompli*, the Council retaliated in the only way it could, by proroguing the Assembly to May 1--a rather futile gesture.[19]

Lloyd had won a small point, but he was still frustrated in his desire to render into law the land reform schemes he had envisioned in his rejected draft of a charter of property. Penn's anticipated sale of Pennsylvania to the Crown did not materialize, however, because of the objections of the Board of Trade to his demands,[20] and Lloyd's fears for the property rights of the colonists, not to mention his own, were, for the time being, allayed. Property-rights legislation, therefore, could be postponed.

Lloyd, moreover, had not quite succeeded in achieving the legislative separation of the Lower Counties from Pennsylvania. The *fait accompli* which he and his friends had presented the Council in the election of October 1 had not resulted in legislative action, because of the refusal of the Council to cooperate. Lloyd's legislative plans could not be achieved until the separation issue had been satisfactorily resolved.

Penn, meanwhile, took steps to protect his interests in Pennsylvania and the Lower Counties against the encroachments of Lloyd and his following. Negotiations with the Crown were, for the time being, at a standstill, and Penn was eager to improve his relations with Whitehall. Accordingly, he chose a Deputy Governor who had the confidence of Queen Anne--a young army colonel, still in his twenties, who was a staunch protagonist of royal prerogatives. This young man, Colonel John Evans, arrived in Philadelphia on February 2, 1703/4, bearing the approval of the Queen-in-Council and instructions from Penn to "maintain to the utmost the powers of my [Penn's] grant, and the authority of the laws. . . ."[21] Lloyd soon found Evans to be the strongest and most aggressive political oppo-

nent he had faced since the administration of Governor Fletcher.

The change in the administration did not improve Lloyd's
chances of achieving the legislative separation of the Lower
Counties from Pennsylvania. Deputy Governor Evans and the
Council resolved, a few days after Evans' arrival, that "all
Endeavours should be used to keep the whole still united to-
gether, as well in Legislation as administration."[22] Evans
acted immediately to carry out his instructions from both
Penn and the Queen-in-Council to keep the province and the
Lower Counties legislatively united. He enlarged the Council
by appointing two members from Sussex and Kent Counties
to give the Lower Counties greater representation in that body.
Moreover, he added to the Council the Proprietor's secretary,
Logan, the new Attorney General, Roger Mompesson, who
was also the new Judge of the Court of Vice-Admiralty and the
new Chief Justice of the Supreme Provincial Court, and two
rich Philadelphia merchants, William Trent and Richard Hill.[23]
Lloyd had, therefore, to contend with a stronger Provincial
Council, as well as with a stronger Deputy Governor who was,
furthermore, armed with proprietary and Crown instructions
to prevent Lloyd and his followers from achieving their ends.

Lloyd, however, was assisted by Penn's past mistakes and
the reluctance of the Lower Counties to join the Province in a
single legislature. The Lower Counties had not forgotten Penn's
promise, in 1701, to grant them a charter of property, similar
to the draft which Lloyd had prepared for Pennsylvania, and
they wanted land reforms for themselves as much as Lloyd
wanted them for Pennsylvania. The Lower Counties hoped to
achieve land reform through a legislature of their own. Logan
observed this fact and warned Penn that "that unhappy charter
thou granted . . . will, most certainly, utterly separate the
province and territories [Lower Counties], I doubt to our confusion."[24] There was, however, an articulate proproprietary
element in the Lower Counties which encouraged Evans to
make an effort to restore the legislative union of the sections.[25]

Evans, in April, arranged a conference of the provincial
assemblymen and representatives from the Lower Counties
who had been elected by the Deputy Governor's writs. Lloyd,

however, vigorously resisted legislative reunion, and the conference proved a failure. The Lower Counties representatives,
greatly influenced by their proproprietary colleague, James
Coutts, were now willing to accept the Frame of 1701, if they
could have representation in the Assembly equal to that from
the province. Lloyd stoutly opposed their compromise offer. He
asserted that the Pennsylvania assemblymen "were a House of
themselves, & it might they feared infringe their Priviledges
to admit any other."[26] He was unmoved by Evans' warning that
"her Majesty Considers both this province and Territories as
one Intire Governm[en]t, and both the Royal approbation and
my Commission tell me that I ought to use my utmost endeavour to keep them so."[27] Lloyd was, furthermore, unimpressed
by Evans' assertion that "Unity and Concord are the greatest
Cement of Publick Happiness and tis no small part at this time
of the Glory of England, that in the Legislative Powers there
the Parliament is in harmony and Union."[28] In an exchange of
messages, Lloyd and his following urged the Lower Counties
to form a separate assembly of their own.[29] Evans, subsequently, gave up all hope of reuniting Pennsylvania and the
Lower Counties in a single legislature. Advised by Judge Mompesson that the Lower Counties could legally elect a separate
assembly by writs, Evans permitted the sections to separate
legislatively, after recommending that they improve their relations with each other and work toward reunion at some time
in the future.[30]

Lloyd subsequently blamed the Lower Counties for the legislative separation of the sections,[31] but his own persistent efforts to achieve separation so that he might organize an effective legislature in Pennsylvania were the chief cause of the sectional split. He had refused to accept the compromise offer of the Lower Counties and had urged them to form an assembly of their own. Having achieved this goal, Lloyd was now
able to organize his power in the provincial Assembly and to
prepare legislation without obstruction by the Lower Counties.
Other obstacles to the enactment of the legislation he desired
remained, however, to be cleared away.

# 12. The Struggle for Power

Lloyd had already begun to organize his power in the Assembly. At the beginning of the session of 1703-4 he and his followers had formulated rules of parliamentary procedure, modeled upon those of the House of Commons in England, which gave the Assembly a discipline it had not theretofore known. No Speaker before 1704 had enjoyed such powers as those wielded by Lloyd. Earlier nothing had prevented the Assembly from degenerating into a cacophonous Babel, everybody speaking at once in the heat of a passionate and undisciplined debate. Now an orderly procedure during debates obtained. A member who wished to speak arose, addressed the chair, spoke pertinently to the occasion, and upon concluding his speech sat down. No member could speak more than twice on any one matter without the Speaker's express permission. The Speaker tolerated no interruptions while a member held the floor. The rules forbade any member to pervert the sense of another's speech, and the Speaker could require any offending member to stand at the bar and to receive the censure of the Assembly. Members were expressly forbidden by the rules to divulge publicly the debates or secrets of the Assembly.

The rules, furthermore, required every member of the Assembly to respect the person of the Speaker. No member could enter or leave the Assembly room before the Speaker or depart without the Speaker's permission. Members who cast reflections upon or behaved insultingly toward the Speaker or toward any other member could be punished by fines not exceeding ten shillings each. Acts and resolutions were to be passed or defeated by a majority of votes; any matter being debated could be brought to a vote by the request of any four members, and the assemblymen were to vote by standing and by saying yea or nay; but in the event of a tie the Speaker cast the deciding vote.

The Speaker, moreover, was authorized to nominate all committees of the Assembly, and members so nominated were barred by the rules from refusing service. The Speaker, however, could not appoint any member, who was known to oppose a certain bill, to a committee which had that bill under consideration. The rules provided for standing committees to be appointed by the Speaker immediately after election. These were committees to consider commands of the Crown, commands of the Governor, the safety of the government, the preservation of liberty and property, grievances, public and private bills, and petitions.

In June, 1704, Lloyd added to these rules by ordering that all legislative bills should, upon first reading, be committed to the perusal of certain members appointed by the Speaker. These members were to report suggested amendments to the floor of the Assembly, and such amendments were to be adopted only by a majority vote of the Assembly. Amended bills were then to be read a second time, engrossed, and sent to the Deputy Governor. Amendments recommended by the Deputy Governor were to be considered by the Assembly before the third reading of the bill.[1] This ruling enabled Lloyd to achieve an even greater control over legislation than any Speaker had theretofore enjoyed.

Lloyd exercised his power of appointment to consolidate his personal influence over the Assembly's business. He appointed as chairman of important committees such stanch partisans as Anthony Morris, Joseph Growdon, William Biles, a former sheriff of Bucks County who had refused to collect the proprietary tax, and Joseph Wood, a former sheriff of New Castle County who had long been an advocate of the legislative separation of the Lower Counties from Pennsylvania. Lloyd, moreover, did not have the Assembly appoint a clerk, but kept the minutes and performed all the clerical work of the Assembly

himself, thereby further enabling himself to maintain a firm
control over lawmaking and other Assembly business. [2]

Lloyd, however, faced a growing opposition to his challenge
of proprietary authority. The judicial reform, which he had
made the law of the province in 1701, was seriously compro-
mised by an order of the Queen-in-Council, dated January 21,
1702/3, which required all judges to swear and to administer
oaths or solemn affirmations. The order of the Queen-in-
Council further required judges to administer oaths to whoso-
ever wished to swear them. [3] Quaker justices in Pennsylvania
were unable to comply with this order because of their religious scruples, and for that reason the courts were prevented
from proceeding to business. The Bucks and Chester County
courts were completely halted because their justices were all
Quakers. In the Philadelphia County court all the Quaker justices, led by Griffith Jones, had quit the bench in 1703 when
oaths were about to be administered, and only the Anglican justices remained. [4] Lloyd had the Assembly remonstrate to the
Queen that her order effectively excluded the Quakers from
the bench and that, because the Quakers were the most considerable in numbers and estates in Pennsylvania, they could
not afford to lose control of the courts. The Assembly, therefore, asked that the solemn affirmation, as a substitute for
the oath, be required of all persons in Pennsylvania, regardless of their religious faith. [5] The Assembly's remonstrance,
however, was ignored at Whitehall.

Deputy Governor Evans employed the opportunity afforded
by the order of the Queen-in-Council to appoint his Anglican
friends to replace Quakers in the Supreme Provincial Court
and in the Philadelphia County courts. Nevertheless, Lloyd
prepared a legislative bill for the universal substitution of the
solemn affirmation for the oath in Pennsylvania and submitted
it to the Deputy Governor. While Evans was considering the
bill, a letter from Penn arrived, urging the Quaker colonists
to stand up for their privileges in religious matters. "Tho I
would not have my officers & Magistrates walk So near the
Edges & Ridges of the Powers of my Patent & Laws of the
Countrey," Penn wrote, "So neither would I have them be
cowed, while they keep within Compass thereof in the just
Execution of their offices, but assert the powers of my Grant,

& Authority of their Laws, as with wisdom so with Resolution. . . . "[6] The general tenor of Penn's letter indicated that
the Proprietor would support Lloyd's bill for the universal
substitution of the affirmation for the oath, and Evans expressed no aversion to it. Lloyd, however, had presented
the bill as a clause in a larger bill for the regulation of the
courts, and it was only too evident that he was attempting not
only to restore the judicial reforms of 1701 but to increase
local autonomy in the regulation of the Pennsylvania judicature.
Consequently, Evans requested that the bill for the universal
substitution of the affirmation for the oath be presented as
entirely separate legislation, and he promised "to use his Endeavours to get such a Bill to pass at home. "[7] Responsibility
for persuading the Crown to approve the universal substitution of the affirmation for the oath was subsequently passed
on to Penn, who had little luck with it. [8]

Another formidable obstacle to Lloyd's efforts to organize
his power, to increase the autonomous control of Pennsylvania's institutions, and to enact his legislative program, was
Penn's claim to a veto power in legislation. There was no provision for such a veto power in either the Frame of 1701 or
provincial law. A clause in Evans' commission, however, reserved to the Proprietor veto power over all provincial legislation. This was an effective barrier to any acts of Assembly
Lloyd might attempt to secure, for such legislation would have
to pass the test of three veto powers--that of the Deputy Governor, that of the Proprietor, and that of the Queen-in-Council.
Logan had rightly predicted that Penn's claim to a veto power
would cause trouble, although he had felt that the Proprietor
should exercise such power over legislative bills which concerned his own property rights. [9]

Lloyd, on May 12, 1704, convened the Assembly as a committee of the whole, and, mounting the rostrum as its chairman, he expostulated at length concerning Penn's assumed
veto power. It seemed hard enough to him that all legislation
had to be sent to England anyway for royal confirmation. That
acts of Assembly would have to be submitted to proprietary
review before they could be reviewed by the Queen-in-Council,
he argued, would only increase delay and uncertainty in provincial legislation. Gubernatorial commissions, he asserted,

were of the nature of royal writs, and no part of them could be voided without the whole being voided. [10] Lloyd appeared to be hoping that the invalidity of the veto clause would vacate Evans' commission entirely.

Judge Mompesson entered the meeting house when Lloyd was speaking to the committee of the whole. He thought the procedure employed by the Speaker in convening the Assembly as a committee of the whole highly irregular, but he heard Lloyd's speech through and reported it to Evans. Evans discussed the matter with his Council, and the latter concluded that the clause in the Deputy Governor's commission, which reserved to Penn a veto power in legislation, was null and void, but it denied Lloyd's argument that the entire commission was vacated on that account.

Lloyd, meanwhile, obtained from the Assembly a resolution to the Deputy Governor and Council which requested the Council's opinion in writing as to the validity of the controverted clause. The Assembly also wanted to know whether Penn, after having approved and sealed legislation, could subsequently vacate and annul such legislation. The Council put the conclusion it had already reached into writing and added that Penn could not lawfully vacate laws which he had already approved and sealed. Among those who signed this opinion were Logan, Mompesson, and William Penn, Jr. Evans abstained. [11]

Armed with the Council's written opinion, Lloyd appointed his father-in-law and another member of the Assembly to prepare an address to Penn complaining of the veto clause in Evans' commission. The address indicated that Lloyd wanted Penn to forego any further claim to a veto power in legislation and that he did not intend to press for the vacation of Evans' commission because of the voided clause. The address indicated further that Lloyd wanted Penn to use his influence to secure the Queen's approval of the laws passed in 1701 and that he especially desired the Queen's allowance of the universal substitution of the affirmation for the oath in Pennsylvania. [12] Penn made no further effort to assert his claim to a veto power in legislation.

By May, 1704, the artisans, tradesmen, and farmers of Pennsylvania generally regarded Lloyd as their leader, and they turned to him and his following in the Assembly for the

redress of their grievances and for the protection of their
economic interests. Philadelphia shoemakers and saddlers
requested a law prohibiting the exportation of leather, and
feltmakers asked for legal protection against the exportation
of beaver and raccoon matchcoats and other furs. Other Philadelphians protested against the shipment abroad of deerskin dressed in the hair and requested that a duty be placed
on all foreign hops imported into Philadelphia. The farmers
complained to the Assembly of irregularities and injustices in
the administration of the proprietary land policy. Philadelphia
tradesmen even petitioned the Assembly to perform business
which was ordinarily that of the City Corporation of Philadelphia, for example, the destruction of an old prison wall and the
erection of a new prison and courthouse in the city. [13]

Lloyd was highly responsive to the colonists' requests. He
ordered the Assembly to prepare legislation prohibiting the
exportation of raw hides and deerskin and imposing a duty on
imported hops and recommended that the feltmakers submit
a legislative bill of their own writing for the prohibition of
the export of fur. The depression continued unabated, and
Lloyd agreed with many colonists that Pennsylvania should
develop her own manufactures and strive for economic self-
sufficiency. Penn himself had suggested that the colony might
either have to develop a new commodity for trade in England
that would pay debts there or endeavor to become economically
self-sufficient. [14]

Lloyd, however, had several important matters to take into
account before he could further develop his legislative program
for Pennsylvania. One was the need for revenue to finance the
operations of the Pennsylvania government. The colonists continued to balk at paying the £2, 000 proprietary tax, and, when
Evans attempted to secure an appropriation for the military
defense of the colonies, Lloyd turned him away with a reminder that "we have our own back Settlem[en]ts to secure,
and our friend[ly] Indians to engage."[15] Nevertheless, Lloyd
obtained from the Assembly a resolution that the freemen of
Pennsylvania be taxed not less than £1, 000 for the support of
the government--£400 for the Deputy Governor's salary, £100
for Indian relations, and the balance for the normal operations
of government. [16] It was no more than a resolution; no appro-

priation law was enacted. The question was how any revenue was to be collected, economic conditions being what they were. Virtually all the hard money in the province was in the possession of the city merchants, and "wheat, the farmer's dependence," as Logan wrote, bore no price.[17] As things turned out, the Assembly made no attempt to collect revenue from the hard-pressed colonists, and the Deputy Governor had to depend on Logan for his compensation.[18]

Another problem which troubled Lloyd was the fact that the Queen-in-Council had not yet approved of the laws enacted in 1701, the Frame of 1701, and other proprietary grants given by Penn before his return to England. The Frame of 1701 and the Philadelphia City Charter were particularly under attack by Crown officers, and the Board of Trade was scrutinizing both documents. Logan had advised Penn to instruct Deputy Governor Evans "to act in legislation by advice and consent of the council"--an instruction which would have, in effect, amended the Frame of 1701 by including the Council in the legislative power.[19] Lloyd, therefore, moved to protect the reforms of 1701 by having them passed as new acts of Assembly--a move which would have guaranteed the continuance of the Frame of 1701 and the Philadelphia City Charter for at least five more years, considering how slowly the Queen-in-Council acted in reviewing colonial legislation.

In June Lloyd prepared and submitted to the Assembly bills for the confirmation of the Philadelphia City Charter and for the confirmation of the Frame of 1701.[20] By so doing, he followed a precedent established in 1697 when the Assembly had passed an act confirming the Frame of 1696.[21] The bill confirming the Frame of 1701, however, was more than just a bill of confirmation; it was an attempt to achieve for the Assembly more parliamentary privileges than Penn had granted it in 1701. Lloyd included provisions to clarify and to render into law the Assembly's position that it could adjourn itself for any length of time within the year of its session. The Assembly passed Lloyd's bill, with some minor amendments, and submitted it to Deputy Governor Evans, who immediately pounced upon the clause defining the Assembly's adjournment privileges. He believed that Penn had never intended to surrender the executive power to dissolve and prorogue the Assembly, and he wanted the Assembly to recognize this power as inherent in the prerogative of the Proprietor as chief Governor and of his deputy. The Assembly refused to do this. [22]

Lloyd appointed Joseph Wilcox, who was rapidly becoming his chief lieutenant in the Assembly, to prepare the Assembly's reply to Evans' affirmation of the executive power of the prorogation and dissolution. Wilcox's statement aptly reflected the opinion of Lloyd and his partisans. It asserted

> That to admitt of the Power of Dissolution of Prorogation in the Governor, will manifestly destroy or frustrate the Elections settled by the Charter [i. e., the Frame of 1701], which is a perpetual writt supported by the Legislative authority of this Government, & will make way for Elections by writts, grounded upon a Prerogative or rather Preeminence, which the Propr[ietar]y or his Deputy are by Charter [Frame of 1701] debarred to resume. [23]

Evans' proposal that the bill confirming the Frame of 1701 be amended so as to recognize the executive prerogative in proroguing and dissolving the Assembly was construed by Lloyd and his partisans as "destructive to the present Constitution. "[24] The Assembly offered to compromise by inserting a clause in the bill which would limit the session of the Assembly to twenty days annually, beginning on October 14, unless the Deputy Governor should agree to a longer session, and which would fix the time of adjournment at not less than three months. [25] This was not what Evans wanted. He wanted to be able to dissolve the Assembly whenever it conflicted with his and Penn's wishes in legislation. The compromise suggested by Lloyd and his partisans would have crystallized in the form of a law the existing procedure followed by the Assembly in adjournments and would have left Evans without freedom of action in his handling of an unruly legislature. Evans obtained from Mompesson the legal opinion that the power of dissolution and prorogation could not be granted away by the Deputy Governor, unless the Proprietor himself did so. [26] The question remained, however, whether or not Penn had granted away that power in the Frame of 1701. Evans, in a subsequent message to the Assembly, argued that Penn had not; therefore, he believed that he, as the Proprietor's deputy,

could not grant away a power which Penn had not himself granted away. Lloyd and his partisans, however, maintained that
the Frame of 1701 gave the Assembly exclusive authority
over its own adjournments, and they rejected Evans' offer to
refer the question to Penn in England. [27] Lloyd was mistaken
in his interpretation of the Frame of 1701. The Frame gave
the Assembly the privilege of sitting on its own adjournments,
but there was nothing in it to indicate that Penn had ever intended that privilege to be as sweeping as Lloyd supposed. [28]
Evans and the Assembly never reached any agreement on adjournments during 1704.

Lloyd, upon writing the bill for the confirmation of the Frame
of 1701, had included a statement that the Assembly constituted
the sole legislature in Pennsylvania and that the Council was
therefore excluded from the legislative authority. This was
a corroboration of the Council's own decision, made after
Evans had become the Deputy Governor, that it had no power
in legislation. [29] Logan, however, was actively campaigning
for greater conciliar authority in legislation, and Evans asked
the Assembly for an amendment to Lloyd's bill which would
have restored the Council as the upper house of a bicameral
legislature. Lloyd and his followers thereupon resolved that
it was inconsistent with Penn's charter and the Frame of 1701
"that the Council (as now chosen) should have a Share in the
Legislation, unless it be when the Government is in the Council."[30] Penn's charter, of course, did not specify a unicameral
legislature for Pennsylvania, any more than did any other proprietary charter. It required only that Penn or his deputies
make laws for the colony "by and with the advice, assent and
approbacon of the freemen of the said Countrey, or of their
Delegates or Deputies."[31] Lloyd's intention was to deny the
Council appointed by Penn any share in the legislative authority.

Evans proposed an amendment to Lloyd's bill which stipulated
that the Governor or Deputy Governor should pass legislative
bills only when he was in consultation with his Council, but
Lloyd and his followers considered it a superfluity. They did
not care if Evans passed laws in the presence or in the absence of the Council and by no means denied the Council the
right to advise the Deputy Governor in legislative matters.

They simply did not want the restoration of the pre-1701 legislative Council. [32]

Evans neither passed nor entirely rejected Lloyd's bills
confirming the Frame of 1701 and the Philadelphia City Charter. He and his Council tabled them and made no effort to act
upon them during the remainder of the session. [33] Logan wrote
to Penn of the bills and asserted that the colonists "think privileges their due, and all that can be grasped to be their native
right. . . ." In an obvious allusion to Lloyd, Logan added that
"some people's brains are as soon intoxicated with power as
the natives are with their beloved liquor, and as little to be
trusted with it." He warned that "property and commonwealth
men invested with power, have been seen to prove the greatest
tyrants." [34] Even while Logan's letter was on the way to England, Penn was urging Logan not to let the colonists use the
Frame of 1701 against him and asserting that he had only
granted it as a protection to the colonists at a time when he
had feared losing the government of Pennsylvania. [35]

Lloyd had failed to secure enactment of legislation confirming the Frame of 1701 and the Philadelphia City Charter, but
he had greatly increased his popularity among the colonists.
When Thomas Story resigned from the City Corporation of
Philadelphia in July, the corporation chose Lloyd to replace
him as city recorder, a position which also made Lloyd the
presiding judge of the City Court of Philadelphia, a justice
of the peace, and a justice in the Philadelphia Court of Oyer
and Terminer and in the Philadelphia County courts. [36]

Not only did Lloyd increase his influence in the city of Philadelphia, the farmers in the countryside also looked to him for
the security of their property rights and for the autonomous
control of the Pennsylvania Land Office. Land reform, of
course, had long been Lloyd's chief goal, but there was no
reason to believe, in the summer of 1704, that land reform
legislation would fare any better than had Lloyd's bills for the
confirmation of the Frame of 1701 and the Philadelphia City
Charter. By August, however, the Assembly had received
from the farmers so many petitions and complaints about property matters that remedial legislation seemed clearly necessary. [37] Lloyd, however, looked beyond mere remedial legis-

lation to the enactment of the ideas expressed in the draft of
a charter of property which Penn had rejected in 1701/2.

Early in August Lloyd wrote a "Bill for regulating the Act-
ings and Proceedings of the Commissioners of Property, Surveyor General's Office, and Secretary's Office, " which Anthony Morris, chairman of the Assembly's grievance committee, boasted would "prevent those Enormities [alleged
abuses of which the farmers had complained to the Assembly]
for the future. . . ."[38] The contents of the bill, with the exception of one clause, were unfortunately not given in the journal of the Assembly, and the bill itself is no longer extant. The
only clause mentioned in the journal of the Assembly stated
that one purpose of the bill was "to ascertain and settle the
Bounds of each County in this Province."[39] The bill, however,
appeared to have been in the spirit of Lloyd's draft of a charter
of property. The title strongly indicated that Lloyd's intention
was to gain control of the Commissioners of Property, the
Surveyor General's Office, and Logan's office of Provincial
Secretary. The Assembly passed the bill and submitted it to
Deputy Governor Evans, who had no intention of approving it.[40]

Securing control of proprietary land offices, however, was
not enough to solve the farmers' problems, as Lloyd well
knew. The farmers were indebted to the Philadelphia merchants, and most of them were unable to pay their debts.[41]
Consequently, they were threatened with imprisonment by
angry city creditors, even for nonpayment of small debts.
Lloyd and his partisans, therefore, prepared a judiciary bill
which included clauses intended to protect debtors against
unjust arrest and imprisonment. One clause prohibited the
courts from issuing writs of arrest *(capias ad respondendum)*
for debt against any freeholder who was enabled by the constitution of the provincial government to elect or to be elected a
member of the Assembly. That, of course, meant all male
freeholders twenty-one years of age or older who believed in
God and who were English citizens. Another clause prohibited
the courts from issuing an execution *(capias ad satisfaciendum)*
"against the Body of any Person in this Province . . . unless
it be first testified [by appropriate writs] that the Party hath
no Lands, Goods or Chattels in the respective Counties where

those Writs or Testatums [Testata] are to be executed.'"⁴² The
Assembly, by unanimous resolution, added still another clause
which was intended to enable the courts of common pleas for
the counties and the City Corporation of Philadelphia to try
all actions for debt or damages without any limitation as to the
money value of the case. ⁴³ The purpose of these clauses was
to benefit the farmers and artisans, the debtor classes of
Pennsylvania.

Lloyd and his partisans believed, also, that Pennsylvania
freeholders were being gouged by proprietary officials who,
as Lloyd subsequently alleged, charged exorbitant fees for
services performed in connection with land sales, patents,
and surveys. Penn, in 1701, had rejected a bill for the regulation of fees, and Lloyd had never forgiven him for it. ⁴⁴ The
regulation of official fees and salaries was essential to the
achievement of political autonomy, as well as to the protection
of the freeholders' interests. For these reasons Lloyd and his
followers prepared a legislative bill for the regulation of officers' fees and salaries. ⁴⁵

The legislative bills prepared by Lloyd and his followers in
August, 1704, reflected the demands made upon the Assembly
by the farmers and artisans of Pennsylvania; they also reflected Lloyd's intention of furthering legislative supremacy
and of gaining control of the entire provincial government
through his personal control of the Assembly. Lloyd appointed
his father-in-law chairman of the committee of the whole to
prepare legislation appropriating £100 of tax revenue for the
maintenance of agents in London who were to solicit the Queen's
approval of provincial laws. Also, Lloyd and his partisans,
late in August, added clauses to the judiciary bill which would
have transferred the functions of the Register General of Wills
to the county courts and which would have prescribed a method
for suits brought against the Proprietor by the colonists. ⁴⁶
This legislation, along with the other bills drawn up by the
Assembly, was motivated by a desire on Lloyd's part to take
from Penn nearly all of his prerogatives, even the prerogative of representing Pennsylvania at the court of Queen Anne.

The legislative activities of Lloyd and his following in the
Assembly met with the approval of most artisans, farmers,
and tradesmen, but the merchants in the Council were not as

favorably impressed. John Guest, one of the Council's most vociferous critics of the Assembly, ridiculed the Assembly's legislative bills as "absurd, unreasonable and monstrous"-- an attack which moved Lloyd to appoint Wood, Wilcox, and Norris to request that Evans rebuke Guest for contempt of the Assembly. [47] Evans learned from the Commissioners of Property that the bill for the regulation of proprietary land offices was based on Lloyd's draft of a charter of property, and he turned it over to Logan for study and report. Logan kept the bill and took no action on it during the remainder of the session. He wrote to Penn that "such is the confusion here, that if thou canst make a good bargain for thyself 'tis what thy best friends will advise. I see nothing here that should incline thee to defer good terms one hour after they are offered. "[48]

Lloyd had not the slightest chance of getting any part of his legislative program enacted into law. Evans persisted in claiming the prerogative of dissolving the Assembly, and the Assembly as obstinately denied his claim. [49] Lloyd, in an apparent effort to reconcile differences between the Assembly and the Council, appointed himself, Wilcox, and Wood a committee of three to consult with Judge Mompesson "in order to clear what Objections may be raised upon those Bills which he has to peruse. "[50] The conference did not succeed. Mompesson was in full agreement with Evans as to his power of dissolving or proroguing the Assembly, and Lloyd resolved to adjourn the Assembly rather than admit such a prerogative in the Deputy Governor.

Lloyd believed that Penn was the cause of his difficulties with Deputy Governor Evans and the Provincial Council, and he did not adjourn the Assembly before he had taken a parting shot at the Proprietor. On August 25 he appointed himself, Wilcox, and Norris a committee of three to prepare a representation to Penn. After haggling over the wording of the "Remonstrance" all night, the committee failed to make progress, and Norris, repulsed by Lloyd's intense hatred of Penn, refrained from any further connection with the project. According to the journal, the Assembly resolved on the subject matter of the "Remonstrance" just before it adjourned on August 27, and the document was subsequently written up on that basis. [51] The journal does not record that the finished "Remonstrance" was reported to the Assembly or that the Assembly voted on it. Lloyd, as he testified five years later, appointed seven assemblymen[52] to read the prepared "Remonstrance. " With the exception of three members the reading committee and other assemblymen read and approved the document. More work was done on the "Remonstrance, " however, and the final draft was read and examined by five assemblymen before it was sent to England. [53] Apparently, all this work was done after the Assembly had adjourned on August 27.

Norris subsequently told Logan a slightly different version of what had happened. The reading committee, he said, had never met. He did not know exactly who had written the "Remonstrance, " but thought Wilcox had written it with Lloyd's assistance and with Jones's and Wood's approval. Aside from those four, Norris said, only Richardson had seen the document, and he had not liked it.

Logan, who reported Norris' account to Penn, disagreed with Norris as to the authorship of the "Remonstrance." He thought Lloyd was the sole author, and he relayed to Penn the information given him by other assemblymen that Lloyd had owned the writing of the "Remonstrance" as his own proper act, and therefore pleaded as such it was not subject to the house nor any other power. "[54]

The substance of Norris' and Logan's testimonies was that Lloyd and a tiny clique of his own intimate associates had prepared and approved the "Remonstrance" without the approval of the majority of the assemblymen, most of whom did not know its contents. Undoubtedly Lloyd was the prime mover and perhaps the chief author of the "Remonstrance." Certainly his method of conducting the business of the Assembly just before and even after its adjournment was questionable on ethical grounds. No legislative official--speaker, senate president, or other parliamentary leader--today could get away with it. Nevertheless, the "Remonstrance" and Lloyd's proceedings in preparing and sending it to England very evidently had the support of most assemblymen. [55]

The "Remonstrance" was the boldest attack ever made on the Proprietor in the history of the province. Lloyd and whoever assisted him in writing the document spared nothing in their verbal assault on Penn. When Pennsylvania was first

settled, they wrote, Penn had "promised large Privileges,
and granted several Charters [Frames of government] to the
People." But since those early days of the "Holy Experiment"
Penn had changed his mind. The Utopian of 1682 had become a
"Tyrant," and "by his Artifices," Lloyd and his partisans asserted, he had brought all his early promises and frames of
government "at his will and Pleasure to Defeat." They implied
strongly that Penn had never had the right to dissolve or prorogue the Assembly or to issue writs of election or to authorize
his deputies or commissioners of state to do the same. By
doing those things, they charged, Penn had violated every
frame of government since 1682.[56]

The charges, to be sure, were unfair. The Frames of 1682
and 1683 had not precluded the Proprietor or his deputies
from proroguing and dissolving the Assembly and from issuing
writs for the election of assemblymen. The standard of liberties had changed since the early years of the province. What
had seemed proper in 1683 now seemed tyrannical to Lloyd
and his partisans who were seeking to broaden their powers.

Lloyd and his lieutenants also inveighed against Penn for
his failure to obtain the confirmation of provincial laws by the
Queen-in-Council and for his refusal in 1701 to pass a legislative bill which would have regulated officers' fees and salaries. They charged that the absence of a law regulating officers' fees and salaries had resulted in great corruption on
the part of surveyors and other officers concerned in property. They pointed out that there had been no Surveyor General in the province since the death of Edward Pennington
and asserted that there had been abuses and extortions by
surveyors and other officials connected with the Land Office.[57]
This was a thinly disguised attack on Logan who was in full
charge of the land and Surveyor General's offices, although
the articles of the "Remonstrance" which appeared in the
journal of the Assembly did not mention him by name.[58]

Lloyd and his partisans aimed thair shafts more directly
at Evans, his Council, the Philadelphia town clerk, the justices, sheriffs, the Commissioners of Property, and other
officers of the government who held proprietary commissions.
They complained that obstructionism on the part of Evans and
his Council deprived the colonists of any remedy in matters

which had not been specifically granted by the Proprietor. They
thought it wrong that the clerk of the Philadelphia County court
and the justices were of proprietary appointment. Whenever
colonists wished to take legal action against the Proprietor
for some alleged infringement of their civil rights, Lloyd and
his partisans said, the clerk of the Philadelphia County Court
of Common Pleas, Robert Assheton, refused to make out any
process. They believed that, because the clerk and justices
held office by proprietary commission, the Proprietor tended
to become a "Judge in his own Case, which is against natural
Equity."[59] They were also disturbed that sheriffs and other
officers who had been commissioned by Penn were "men of
no visible Estates," that is, that they were not property owners
in the province. Elected officials had to be property owners,
so why not appointed officials? Besides, the men whom Penn
had commissioned were not bonded, and the colonists therefore were not protected against the abuses and frauds which
Lloyd and his partisans alleged were committed by these officials. They also alleged that the Commissioners of Property,
who were agents of the Proprietor, had deliberately neglected
to satisfy the demands of colonists who believed that they had
not received their full quantity of land as described in their
instruments of purchase.[60]

This verbal assault on the Proprietor and on his commissioned officers in the provincial government did not, however,
arise from a desire on the part of Lloyd and his partisans to
do away with proprietary government altogether. They wanted
increased local control of local affairs and that involved the
virtual eradication of the old feudal relationship between lord
and tenants, but they wanted at the same time to keep the
framework of proprietary government. The trend throughout
the colonies was toward royal government; neighboring East
and West New Jersay had become a royal province in 1702;
and everybody in Pennsylvania knew by this time that Penn
was negotiating for the sale of the provincial government to
the Crown. Lloyd and his partisans feared that political autonomy would be virtually unobtainable under royal government. Therefore, they concluded the "Remonstrance" with
an entreaty to the Proprietor not to surrender the Pennsylvania government to the Crown.[61]

Apparently Lloyd intended the "Remonstrance" not so much for Penn's eyes as for those of the Proprietor's Quaker critics in England. About October 3, after Lloyd had signed the "Remonstrance" as the Speaker of the adjourned Assembly, he sent it under the care of Robert Barber, a resident of Chester County, to three leading Quakers in England, George Whitehead, William Mead, and Thomas Lower. Whitehead was a Quaker missionary who had traveled in America. Mead had been a close friend of Penn in their youth. They had been arrested together under the Conventicle Acts in 1670, and Mead had stood by Penn at the famous courtroom trial in which Penn had made his historic appeal for the independence of juries from the arbitrariness of tyrannical judges. In his later years, however, Mead had become estranged from Penn. Lower, whose legal interests in Pennsylvania Lloyd represented, had long been critical of Penn. Apparently Lloyd's reason for sending the "Remonstrance" to Whitehead, Mead, and Lower was to influence Quaker public opinion in England against Penn so that Penn would be compelled by the pressure of that public opinion to yield to the demands of the Assembly radicals in Pennsylvania.

With the "Remonstrance" Lloyd enclosed a letter to Whitehead, Mead, and Lower and a copy of the Assembly's bill to substitute the affirmation for the oath universally in Pennsylvania. He informed the English Quakers of the judicial situation in the province and asked them to solicit the Queen for her approval of the universal substitution of the affirmation for the oath in Pennsylvania, as he did not think Penn had made any effort in that respect. He also asked Whitehead, Mead, and Lower to influence Penn to do something about alleviating unsatisfactory conditions in the provincial government and offered the English Quakers £100 per annum, which he supposed the Assembly would make an annual fund at its next session, "to defray the charge of a correspondence which they [the assemblymen] desire to have settled for negotiating the affairs of the province, for you now see how we have been abused trusting to William Penn." He particularly requested that the English Quakers, as the Assembly's agents, find "an able counsellor at law that were a person of sobriety and moderation, but not in William Penn's interest." He thought that such a person would receive £400 or £500 per annum plus fees and other perquisites from the colonists of Pennsylvania, the Lower Counties, and the Jerseys as their Chief Justice, should he receive the Queen's commission. Lloyd had thought of Judge Mompesson for this position but had rejected him because he was Judge of the Vice-Admiralty Court and Chief Justice of the Supreme Court of New York. The fact that Mompesson was too much in Penn's interest also influenced Lloyd's decision against him, as did his alleged taste for liquor. Lloyd did not trust anyone who indulged in alcoholic beverages. [62]

Lloyd concluded his letter to Whitehead, Mead, and Lower with the plea, "Friends, it's the public cries for your assistance."[63] However questionable his conduct of the Assembly's business in the late days of August might have been on ethical grounds, however few his confederates in drawing up the "Remonstrance" were, Lloyd honestly believed that what he had done was entirely consistent with the desires and best interests of the majority of Pennsylvania colonists.

# 13. The Reaction against Lloyd

The "Remonstrance" had no immediate effect on Lloyd's political fortunes. Lloyd kept the document in his possession until after the election of October 1, 1704, and the rules of the Assembly prohibited members from divulging publicly the secrets of the Assembly, and even those assemblymen who disapproved of the "Remonstrance"--Norris, Richardson, and Waln--maintained a discreet silence during the election. Deputy Governor Evans knew nothing of it until several weeks after the election, and Logan was unaware of it until October 26.[1] Consequently, the "Remonstrance" was not a factor in the election of October 1, 1704.

A more influential factor, one which redounded to Lloyd's advantage, was the unfavorable public reaction to the after-dark escapades of Deputy Governor Evans and William Penn, Jr., whose sensualism conflicted with the severe moral code of the Pennsylvania community. During the summer of 1704 the town constable of Philadelphia had discovered Evans and young Penn on one of their escapades in what was apparently a drinking house. The constable's attempt to arrest the pair for disorderly conduct had been met by violent resistance, and in the scuffle that ensued Evans and young Penn had handled the law enforcement officer more roughly than the latter had been accustomed to. Subsequently young Penn was presented by the grand jury for assault and was arraigned before the Mayor's Court of the City of Philadelphia. Although he was not punished, the Quaker-dominated Mayor's

Court reprimanded him harshly and his dignity suffered in
the process.

Evans' and Penn's escapade had disgusted the colonists.
Norris had written that he wished young Penn had never come
to America.[2] Lloyd had taken the matter very seriously, saying, "This poor province is brought to poor condition by the
revels and disorders which young Penn and his gang of loose
fellows are found in here, to the great grief of Friends and
others here."[3] Young Penn had been released out of respect
for his father, and Evans had not been arraigned out of respect for his office, but the Mayor's Court had imposed a sentence on the keeper of the house in which the constable had
discovered the young revelers. Evans had later issued an order nullifying the sentence, and the Mayor and aldermen had
remonstrated against the Deputy Governor's broad-mindedness
in setting free one whom they considered a purveyor of vice
and corrupter of youth.[4] The incident did not help the Proprietor's cause in Pennsylvania.

In the election of October 1, 1704, Lloyd and his followers
strengthened their position both in the provincial Assembly
and in the City Corporation of Philadelphia. Lloyd and Wilcox
were re-elected to the Assembly from Philadelphia County, and
they were joined by Joshua Carpenter and Francis Rawle, two
Philadelphia merchants of pronounced Lloydian views. Norris,
Richardson, and Waln, because of their opposition to the "Remonstrance," no longer identified themselves with the Lloydians, and either they did not seek re-election or they were
defeated. In the City Corporation of Philadelphia, where Lloyd
continued to be the recorder, Griffith Jones was elected may-
or.[5] Lloyd now controlled a considerable political machine both
in the Assembly and in the city.

Lloyd was politically astute enough to withhold sending the
"Remonstrance" to England until after the election, but his
bitterness toward Penn was too great to be entirely concealed.
On several occasions he reputedly accused Penn of having
taken "his bread from him," and Logan, informing Penn of
Lloyd's unguarded remarks, gave his opinion that Lloyd was
"truly a promoter of discord, but with more bitterness, with the
deepest artifice under the smoothest language and pretences."[6]

After the election was over, Lloyd sealed in a packet the "Remonstrance," his letter to Whitehead, Lower, and Mead, and a copy of the bill substituting universally the affirmation for the oath and gave the packet to one of his Chester tenants, Robert Barber, to take to England. Barber never reached England. The ship on which he sailed was captured by a French privateer, and Barber was subsequently imprisoned in France. A fellow prisoner, who, by peculiar coincidence turned out to be a personal friend of William Penn, relieved Barber of the packet, and, after he had been released from imprisonment and had returned to England, he delivered the packet and its contents to Penn. [7] Lloyd knew nothing of these developments until months after Barber had sailed from Pennsylvania.

Lloyd was re-elected Speaker by the Assembly, which convened in Philadelphia on October 14, and he renewed his efforts to secure enactment of the legislative program which he and his partisans had initiated in the previous session of the Assembly. Evans, however, refused to consider any legislation other than that promulgated by the current session of the Assembly, and Lloyd subsequently had messengers take to the Deputy Governor bills to confirm the Frame of 1701, to reform proprietary land administration, and to substitute universally the affirmation for the oath--all of them identical with the bills initiated earlier in the year. [8] Further action was temporarily delayed, however, as Evans had to go to New Castle, where the Assembly for the Lower Counties was in session, and the provincial Assembly adjourned for a few days. Probably Evans knew of the "Remonstrance" even before he went down to New Castle. Word of it was getting around among the conservatives in the Council when Logan returned from a visit in New York and was "surprised to hear" of it. Norris, thoroughly disaffected from Lloyd, had broken his silence, and he told Logan as much as he knew of the circumstances which had surrounded the writing of the "Remonstrance." Logan immediately passed on Norris' testimony to Penn. [9]

When Evans returned to Philadelphia from New Castle, he and his Council were even less inclined to accept the Assembly's legislation than they had been. Lloyd suggested a grand conference of assemblymen and councilmen to iron out the

differences between them over legislation, but Evans refused.[10]
There seemed no possibility of cooperation between Lloyd and
Evans and between the Assembly and the Council.

Just as Evans refused to consider Lloyd's legislative program, so Lloyd resisted Evans' continued demands for recognition of his power to dissolve or prorogue the Assembly and
for a tax bill appropriating money for the defense of New York
and for the organization of a militia in the province and Lower
Counties. When Evans inveighed against the procedure followed
by the Assembly in conducting its business, Lloyd replied that
the Assembly based its procedure on precedents established by
the Parliament in England and that Penn's charter granted the
colonists parliamentary privileges. Evans ridiculed this claim,
and Logan wrote that Lloyd and his followers were imitating
the English Parliament of 1641 which in attacking the royal
prerogative had plunged England into civil war. Evans warned
Lloyd and his partisans that "no Government Can be happy but
where there is an Union between its parts, and that the real
Interest of Both Governments and the Governed are Interwoven."[11] Lloyd and Evans, however, did not agree as to what
that "real Interest" was.

Early in the winter of 1704 Evans received a letter from
Penn, and in an irate address to the Assembly he told of Penn's
indignation and demanded a copy of the "Remonstrance" that
he might peruse its contents.[12] Lloyd, who did not as yet know
of Barber's capture by the French, must have realized after
hearing Evans' harangue that something had gone wrong, and
his subsequent actions showed that he was clearly on the defensive. He urged the Assembly not to submit the document
requested except by an act of Assembly.[13] This, however, was
an unusual procedure, for the Assembly had in the past provided the Deputy Governor with documents on demand without
any special formality. Many assemblymen evinced a disparag-
ing attitude toward their Speaker, and Lloyd's request was
defeated by a majority vote. Lloyd then denied having a copy
of the "Remonstrance" and made a show of sending to York
for it when, as Logan observed, it was too late. The Philadelphia Monthly Meeting also requested a copy of the "Remonstrance," and Lloyd's reply was the same. He did not have
it.

Most assemblymen, nevertheless, remained loyal to Lloyd, but criticism of the "Remonstrance" was now growing to such an extent that Lloyd's entire political machine was imperiled. Lloyd, apparently, attempted to save his political lieutenants by accepting full responsibility for the assault on Penn. Several assemblymen informed Logan that Lloyd confessed himself the sole author of the "Remonstrance" and "pleaded as such it was not subject to the house [the Assembly] nor any other power."[14] Logan wrote to Penn, furthermore, that Lloyd had falsified the minutes of the Assembly, and committed forgery, and had engaged in clandestine activities in writing the "Remonstrance" after the Assembly had adjourned.[15] Although Lloyd, to be sure, had kept the journal of the Assembly and evidently had omitted from it information which might have proved embarrassing to himself and his partisans, Logan could never prove the charges of falsification and forgery. Nevertheless, he continued to believe them as late as 1709.[16]

Consequently, the "Remonstrance" served only to strengthen the resistance of Penn, Evans, Logan, and the Council to the radical legislative program of Lloyd and his partisans. Logan thought the colony could not be "brought into regular order again till under the Crown." Penn, he believed, had been too generous in bestowing his favors upon the colonists; his proprietary grants had only been used "by ill men as tools for mischief."[17] Penn, who was aware that Lloyd and his followers were only following a trend which was in evidence in the other colonial assemblies of British America, asked Logan, "Will they never be wise? These assemblies, held so absurdly as well as hazardously, will, in the end, subject the whole to laws made for them in Parliament."[18]

Whatever hopes Lloyd still had of achieving enactment of his legislative program vanished. Evans sent to Penn the bills for the confirmation of the Frame of 1701, for the confirmation of the Philadelphia City Charter, and for the reform of proprietary land offices. In England Penn showed the legislative bills to lawyers and other friends who ridiculed them as "great Absurdities," and Penn, in a subsequent letter to Logan, facetiously referred to the land reform bill as "David Lloyd's hedging-in of the Cuckoo by the New Castle charter."[19] Evans warned the Assembly that, even if he had passed the bills, they would have been repealed by the Queen-in-Council. [20]

Even Lloyd's plea to the Proprietor not to surrender the provincial government to the Crown turned sour. Penn, encouraged by Logan's advice, renewed his efforts to sell the Pennsylvania government to the Crown, but his negotiations with the Board of Trade bogged down when he insisted that the Crown guarantee liberty of conscience to all Christian sects in the province. Logan and Evans were confused as to whether or not Penn would come to terms with the Crown, but they resolved nevertheless to employ the talk of the impending surrender of the provincial government to the Crown as a means of discrediting Lloyd and his followers. If the government were surrendered, they hoped the colonists would blame Lloyd for it. Even if Penn retained possession of the government, Logan supposed that Lloyd and his political machine would be "pressed to do business, or be exposed to the Country."[21]

Penn was furious with Lloyd. He expected that Pennsylvania Quakers and the provincial Assembly would make Lloyd "a public example, and turn him out from being a recorder or a practitioner at any of my courts." He thought Lloyd was motivated chiefly by self-interest and inveighed against the colonists who had proved themselves disloyal to the Proprietor by following "such a self-interested tool as David Lloyd, that owed his bread to me too." He wanted Judge Mompesson to demonstrate to the colonists that their proprietary grants could be implemented to exact their obedience as well as to allow them privileges. [22] In a letter to Judge Mompesson, Penn wrote that he had intended the Frame of 1701 to shelter the colonists "against a violent or arbitrary governor imposed" by the Crown upon them. That Lloyd and his following had turned the Frame against him seemed to him "unworthy and provoking." He had read the three legislative bills written by Lloyd, and he warned that if they had been enacted Lloyd "might have spoiled himself," for the Crown would never have approved of them. Passage of the bills, Penn was certain, would have greatly depreciated the value of the government he was trying to sell to the Crown. "What a bargain should I have made for my government with the Crown," he demanded, "after such a bill had taken from me the very power I should dispose of?"[23]

In the face of the reaction against him, Lloyd changed his strategy from one of direct attack to one of discretion and watchful waiting. The result was a temporary subsidence of the political storms of 1704. Griffith Jones conducted himself in the office of mayor of Philadelphia with such moderation and good temper that he surprised Logan. Lloyd maintained a discreet distance between himself and the councilmen. He appeared anxious to allay the rancor against him, but Logan particularly was not to be reconciled to him. Logan thought of Lloyd as a "lurking snake" and hoped to accomplish his political defeat in the next election. When Lloyd went to Maryland on a visit in mid-February, 1704/5, Logan was glad to be rid of him, even if only for a little while. [24]

Lloyd's enemies did not relinquish the initiative they had seized. They planned a letter to Penn remonstrating against Lloyd's conduct in the Assembly in 1704--a letter intended rather for public consumption in Pennsylvania than for Penn's edification. Logan suggested that Penn "write a tender, affectionate, and yet somewhat upbraiding letter, to Friends here, to be read in all their meetings, shewing still a confidence in the honest, guarding against jealousies, &c." He thought that such a letter, properly timed, would have a salutary political effect. [25] When the Assembly reconvened in May, 1705, after a long adjournment, Deputy Governor Evans and his Council resolved to take measures to prosecute Lloyd for forgery in signing the "Remonstrance" to Penn as Speaker after the Assembly had adjourned in 1704. Penn, who had no desire to "turn an enemy of the public," although in a moment of pique he wished that he could ship the colonists back to England a while that they might learn how much better off they were in America than in the homeland, supported the planned prosecution of Lloyd. In a letter reported to the Assembly by Evans Penn warned that if the "Remonstrance" was "the act of the People" then he had sufficient reason "to Cancel all obligations of care over them." If, on the other hand, it had been the work only of Lloyd and his closest lieutenants, Penn expected that the colonists would "purge themselves" of Lloyd and those who persisted in following him. To expedite the prosecution of Lloyd, Penn sent Logan "the letter pretended to be written by the authority of the Assembly, only signed by him."[26]

Lloyd maintained firm control of the Assembly, and, ironi-
cally enough, he was assisted in so doing by the indiscretion of
his enemies in the Council. The Council appointed a committee
of five to inspect the journal of the Assembly and to copy all
minutes and entries relating to the "Remonstrance," but the
Assembly regarded such an investigation as an invasion of
its privileges. Tempers were once again heated, and one of
Lloyd's lieutenants, William Biles, committed the indiscretion of attacking the Deputy Governor verbally within earshot
of one of Evans' friends. Biles was not in the Assembly's
meeting place and was not engaged in the official business of
the Assembly when he committed his indiscretion, and, therefore, his remarks were not privileged. Just what he said is
not clear. According to Logan he said, *"He* [Evans] *is but a
boy; he is not fit to be our Governour. We'll kick him out;
we'll kick him out."*[27] Evans told his Council that Biles had
accused him of opposing the Queen's and the Proprietor's authority. Biles could not remember having spoken the words
attributed to him.[28] Whatever he said, he deeply injured the
feelings of the young Deputy Governor. Evans charged Biles
with subverting "the Peace and Quiet of the Governm[en]t"--
an odd charge, all things considered--and the sheriff attempted
unsuccessfully to serve a summons on Biles while the latter
was in official attendance in the Assembly. Biles ignored the
summons which he considered a breach of his privileges as
an assemblyman while he was in the performance of his official duties. Nevertheless, he appeared anxious to pacify the
angry Deputy Governor, and in a petition to Evans he explained
why he had ignored the summons, denied having spoken the
words attributed to him, and apologized for having said anything offensive to Evans. The Deputy Governor nevertheless
prosecuted Biles in the Philadelphia County court and called
upon the Assembly to oust Biles from his seat as a representative of Bucks County.[29]

Lloyd immediately came to the rescue of his embattled lieutenant. He represented Biles before the Philadelphia County
Court of Quarter Sessions and pleaded with the court to allow
the defendant his privileges as an assemblyman. At the same
time he prepared an Assembly address to the Deputy Governor
which contended that the summoning and prosecution "before

any Secular Judges" of an assemblymen without the permission
of the Assembly in which he was in official attendance violated
what he believed to be the privileges of the representative legislature. Only in cases of treason, felony, or breach of the
peace could assemblymen be arrested and brought into court
during a session of the Assembly, he wrote. He pointed out
that such privileges as immunity from arrest belonged to the
Assembly, "as proper Incidents to the Power of Legislation,
granted to the ffreemen of this Province under the great seal
of England, Without which the Rights of the subject and the
Dignity of this house Cannot be upheld." To be sure, Lloyd
and his partisans disapproved of the language which had been
attributed to Biles, and they assured Evans that, if his charges
were true, there were grounds for the expulsion of Biles from
the Assembly. But they asked that Biles be given an opportunity
to vindicate himself. [30]

Lloyd's efforts on behalf of Biles were in vain. The Philadelphia County Court of Quarter Sessions returned judgment
against Biles, awarding £300 damages to Evans. Evans and
his Council considered the attitude expressed by Lloyd in his
Assembly address rude and absurd and resolved to dismiss
the Assembly until the October election. Evans lectured the
Assembly for what he believed had been a threat to his authority. He denied the right of any assemblyman to oppose the
executive and insisted that in England there were "no such
Priviledges as you pretend to" and, if there were, "yet non
in Am[er]i[c]a has such an inherent Right to them." [31]

Rather than permit Evans to dissolve the Assembly, Lloyd
adjourned the Assembly sine die, but his enemies struck one
more blow at him, before the Assembly disbanded. Griffith
Owen, Caleb Pusey, and Richard Hill, wealthy merchants and
members of the Council, managed the preparation of a remonstrance against Lloyd, which, as Logan told Penn, was
"drawn up in great haste at the rising of the Assembly, that
the honest members of it might sign it before they went out of
town." [32] The contents of the anti-Lloyd remonstrance are unknown. The only signers mentioned by Logan were Owen, Pusey, Hill, and Joseph Growdon, Lloyd's father-in-law, and only
Growdon was a member of the Assembly. Logan mentioned
no other assemblyman as a signer of the remonstrance against

Lloyd. Although Logan denied having participated in drawing up the remonstrance, he sent it to Penn himself.[33]

The disaffection of Lloyd's father-in-law in June, 1705, marked the nadir of Lloyd's fortunes that year. For about a year Growdon had regarded his son-in-law's political activities and obvious hatred of Penn with increasing disfavor, and he had secretly been bargaining with Lloyd's enemies.[34] His signing of the anti-Lloyd remonstrance represented the final consummation of his disaffection from Lloyd. Thereafter Growdon emerged as a leader of political forces opposing Lloyd.

The anti-Lloyd reaction and the disaffection of Growdon, however, did not silence Lloyd. Shortly after the adjournment of the Assembly, Lloyd, Isaac Norris, and John Moore received a letter from the Ford family in England, authorizing them to act as the Fords' legal representatives in Pennsylvania. Penn had never paid off the principal and interest on the mortgage, which Philip Ford had held against the province since 1697, and by 1705 Penn's debt to the Ford family had increased to £13,000, a sizable sum. Early in 1705, therefore, the Fords, in spite of Philip's earlier agreement with Penn not to do such a thing, had resolved to take over the province. For this reason they appointed Lloyd, Norris, and Moore to represent their interests. Norris refused to participate in any action against Penn, and the Fords sent Lloyd and Moore a power of attorney and instructed them to advise colonists not to pay quitrents until further notice. Lloyd, Moore, and Norris took the Ford letter to the Commissioners of Property, and, although they reputedly agreed to keep the matter a secret until the power of attorney had arrived, Lloyd made the Ford letter public.[35]

From Lloyd's point of view the Ford letter seemed a political windfall in the midst of adversity. Here was proof that Penn had been meddling in the government of a province which he had mortgaged and which he might not even own because of his failure to meet the terms of the mortgage! Lloyd and his lieutenants made great use of the Ford letter, and news of it spread rapidly throughout Pennsylvania. Norris fully expected the Lloydians to profit from the affair.[36]

The Ford letter, however, had just the opposite effect from that which Lloyd and Norris expected. It resulted in a wave of popular sympathy for Penn which manifested itself in the election of October 1, 1705. Lloyd's political machine was overwhelmingly repudiated in the counties, and Lloyd himself was defeated in his bid for re-election in Philadelphia County. Only in Bucks County did three or four pro-Lloyd assemblymen win election. Four members of the Council, all wealthy merchants, were elected to the Assembly from Philadelphia County, as were Norris and Growdon. Lloyd, however, still retained control of the City Corporation of Philadelphia, and his partisans in that body chose him as their representative in the Assembly. "It was unfair play that got him in, " lamented Logan, "our party was so strong. "[37]

# 14. Lloyd Regains His Popularity

Lloyd's fall from popular favor was temporary. His skill as a lawmaker soon proved indispensable even to an anti-Lloyd Assembly. By July, 1706, Logan was compelled to admit that "there are many excellent laboured laws, which . . . are chiefly owing to David Lloyd."[1] Penn urged Deputy Governor Evans and Logan to have Lloyd "brought on his knees" and accused Lloyd of having maladministered the offices of Master of the Rolls and Clerk of the Philadelphia County Court of Common Pleas in 1698, but Evans and Logan hesitated to initiate legal proceedings against Lloyd. They had no case against Lloyd that would stand up in court; they needed his lawmaking talents in the Assembly, as long as he was in a subordinate position in that body; and Lloyd was rapidly returning to popular favor in both Philadelphia and the countryside.[2]

Lloyd's return to popularity was in direct ratio to Evans' growing unpopularity. Evans estranged even the Quakers in the Council by refusing to pass an act of Assembly substituting universally the affirmation for the oath until a clause had been added to it rendering the act ineffective pending the Queen's allowance. Moreover, Evans and his Anglican friends in the Council overrode the Quakers by issuing a proclamation ordering a general muster throughout the province and an inspection of all available arms and ammunition. To lend force to the proclamation, Evans collaborated with friends in Philadelphia and the Lower Counties in spreading a false report of an imminent French naval invasion of the province as a test

of the colonists' willingness to defend themselves. He succeeded, however, only in arousing the resentment of the Quakers, when they discovered that the invasion was a hoax. Few
heeded the proclamation. Realizing that the proclamation was
ineffectual without an act of Assembly, Evans asked the Assembly for a law to raise and regulate a militia and for a provincial tax to pay the cost of organizing the military defense
of Pennsylvania. As he ought to have expected, he was promptly rebuked. The Assembly was proprietary and conservative, but it had a Quaker majority, which was not at all willing
to do business with Evans on the terms he desired. The Assembly, on its own motion, was dismissed by the Deputy Governor
and Council for harvesting. [3]

Lloyd capitalized not only on Evans' unsuccessful efforts to
militarize Pennsylvania but on the Deputy Governor's imprisonment of William Biles because of Biles's alleged libel against
him the previous year. Even Logan fell out with Evans over this
extreme treatment of Biles. [4] The reaction against Evans and
his Anglican friends enabled Lloyd to strengthen his position
in the City Corporation of Philadelphia, where Joseph Wilcox,
now recognized as Lloyd's most trusted lieutenant, was the
new mayor. Logan was so distressed by Lloyd's ascendancy in
Philadelphia that he urged Penn to "destroy or humble the Corporation, thy most backward friends in the Government. . . ."[5]

The fact that the proprietary victory of 1705 had failed
to improve economic conditions also redounded to Lloyd's advantage. Even such a wealthy merchant as Samuel Carpenter
was compelled to sell much of his property, including his
mills, in order to raise money. Many colonists were dissatisfied with acts of Assembly altering the value of coin and imposing a tax on freemen. An anonymous letter writer expressed
the opinion of many colonists when he reminded the Assembly
"th[a]t you derive your power from the people & th[a]t you are
or ought to be their sarvants and Consequently ought before
you perfected any bus[i]ness of moment to give your Masters
an account of it by making publicke all notes & bills th[a]t came
before you as the Representatives of the people."[6] Asserting
that the Assembly was packed with Evans' cronies, the writer
suggested that some of the laws passed by the Assembly were
contrary to the Magna Charta and had no precedent in America.

He was convinced that the Assembly had been elected only for a single purpose and did not care to observe its responsibilities to its constituents, the freemen of Pennsylvania.[7]

Lloyd had little influence in forming the proprietary Assembly's legislative program, to be sure, but he nevertheless authored a watered-down version of his much-maligned bill for the confirmation of the Frame of 1701. The conservative Assembly would never accept the radical proposals contained in Lloyd's original bill, but it did pass, with amendments, Lloyd's "Act to Ascertain the Number of Assemblymen." This act confirmed only so much of the Frame of 1701 as dealt with the annual election of assemblymen, and it recognized the *status quo* which had existed since the establishment of a separate Assembly in the Lower Counties. Moreover, it contained a liberalization of the suffrage qualifications. Voters were to be natural-born or naturalized subjects of England, twenty-one years of age or more, who possessed "fifty acres of land or more well-seated, and twelve acres thereof or more cleared and improved; or be otherwise worth fifty pounds, lawful money of this province, clear estate, and have been resident therein for the space of two years before such election."[8]

The revival of Lloyd's popularity became particularly pronounced in September, 1706, when Evans and the conservative Assembly fell out over the organization of the courts. The courts were at a standstill because of the repeal of the judiciary act of 1701 by the Queen-in-Council.[9] The Assembly prepared a judiciary act which gave the Deputy Governor powers to hold a court of equity and to issue special commissions "of Oyer and Terminer & Gaol Delivery" for the trial of capital offenses.[10] Evans, however, was dissatisfied and demanded restrictions upon the county courts and the Philadelphia city courts which the Assembly would not grant. When Evans threatened to establish courts by executive ordinance, Lloyd joined three conservative assemblymen in urging the Deputy Governor to defer such action until after the election of October 1. Evans and his Council, accordingly, suspended further action until after the election and prepared a new judiciary bill to submit to the new Assembly.[11] Evans' threat to establish courts by his executive ordinance was one of the important factors which influenced the election of October 1, 1706.

The election of October 1 was a sweeping victory for Lloyd.
Lloyd, Wilcox, Jones, Francis Rawle, and Joshua Carpenter
were returned to the Assembly by the freemen of Philadelphia
County, and the great majority of assemblymen were Lloydians. The only assemblyman elected from Philadelphia County
who could at all be considered proproprietary was Samuel
Richardson, and Logan deemed him "very rough." Logan wrote
that the election was the worst he had seen in the province,
and he advised Penn that he and Deputy Governor Evans would
"use all possible means to make their [the Lloydians'] sessions short and abortive."[12]

The election victory gave Lloyd the opportunity he needed
to restore the judicial reforms which he had initiated five years
before and which had been jeopardized by the Queen's repeal of
the judiciary act of 1701 and by Evans' threat to establish
courts by executive ordinance. As October 14 drew near, he
prepared for the coming battle for the control of Pennsylvania's
judiciary system.

# 15. The Judiciary Controversy

Lloyd had no intention of permitting the judiciary bill, written by Evans and his Council just before the election, to be enacted into law. By writing such a legislative bill, Evans and his Council were claiming a legislative power for the Council that contradicted the interpretation of the Frame of 1701 to which Lloyd was committed. Moreover, the bill called for the establishment of the court of equity in the Deputy Governor and Council, thereby denying the county courts the equity jurisdiction they had formerly enjoyed, and it was so worded that fictions, such as the declaration of ejectment which Lloyd vigorously opposed, could be entered in any court in Pennsylvania.[1]

Lloyd received Evans' judiciary bill when the Assembly convened on October 14, but he immediately shelved it. He constituted the Assembly as a committee of the whole to consider the preparation of a new judiciary bill and appointed Wilcox to be its chairman. The committee of the whole passed a number of resolutions which it desired Lloyd to write up in the form of a judiciary bill. Lloyd wrote the bill, and, after it had been amended by the committee of the whole, the Assembly passed it and submitted it to the Deputy Governor for approval.[2]

The Lloydian bill was just the opposite of Evans'. It would have excluded the Deputy Governor and Council entirely from the equity jurisdiction and would have given equity powers to the county courts of common pleas and to the Supreme Provincial Court. Moreover, it would have protected and broadened the judicial powers of the City Corporation of Philadelphia, which Evans wanted to restrict, by authorizing the corporation to commence actions in the Supreme Provincial Court and by prohibiting county courts from interfering with the jurisdiction of the corporation as a judicial body. It would have authorized the county courts to collect fines and forfeitures for the payment of county justices' salaries and fees, thereby depriving Penn of one of his sources of revenue. It would also have established legal protection for debtors by providing that no person should be arrested and imprisoned for debt, unless he was about to leave the province, or had absconded, or had refused to give security to the reasonable demands of the creditor. Furthermore, for the first time in the history of Pennsylvania, the proposed act would have recognized the existence of a professional class of legal practitioners by making specific requirements for admission to the bar. It required that "such Persons who shall be admitted to practice as Lawyers in the Courts of this Province, shall be learned in the Laws of *England,* and of this Government, and of known Integrity. "[3]

All these reforms would have been carried out had the Lloydian bill become law. Evans and his Council, however, regarded it with disgust, terming it "a long and tedious bill. "[4] The purpose of the bill, only too obviously, was to transfer considerable control of the courts from Penn and his deputies to the colonists through their representatives in the Assembly.

The Lloydian judiciary bill aroused a storm of controversy between the Deputy Governor and his Council, on the one hand, and Lloyd and his followers, on the other. Evans had no intention of granting away prerogatives which he thought "Indisputably belong to the Gov[erno]r in Chief or his Lieut[enant], such as the putting in & turning out of officers as he shall see occasion, fines & forfeitures, & the perquisites arising from the Licensing of Publick Houses. " He sent the bill back to the Assembly with a warning that unless the Assembly passed the bill he had recommended to it at the beginning of the session he would establish courts by ordinance.[5] In a message to the Assembly on November 28, 1706, Evans stated more clearly his principal objections to the Lloydian bill.

"The case is short and plain, " he said, "the Assembly requests several things to be granted away from the Propr[ietor] & Gov-[erno]r which are now his, and to this he will not agree; they desire some other new matters to be Enacted that were never known here before, which he thinks not safe for the Countrey, & therefore cannot assent to. " Evans stated his conviction that the whole purpose of the Lloydian bill was "to divest the Gov-[erno]r of his power and render him as useless as they would the Council. "[6]

Lloyd, who wrote subsequent Assembly messages to Evans, answered that the Assembly's judiciary bill was based "upon the best Constitution we could find, to witt: the common and statute Laws of England. "[7] He admitted that some parts of Evans' proposals which had been rejected by the Assembly agreed in some ways with the judiciary systems in neighboring colonies, but he warned that they might, if enacted, "produce the like Inconveniences as theirs do. "[8] He referred to the laws of England to justify clauses in the Assembly's judiciary bill which provided for the granting of licenses by the county justices and for the payment of justices' salaries and fees out of fines collected by them. The right of magistrates to set fines, he asserted, was guaranteed by English law and precedent, and he referred specifically to a passage in *The Reports of Sir Peyton Ventris* as proof. [9] What Lloyd wanted was the practice in England and in some of the royal colonies in America. In fact, he insisted that the Assembly demanded nothing of the Proprietor that had not earlier been granted by him. He reminded Evans that Pennsylvania

. . . was not at first settled as some others were, either at the Charge of the Crown of England or of any private man, nor was it peopled with the purges of English prisons, but by men of Sobriety and substance, who were Induced Chiefly by the Constitution, which by Compact with the Proprietary, was to be so Established as that the purchasers and adventurers were to have greater Privileges than they Enjoyed in their native Countreys, Which however, we have been deprived of, we think the Proprietary in duty and Conscience obliged to endeavour to restore unto us instead of surrendering. [10]

To be sure, Lloyd's insistence on greater control of Pennsylvania institutions by the colonists at the expense of proprietary prerogative did not mean that he and his followers were not loyal Englishmen. Lloyd acknowledged that the governments of England and of the English colonies were the best in the world "when under a good ministration." He assured Evans that it was not the Assembly's intention to deprive the Deputy Governor of power and support. He warned, however, that "if a Gov[erno]r would divest or deprive the Queen's Liege people in her particular Governm[en]ts of the Privileges, that by the Statute Laws which are made for the Publick good, as well as by the Common Law . . . That such a Gov[erno]r can not expect the people with Cheerfulness to support him."[11]

Lloyd cited, as warning, an act of Parliament, passed during the reign of William III, which provided for the punishment of colonial governors who oppressed English subjects or who violated the laws either of England or of the colonies they governed. He observed that there were people who held the opinion that "the privileges of the subject in the Plantations are merely Dative & at the will of the Prince." Such an opinion, he said, had been propagated earlier in the history of Pennsylvania--presumably he meant by Blackwell--but it had long since been exploded. Several legal authorities, whom he did not name, had been introduced into the Assembly, he asserted, which showed "that the subjects coming into the Queens Plantations abroad, barrs not their Claim to their native English rights." Lloyd and his followers wanted specific guarantees that their rights as freeborn Englishmen would not be violated by an arbitrary governor on New World soil. "We are not striving for Grants of Power," Lloyd explained, "but what are essential to the Administracon of Justice, and aggreeable to an English Constitution. . . ."[12] Lloyd's explanation was sincere, but his fanatic devotion to the cause of legislative supremacy blinded him to the all-important fact that he and his partisans were actually seeking "Grants of Power" for the Assembly greater than those to which the Assembly was legally entitled. Lloyd, moreover, did not always follow the English constitution when he prepared legislative bills, as the innovations in his judiciary bill attest.

One of the innovations in Lloyd's judiciary bill, which Evans was at a loss to understand, was the idea of a supreme appellate court of law and equity to rule on the regularity of proceed-

ings in the lower courts. Such a court, it seemed to Evans,
would only prolong and complicate the judicial process and,
rather than relieve the colonists, would in fact oppress them.
The Deputy Governor thought Lloyd's supreme court idea novel.
In appearance it would have combined within the supreme court
the powers of the great common law courts of King's Bench
and Common Pleas at Westminster Hall. Yet it was unlike both
in that it would not have initiated proceedings but would have
been a supreme appellate court within the province with authority only to pass judgment on the regularity of proceedings
in the lower courts when appeals were made to it in specific
cases. Evans compared it with the Courts of King's Bench and
Common Pleas in England, but he could not understand the
detailed definition of the supreme court's powers which Lloyd's
judiciary bill contained. He thought such a definition of powers
unsafe.[13] The definition of the supreme court's powers by law
involved a serious limitation of the proprietary prerogative in
the administration of Pennsylvania jurisprudence.

Evans, furthermore, was averse to any proposition that the
Governor and Council be deprived of the equity jurisdiction. He
thought that the Lloydian judiciary bill conflicted with acts of
Parliament which had granted equity powers to the President
and Council of Wales. Lloyd replied that the "acts of Parliament" to which Evans had referred were the Ordinance of Wales
which had, among other things, given the President and Council
of Wales authority to act as a court of chancery. He added,
however, that the establishment of equity powers in the President and Council of Wales had been rebuked there as "a burthen
to the subject and a means to Introduce Arbitrary Power,"
and that it had been suppressed by a statute of 1 William and
Mary, chapter 27. From the reign of Henry VIII, Lloyd reminded Evans, the equity jurisdiction in Wales had been established in the county courts.[14] Lloyd was willing to compromise by lodging a centralized court of equity in commissioners
appointed by the Deputy Governor. He desired primarily, he
said, to prevent the Council's "assuming unto itself a power
to Intermeddle in Civil Causes, and matters only of private
Interest between party and party which the Parliament of England thought fitt to stop there, and from that Example we think
it our duty to oppose the same mischiefs here."[15] Evans, un-

willing to accept even this compromise, insisted that the establishment of a court of equity in the Governor and Council was the practice in New York, Maryland, Virginia, and other colonies by the express direction of the Queen herself. [16] Lloyd, however, was not of a mind to copy institutions in the royal provinces which conflicted with the autonomous interests of the colonists of Pennsylvania.

Lloyd was disturbed by the fact that Evans' judiciary bill had been promulgated in the Council before the Assembly had convened, and he was aware that the Council had helped Evans prepare his objections to the Assembly's judiciary bill. Lloyd and his partisans were willing to consider recommendations by the Deputy Governor and Council, but they would not allow the Council any share in the legislative power. The Deputy Governor, Lloyd explained, might consult his Council in legislative matters, but the Pennsylvania Council did not have the authority of "Councils in Gov[ern]m[en]ts immediately under the Crown, where the Queen Gives them their share in Legislation, as well as the Govern[o]rs, by Express powers." [17] Evans replied that his Council had the same share in the legislative power as the Attorney General and "divers others" in England who made objections to legislation passed by the Assembly. He pointed out that the Queen herself shared in the legislative power, since her authority alone confirmed or repealed the provincial laws. Evans reiterated the position that Penn had taken prior to his grant of the Frame of 1701, when he asserted that the colonists through their Assembly had only the right of concurrence in the making of laws. He believed that only the Governor or his deputy had the right to promulgate and approve legislation. It seemed to him that Lloyd and his partisans in the Assembly were only using the judiciary controversy as a means of amending the provincial constitution so as to extend their own power at the expense of the Proprietor's and his deputy's. Evans argued that if constitutions were always to be altered, "all constitutions would be entirely changed in a very few years, and there would remain no ancient Rights to be asserted, all would be soon bought and swallowed up by the People, who yet would never find themselves the more happy, tho' they might perhaps be more licentious in Government." [18] Evans' arguments failed, however, to move

Lloyd and his partisans, and Lloyd repeated his earlier objections to the assumption of legislative power by the Council. [19]

Lloyd and his followers firmly resisted Evans' threat to establish courts by his executive ordinance. Lloyd contended
that Evans could issue an executive ordinance only with the
advice and consent of the Assembly. He warned that if Evans
nevertheless issued such an ordinance without the Assembly's
consent then the Assembly would feel "obliged to take such
measures as may be proper for our own Vindication, and to
discharge the Trust in us reposed by those we Represent."[20]
Evans wanted to issue the ordinance anyway, but he was restrained by his Council. The Council agreed with Evans that
Penn's charter permitted him or his deputy to erect courts
without the concurrence of the Assembly, but it preferred to
have the judiciary settled by an act of Assembly rather than
by executive decree. [21] Conservative as were the men in the
Council, they were nevertheless predisposed in favor of a
government of laws, rather than of men.

So the controversy resulted in an impasse. Lloyd was angry
with Evans, but he was convinced that Logan was chiefly responsible for Evans' persistent refusal to accept the Assembly's judiciary bill, [22] and he plotted to rid Pennsylvania of
both men. During the Assembly's adjournment he and several
of his partisans wrote to Whitehead, Mead, and Lower, complaining of Evans' and Logan's conduct in the provincial government. They authorized the three English Quakers to represent the Assembly before the Queen-in-Council and the Board
of Trade as the colonial agents of Pennsylvania and requested
that they intercede with Penn on behalf of the Assembly to obtain the removal of Evans and Logan from the government of
the province. If Penn should refuse to remove Evans and Logan,
then Lloyd and his friends requested that their appointed agents
urge the Proprietor to give the Deputy Governor and Provincial
Secretary "positive orders to Comply with our Just demands or
otherwise to procure an honest grave Sober man to be his
Lieuten[an]t with positive directions to Restore us to the Rights
& privileges which were promised us So farr as they are practicable and allowed so to be in other Colonies." They did not
want Penn to surrender the Pennsylvania government to the

Crown, and they were willing "to Contribute to Support the Governm[en]t under Such an Administration as will protect them [the colonists] in their Just Rights & Liberties." Should negotiations with Penn fail, Whitehead, Mead, and Lower were to seek the advice of the Meeting for Sufferings in London. [23] Lloyd and his partisans said nothing of their efforts to seize more power for themselves than they were legally entitled to by the laws of both England and Pennsylvania.

Evans did not appear to know of the Lloydians' correspondence with Whitehead, Mead, and Lower until May, 1707, when Isaac Norris, visiting in London, informed Richard Hill, a member of the Provincial Council, of it. [24] Evans, however, already had the impression that Lloyd was endeavoring to enact his judiciary bill as a security against the possible conversion of Pennsylvania into a royal colony. When the Assembly reconvened in February, 1706/7, Evans warned that if the Proprietor surrendered the provincial government to the Crown the Queen was very likely to repeal all the provincial laws. He was certain that the Queen would not consent to a constitution which was very different from those in her other dominions. Evans, tired of the written debates with Lloyd, which had taken up so much of the legislative session, asked for a conference with the Assembly to discuss judiciary legislation. He would not even give the Assembly a copy of his address for fear that Lloyd would spend several days preparing an answer to it.

Lloyd was not opposed to a conference, but he had no intention of compromising or of yielding to Evans. The conference was held, but it turned out to be only a continuation of the controversy between Lloyd and Evans. Lloyd argued that, although the Proprietor and his deputy had the right of appointment, the Assembly should have the power to remove judges "when they are proved Guilty of Official misbehaviour." He explained that Judge Mompesson himself had recommended such a provision in a provincial judiciary law and that the legal precedent for it was an act of Parliament passed in 1701 which had based judicial tenure in England on good behavior rather than on the King's or Queen's pleasure. Under the English statute judges could be removed only by an address from the throne to both houses of Parliament. [25]

Evans replied that the English Act of Succession did not necessarily apply to colonies in America where circumstances,
different from those in the homeland, prevailed. Moreover, he
contended that judges' commissions had always been *"durante
bene placito,"* that is, during the Proprietor's pleasure. Lloyd,
however, based his argument not only on the English Act of
Succession and on Judge Mompesson's recommendation but
on section eighteen of the Frame of 1682 which had provided
that the Proprietor should grant commissions to justices "for
so long a time as every such person shall well behave himself in the office."[26] The Frame of 1682 was not in force, to
be sure, but the section to which Lloyd referred nevertheless
constituted a legal precedent.

Evans knew that Lloyd's purpose was to use an act of Parliament as a means of depriving the Proprietor and his deputy of
much of their prerogative in the administration of Pennsylvania
courts, and, rather than argue the matter further with Lloyd,
he turned the conference into a personal attack on the Speaker.
Throughout the conference Lloyd had remained in his seat
while speaking. Evans felt that Lloyd had been purposely dis-
respectful toward him by so doing, and he insisted that Lloyd
stand up when he addressed the Deputy Governor. Lloyd's independent spirit rebelled against this tactless directive. Remaining in his seat, Lloyd replied that as Speaker of the Assembly he was "the mouth of the Countrey" and that he would
take his orders from the people. When Evans continued to
demand that he stand up, Lloyd finally arose and declared that
he was "a free agent, and ought not to be directed by any but
the House [i.e., the Assembly]." He then led the Assembly
out of the conference.[27]

Lloyd's temper had gotten the better of him. The day after
the conference either he was sorry or his friends persuaded
him to soothe the Deputy Governor's ruffled feelings. Lloyd
and his followers sent messages to Evans in an effort to pour
oil on troubled waters and to revive the interrupted conference.
The Assembly, said the messages, regretted the misunderstanding between the Speaker and Evans. The Speaker, in walking out of the conference, had not acted by order of the Assembly. The messages explained that the Speaker's privilege of
remaining seated in the presence of the Deputy Governor had

always been observed on such occasions and that Lloyd had intended no offense to Evans. Lloyd and his followers proposed that a joint committee of the Assembly and Council be set up to establish rules of procedure for a future conference.

Evans, however, was in no mood to compromise. His dignity had suffered, and he demanded satisfaction. He asserted "That it is no Priviledge of any Representative of the People, either in England or elsewhere, to sitt when he speaks to the superior of that People. . . ." He construed Lloyd's affront to him as an affront to the Queen of England, inasmuch as he considered himself the Queen's deputy as much as Penn's. Evans desired to resume the conference, but he warned that if the Assembly continued to defend the conduct of its Speaker he would have to exercise his prerogative to reopen the courts by executive ordinance.[28]

Evans, apparently confident that Lloyd would yield, named the place and date for the resumption of the conference. He and his Council waited two hours in vain for the Assembly to appear. Lloyd had drawn the line, and there was to be no conference. Instead he offered as a substitute the establishment of a joint committee of the Assembly and Council. Otherwise he wanted a written statement of Evans' objections to the judiciary bill. Evans chose the latter course, but he merely reiterated the objections he had made before. Lloyd responded by preparing a representation which contained a history of the judiciary controversy and a proposal that so much of the judiciary bill as related to the appointment and removal of judges be extracted and made the subject of separate legislation. He submitted a copy of the representation to Evans and his Council, who greeted it with scorn. Evans subsequently issued a proclamation to enforce an executive ordinance which he and his Council drew up in such a manner as to agree "as far as may be" with the Lloydian judiciary bill. At the same time they prepared a legislative bill to continue the legal processes which had prevailed before the Queen's repeal of the judiciary act of 1701, but Lloyd and his followers promptly rejected it. Lloyd warned that if Evans would not concur in the establishment of courts by law then he and the Assembly would "represent the whole matter to his and our superiors."[29] Evans

ignored this warning, and Lloyd sent a copy of his representation to Whitehead, Mead, and Lower.[30]

Thus Lloyd's struggle to revive and expand the judicial reforms, which he had initiated six years earlier, ended in apparent defeat. Lloyd, however, did not give up the fight. Determined to persevere in the face of adversity, he attempted
once more to drive from the provincial government the man
whom he considered the chief obstacle to his legislative pro-
gram--James Logan.

# 16. Charges and Countercharges

Lloyd, convinced that Logan was chiefly responsible for Evans' opening of the courts by executive ordinance, submitted to Evans, by order of the Assembly, articles of impeachment against the Provincial Secretary. The articles of impeachment covered much more than the judiciary controversy. All the grievances of the colonists, particularly those concerning land, were charged against Logan. Lloyd and his followers accused Logan of having

. . . wickedly Endeavored to deprive the Queens Subjects in this province of the priviledges and benefits w[hi]ch they ought to Enjoy by the fundamental Laws of England and Establisht Constitutions of this Government and instead thereof to Introduce an arbitrary Governm[en]t ag[ains]t Law w[hi]ch he has declared by divers words opinions practices & actions.

Logan, they said, had committed this grievous wrong in several ways, violating the law of Pennsylvania in matters of government and property. [1]

Some of the charges were unfair. The Lloydians accused Logan of having violated Penn's charter and the Frame of 1701 by inserting clauses in Evans' commission reserving to the Proprietor an absolute veto power over all acts of Assembly and authorizing Evans to call assemblies by his writs and to prorogue them at his pleasure. [2] Logan actually had opposed the clause in Evans' commission which reserved a veto power to Penn. [3] He asserted, in his reply to the articles of impeach-

*177*

ment, that the commission had been written in England. He admitted that he had sent Penn copies of all public grants, charters, and Deputy Governor's commissions, including Hamilton's, which, he said, "seems to have been Copied in haste." He denied, however, that he had sent Hamilton's commission to serve as a model for Evans' and insisted that there was no clause in Evans' commission authorizing him to call the Assembly by his writs and to prorogue it at will. The contents of Evans' commission, he explained, were not generally known, because Evans had never thought it necessary to proclaim them. [4]

Lloyd and his followers were more justified in other charges which they made against Logan. Logan admitted the truth of the accusation that he had, in December, 1705, withheld from the Assembly the Board of Trade's objections to certain provincial laws. He explained that he had done so at the instance of several members of the Council and Assembly who had asked him to wait until the next session of the Assembly. He had delivered the objections to the Assembly, after Evans had received the actual repeal of Pennsylvania laws by the Queen-in-Council, but he did not explain why he had withheld such information from a conservative Assembly. As Lloyd and his followers pointed out, Logan's action had made it difficult for the Assembly to prepare laws which the Queen would approve. [5]

The Lloydians also accused Logan of having violated the Frame of 1701 by delaying delivery to the rolls office of the laws passed during the session of 1705/6 so that they might be recorded. Logan explained that he had been "obliged to keep the Laws till I had taken Copies for England and ffor the Counties & then I delev[ere]d them." He denied the allegation that he had ever made public declarations against the Frame of 1701 but admitted that he had contended publicly that the Proprietor had never intended, in the Philadelphia City Charter, to permit the city corporation to set and collect fines in courts in which capital crimes were tried. [6]

Lloyd's attack on Logan was particularly effective when it dealt with Logan's administration of the proprietary land policy. Logan was the subject of wide criticism among the colonists because of his conduct as Penn's agent in charge of surveys, land patents, and quitrent collections. Lloyd and his partisans ac-

cused Logan of having violated the property act of 1700 by imposing "upon divers of the Queens Subjects Certaine Pattents
or Grants of his owne Drawing for the Confirmation of their
lands Refuseing th[e]m Draughts or Copies of those Grants to
advise concerning the validity thereof or the assurance of the
land thereby to be Confirmed."[7]

Logan's reply was rather facetious.

> D[avi]d Ll[oyd] [he said] is against Patents & would have all Grants
> made like other common [mutilated] to be drawn by Such as the Gran-
> tees would employ, I suppose only for his own Benefit[.] [He] pleads
> that 'tis none of my business to draw them[.] We Grant our Patents
> in the Prop[rie]t[ar]ys Name and Stile, as is Practised in all America
> but he would have them in our private Names, Notwithstanding in
> Deeds drawn by himself to be sign'd by attor[ney] he prefers the Meth-
> od of making them the same way viz in the name & Stile of the Con-
> stituents tho but private persons.[8]

Lloyd and his followers charged that Logan had violated the
property act of 1700 also by reserving quitrents for several
years before patentees had definitely located their lands and
that he had compelled freeholders to pay quitrents for land
which had been allowed them by the act of 1700 to make up for
property losses sustained because of road building and discrepancies in surveys. Logan did not deny this charge, but
said that the Proprietor's right to quitrents in such case was
hardly ever disputed. He supposed that the charge had been
occasioned by the refusal of one of Lloyd's partisans to pay
his quitrents.

The Lloydians charged further that Logan had granted warrants for resurveys after the time for resurveys allowed by
the property act of 1700 had lapsed. Logan was not sure that
he had done so, but he knew of "no Law nor Equity against it."
He denied outright the allegation that he had, without the authority of law, surveyed and allotted to claimants lands that
rightfully belonged to others.[9]

Lloyd and his followers complained that Logan was acting as
Surveyor General of Pennsylvania as well as Provincial Secretary and pointed out that the two offices had originally been
intended "to be a mutuall Check upon Each other for the Gen-
erall Securety of the propriet[a]ry & his Tennants."[10] Logan

explained that he had taken the office of Surveyor General without remuneration to save Penn the expense of appointing someone else. [11]

Thus Lloyd and his partisans went far afield from the judiciary controversy in their attack on Logan, and all the constitutional and land problems of the colony became involved.

Lloyd secured from the Assembly not only articles of impeachment against Logan but a remonstrance against Evans'
executive ordinance on the basis of which provincial courts had
been reopened. The only effect, however, was to steel Evans'
and Logan's resistance to Lloyd's frontal assault upon them.
Logan sent his answers to the articles of impeachment to Penn,
and Evans prepared a reply to the remonstrance which he used
as a kind of counterpropaganda. His reply was a warning that
he "would absolutely refuse to pass an act for Courts unless
the House would agree to establish a Militia for the defence of
the Queen's subjects." He argued that conditions in Pennsylvania differed from conditions in England and that laws which
were practicable in the homeland might not be desirable in
Pennsylvania--a curious reversal of the position he had previously held that Pennsylvania should in all things conform to
the institutions, laws, and customs of England. [12] Lloyd, in
an equally curious reversal of his autonomy position, said that,
even though conditions in Pennsylvania differed from those in
England, "to infer from thence that we ought not to have the
Common Rights & privileges of freeborn English subjects . . .
we think as empty an amusement as any thing we have offered. . . ." Whatever the differences in climate might be,
he asserted, "the People are generally averse to any, but an
English Constitution. . . ." [13] He might well have added that
he and his followers demanded rights and privileges greater
than any they had enjoyed in England and institutions and laws
which were not at all a part of the English Constitution.

Lloyd and his partisans continued to press their charges
against Logan, and the question arose as to the judicial powers
of the Deputy Governor in such impeachment proceedings. Not
since the days of Nicholas More and Speaker John White had
the Assembly impeached an official in the provincial government, and the procedure had never been clearly determined.
Evans contended that the proceedings were improper, "since

there is no middle state in it resembling the House of Lords in England, who can judicially hear and determine the Impeachments brought by the House of Commons. "[14] Lloyd replied that Penn's charter granted the Assembly the right to impeach and the Governor or his deputy the right to try persons impeached by the Assembly; these rights had also been established by precedent. He defined the Governor or his deputy as an intermediary between the Assembly and the Crown, holding a position comparable, though inferior to, the House of Lords in England; as such he had the power to act as a judge in the trial of impeached persons. The Council, he added, had no such power; Evans would have to be the sole judge. Lloyd argued that if Evans refused to prosecute Logan on the basis of the articles of impeachment, then the Assembly's right of impeachment would be meaningless. The Assembly's power of raising and appropriating money for the provincial government, he warned, would amount to nothing "without the Power of Impeaching evil ministers that act for the ruin of the nation. " Lloyd thereupon demanded that Evans remove Logan from his Council. [15]

Evans rejected every one of Lloyd's demands, even though Logan petitioned for a speedy hearing that he might clear himself of the charges. [16] Once more Evans and Lloyd were stalemated, and the Assembly went into adjournment without any equitable solution of the judiciary problem having been achieved and without a satisfactory conclusion to the impeachment proceedings. Lloyd, hoping to bring pressure to bear on Penn and his agents from a more authoritative quarter, sent letters to Whitehead, Mead, and Lower, enclosing a remonstrance by the Assembly and City Corporation of Philadelphia against Penn, Logan, and Evans. The English Quakers planned to lay the letters and remonstrance before the Queen. [17]

As the session of 1706-7 drew to a close, Lloyd's popularity remained undiminished. Evans, on the other hand, drew upon himself the increasing ire of the colonists because of his persistent efforts to militarize Pennsylvania. Two hundred twenty merchants and tradesmen, mostly cf Philadelphia, complained to the Assembly that the erection of a fort at New Castle--one of Evans' pet projects--prevented the use of the Delaware River for commerce and trade. Some of the more

intemperate colonists attacked Evans on the street because of
the Delaware fortification. [18]

In the election of October 1, 1707, every member of the Assembly was re-elected, and Lloyd was retained as the Assembly's Speaker. Lloyd promptly rebuked Evans' admonition that
the Assembly consider itself a new body, even though its personnel remained unchanged. Lloyd wanted nothing less than the
speedy passage of his judiciary bill and the removal of Logan
from the Council. Evans accused Lloyd and his followers of
obstructionism and prorogued the Assembly to September 30.
Lloyd, however, had already adjourned the Assembly to November 19. [19]

Lloyd and Evans were in no mood to agree on anything, and
the session of 1707-8 was as unproductive as its predecessor.
The political breach extended even into Quaker meetings in
which Lloyd, as Logan reported to Penn, demanded "a separation and a purging." Young Quakers who followed Lloyd
pushed, said Logan, "for rash measures," while their more
conservative elders remained loyal to "Penn's interest."[20]
Lloyd's efforts to drive Logan out of the provincial government and to purge Quaker meetings of proproprietary influences caused Logan to warn Penn that "David Lloyd's purpose is to throw all into confusion, and these into a surrender
[of the provincial government to the Crown]"--an indication
that he hardly understood Lloyd's real purposes. He advised
Penn to tell Pennsylvania Quakers that unless they took measures "to purge the Assemblies of bad men, thou wilt give them
up, and struggle no longer. . . ."[21] Penn, pressed by other affairs in England, delayed following Logan's advice and thereby
avoided an open clash between himself and the colonists over
Lloyd's supremacy in Pennsylvania politics.

Lloyd did not succeed in driving Logan out of the government
or in purging the Quaker meetings of his political enemies, but
his letters to Whitehead, Mead, and Lower finally bore fruit,
when, in 1709, Penn removed Evans and commissioned Colonel
Charles Gookin to replace him. [22] Even before Gookin arrived
in Philadelphia, Lloyd and his partisans were calling for the
prosecution of Evans for having created false alarms of war
and unnecessary disturbances to the detriment of commercial
shipping in the Delaware River and Bay. [23] Lloyd was relent-

less in his attack on a Deputy Governor who had only tried to carry out the instructions of the Proprietor and of the Queen.

From Lloyd's point of view the change of deputy governors was no improvement. Colonel Gookin proved as obedient to proprietary and Crown instructions as Evans had been, and Penn specifically ordered Gookin not to act in legislation without the advice and consent of the Council. Gookin at once challenged the parliamentary privileges claimed by the Assembly, and he and Lloyd soon clashed over matters of procedure, Lloyd's judiciary bill, Lloyd's effort to pass legislation to protect debtors, and Gookin's proclamation "requiring all men to provide themselves with arms, and forthwith to Inlist themselves under such officers as should be appointed. . . ."[24] Gookin defended Evans against Lloyd's attacks, and Evans accused Lloyd and two or three of his closest partisans of having frustrated his administration of the provincial government.[25]

In September, 1709, when it was clear that Gookin would not cooperate with Lloyd, Lloyd and his partisans submitted a remonstrance to Gookin, attacking the proprietary instruction which prevented the Deputy Governor from acting in legislation without the advice and consent of the Council. Lloyd believed that Logan, as Penn's agent, was the most influential member of the Council, and that all of his difficulties with Evans and Gookin were attributable to Logan. Much of the remonstrance was an attack on Logan, and Lloyd and his partisans charged that Logan had spoken abusively of the Assembly in public. They renewed their demands that Logan be removed from the Council.[26]

Logan retaliated by preparing a "Justification" attacking Lloyd and defending himself. The Provincial Secretary asserted that the Lloydian remonstrance was purely political and demagogic and was timed to answer public criticism of the Assembly on the eve of the election. Much of his attack on Lloyd was a critical history of Lloyd's political life after 1689, and Logan revived many old controversies in his effort to prove that Lloyd's sole motivation in politics was to revenge himself against Penn because twice, in 1689 and 1700, Penn had removed him from positions of trust in the government of Pennsylvania.[27]

Logan's "Justification" had little immediate political effect. Lloyd triumphed again in the election of October 1, 1709, and continued to preside over the Assembly as its Speaker. The "Justification, " however, aroused bitter controversy after the election was over. Gookin told the Assembly that if Logan's charges against Lloyd were true he could not "see th[a]t under this Gov[ern]m[en]t, such a person can be accounted fitt for that station [of Speaker]. "[28] Yet only three days earlier Gookin had approved the Assembly's re-election of Lloyd as its Speaker. Lloyd and his partisans retorted that if Logan's charges against Lloyd "had any Weight, It should have been propounded as an Objection against the Assembly's Choice of him for Speaker. . . ." They resented Gookin's acceptance of Logan's charges against Lloyd, after he had approved Lloyd's re-election.[29]

Lloyd had Logan's "Justification" laid before a committee of the Assembly and read to the entire membership of the legislature. He spoke angrily of the document as "that scandalous paper" and prepared a lengthy "Vindication" of himself to which he attached supporting documents intended to prove the invalidity of Logan's charges. He referred his "Vindication" to a committee of the Assembly which subsequently requested that Logan appear before it and submit proofs of his charges against the Speaker. Logan refused to comply with this request, and the committee resolved that the "Vindication" was sufficiently supported "with undeniable proofs and vouchers, and the rest of it upon very probable circumstances and presumptions. " Therefore the committee concluded that Logan's "Justification" was a scandalous libel "reproaching several good members of the . . . House, and aspersing and contemning the authority, power, and proceedings of the representative body of the people of this Province in Assemblies. "[30]

Neither Logan's allegations of past misconduct on Lloyd's part nor Lloyd's defense and counterattack against Logan had much to do with the real issues: the legislative impasse and the failure of the Deputy Governor and the Lloydian Assembly to agree on judiciary legislation. Lloyd denied every one of Logan's allegations and asserted that behind Logan's animosity toward him was an aversion to the parliamentary privileges

claimed by the Assembly. "I would not willingly suppose, " he
wrote,

> that James Logan is so fond of his beloved Machiavel and those high
> flown statesmen, from whose pernicious rules he seems to take his
> measures in Government; but that he casts an eye sometimes upon
> the proceedings of English Parliaments, where instances are not
> wanting which might satisfy him, if anything that is parliamentary
> could do it, that the methods here taken are not so irregular as he
> would represent them. [31]

Lloyd believed that the parliamentary privileges claimed by
the Assembly were based on precedents and established practices in the English Parliament. "But such is his [Logan's]
aversion to a well-tempered authority, " he continued, "that
he has not been wanting to make divisions in the State influ-
encing the law administration of his Government to connive
at such things as had a tendency to oppress the people, violate
their charters, deny them of their rights and leave them without redress. "[32]

Lloyd followed up his "Vindication" with an attempt to have
Logan arrested and imprisoned in the Philadelphia County
jail, just as the Provincial Secretary was preparing to go to
England to see Penn. Gookin and his Council, however, resolved that the Assembly had no legal authority to arrest and
imprison anyone except one of its own members. When Lloyd
and his partisans demanded outright that Gookin imprison
Logan, Gookin placed the Provincial Secretary under the protection of the Philadelphia County sheriff. [33]

Lloyd's persistent attempts to drive Logan from the provincial government resulted finally in political disaster for
himself and his partisans. Logan went to England and returned
with a letter from Penn exonerating him of Lloyd's charges
and warning that Pennsylvania, because of the radicalism of
Lloyd and his partisans, was getting a bad reputation in Europe.
Penn wanted the Assembly to have privileges equal to those of
assemblies in the royal provinces, but he asserted that the
Lloydians' claim "to a power, to meet, at all times during
the year, without the Governor's concurrence, would be to
distort government, to break the due proportion of the parts

of it, to establish confusion in the place of necessary order,
and make the legislative the executive part of government. "[34]
So far as the judiciary controversy was concerned, he objected to the Assembly's efforts to commit him "to the opinion
of principally one man [Lloyd], whom I cannot think so very
proper to direct in my affairs (for, I believe, the late Assembly have had but that one lawyer amongst them). " He urged
the Assembly to seek the advice of other lawyers, "and I am
freely content, " he wrote, "you should have any law, that, by
proper judges, should be found suitable. "[35] Above all, he
wanted the colonists to signify, in a fair election, if they were
for him or against him. [36]

Isaac Norris published a pamphlet which also proved dam-
aging to Lloyd's cause. The pamphlet, *Friendly Advice to the
Inhabitants of Pennsylvania*, was a reminder to the colonists
that for some years, because of persistent factionalism, little
business had been concluded by the Assembly. Norris thought
that most of the difficulties between Lloyd and his followers,
on the one hand, and the Deputy Governor and Council, on the
other, had arisen from mutual misunderstanding. He urged
the freemen to choose men for the Assembly who would get
down to business and who would not waste time with disputes
and remonstrances, men who would at once cooperate with
the Deputy Governor and protect the colonists' liberties. He
warned that either the colonists would have to support the Proprietor and his deputy or they would have to sustain the loss
of their constitution and privileges in government. If they
failed to cooperate with Gookin, he cautioned, they would probably get a governor less to their liking, for Penn might have
to surrender the provincial government to the Crown. [37] What
both Penn and Norris wanted, in effect, was a vote of confidence in the Proprietor and his deputy.

Lloyd countered Penn's letter and Norris' pamphlet with
a remonstrance against Gookin's failure to proceed in legislation and to imprison Logan. [38] This, however, was only another remonstrance, and the colonists were weary of remonstrances. The legislative impasse had gone on too long, and
the Lloydian Assembly did not seem able to pass necessary
legislation. The city magistrates of Philadelphia wanted laws
to enable them to suppress vice and disorder, and they de-

sired revenue so that they could build a watch house, cage, and workhouse, employ the vagrant poor, and repair public wharves and bridges. [39] The courts remained unsettled. Financial conditions were depressed. The value of currency obtained by trade with Maryland and Virginia was low. The prices of staple commodities had depreciated, and trade was again in a state of decline. Penn still had not paid off the Ford mortgage, and the mortgage had been taken over by the firm of Henry Gouldney, an affluent London merchant and Quaker, whom Logan represented in Pennsylvania. Gouldney's mortgage terms militated against the colonists' property rights and brought land business in Pennsylvania to a virtual standstill. Lloyd was blamed for bringing things to such a pass because of the assistance he had given the Fords in their suit against Penn. [40]

In the election of October 1, 1710, Lloyd and his partisans were decisively defeated, as the freemen of Pennsylvania expressed their sympathy for Penn and their preference for proprietary government by electing assemblymen friendly to Penn, Logan, Gookin, and the Provincial Council. [41]

# 17. A Hard Man in a Courtroom

The election of October 1, 1710, ended, for a time, Lloyd's crusade for reforms in the government, courts, and land administration of Pennsylvania. He and his wife had moved earlier to Chester, where they lived in a house on Edgmont Avenue, built reputedly in 1701,[1] and his life during the next four years was that of a country gentleman or, if the term is properly applicable to colonial Pennsylvania, a landed aristocrat. One of the wealthiest landowners in Pennsylvania, he devoted his time primarily to his business affairs as landlord and speculator in lands. He built houses and sold them, rented out considerable property both in the towns and in the country, and bought up land at a low price to sell at a profit. He was also one of the four professional lawyers in Pennsylvania, and he represented clients particularly in lawsuits involving property rights.[2] He lived comfortably and well, yet not selfishly.

Lloyd was at home in Chester in 1710, when Thomas Chalkley, a leading English Quaker who was traveling through the colonies with his wife, arrived. Chalkley's wife had become gravely ill during their journey from Maryland, and Chalkley, attempting to get her to Philadelphia, carried her "as far as Chester in a horselitter." There Lloyd took them into his home. As Chalkley later wrote, his wife "continued for some months, in much misery, and extreme pain, at the house of our very kind friends, David and Grace Lloyd, whose kindness to us, in that sore, trying, and exercising time, was great, and is not to be forgotten by me, while I live in this world. "[3] Under the ministrations of the Lloyds, Chalkley's wife became well, and the Quaker missionaries continued on their journey. The incident revealed the humanitarian side of Lloyd's character which in large measure balanced his tendency toward unscrupulousness as a politician, land speculator, and lawyer.[4]

In 1710, however, Lloyd was in bad odor among colonists because of his vindictiveness in a law suit brought by him against a Quaker in West New Jersey. Six years earlier David Lloyd had sold a portion of the Thomas Lloyd estate to two New York Quakers, John Rodman and William Hudlestone, but their title had subsequently been challenged by a New York colonist who had produced a bill of sale signed by Thomas Lloyd as proof of his claim. Rodman had thereafter failed to pay the balance of what he owed David Lloyd for the land, and a New York lawyer, to whom David Lloyd had given a power of attorney to collect debts due the Thomas Lloyd estate, had instituted a lawsuit against Rodman.

Throughout 1710 the Flushing Monthly Meeting, of which Rodman was a member, assailed Lloyd for the action he had taken against Rodman and accused him of violating the Quaker testimony of truth. Lloyd, in a written defense transmitted to the Flushing Quakers by the Philadelphia Monthly Meeting, explained that his New York lawyer had acted without his knowledge and that the suit against Rodman was "contrary to his intention and the allowed practice of our communion. And therefore he was sorry for it. "[5] Lloyd's protestations of innocence, however, appeared insincere to the Flushing Quakers, because he had previously refused to submit the dispute to arbitration by a committee of impartial Quakers, although Rodman had requested it. The Flushing Quakers demanded that Lloyd repay the cost of the suit to Rodman as a demonstration of his sincerity.[6] Lloyd, however, allowed the law suit to continue, even though Isaac Norris, the other executor of the Thomas Lloyd estate had earlier reached a verbal agreement with Rodman to settle the matter out of court.[7]

Lloyd also drew upon himself the ire of the German community in Pennsylvania, which had generally supported him politically in the past, because of his involvement in the prolonged litigation between John Henry Sprogel, a German immigrant, and the Frankfort Land Company. With the increase of German immigration after 1708 German purchasers of land in Pennsylvania had pooled their interests in an association known as the Frankfort Land Company. Sprogel, who had arrived in Pennsylvania in 1709, claimed ownership of a considerable number of shares in the company, explaining that he had inherited his father's interest in the company and that he had bought out the interests of other former owners who had decided to remain in Germany. He was unable, however, to prove his claim, because, as he explained, he had been detained by the French on his way to America, and the French had dispossessed him of his papers. The extent of Sprogel's claim is not clear, but it must have been considerable; it was probably a controlling interest in the Frankfort Land Company. Francis Daniel Pastorius, who feared losing his 1,000-acre interest in the company, thought Sprogel's story a tissue of lies.

Lloyd, however, believed Sprogel. He advised the young German to initiate an action of ejectment against the Frankfort Land Company, thereby reversing his earlier expressed aversion to fictitious actions.[8] With the assistance of the company's attorney, a man named Falkner, who also believed Sprogel, Lloyd entered a *fictionem juris ad reipsa detrudendos veros possessores* in the Philadelphia County Court of Common Pleas, and the court returned a judgment in Sprogel's favor. Pastorius, who represented the company, immediately appealed to the Provincial Council, after attempting unsuccessfully to pay Lloyd a small fee in exchange for legal advice.

The result was a flood of accusations against Lloyd. Pastorius charged that Sprogel had retained, by payment of a fee, the "four known Lawyers of this province"--Lloyd, George Lowther, Thomas Clark, and Thomas MacNamara--either to represent him or to silence them. Pastorius complained that he and other members of the company were thereby deprived of expert advice in law. The Council espoused the cause of Pastorius and the Frankfort Land Company and charged that Lloyd was "the principal agent & Contriver of the whole. . . ." The Council asserted that Lloyd had received, as his reward for his services to Sprogel, "a thousand acres of Benjamin

Furley's land which the said Benjamin was so weak as to intrust Sprogel with the disposal of."[9]

In spite of the Council's wishes, the judgment against the Frankfort Land Company was never reversed, and Sprogel retained possession of the lands he had claimed. Nevertheless, the controversy persisted, and it was one of the factors which operated to keep Lloyd out of provincial politics for four years. In 1711 Pastorius wrote an account of the affair, which he entitled "*Exemplum Sine Exemplo;* Or (to borrow the Inscription of one of John Wilson's Plays, ) the CHEATS and the PROJECTORS, " but he could not find a printer who would publish it. [10] In 1713 John Jawert, another member of the company, presented the matter to the Philadelphia Monthly Meeting in an evident attempt to influence the Quakers to condemn Lloyd. He accused Sprogel of having attempted unsuccessfully to bribe him, before Lloyd had entered the action of ejectment on Sprogel's behalf. During the trial in court, Jawert charged further, the lawyer Thomas Clark had become inquisitive as to the proceedings, and Lloyd had said to him, "Thom. hold thy tongue, thou shalt have fourty shillings. " Clark had kept quiet, until Jawert subsequently loosened his tongue by paying him £10 in silver and gold. [11]

How much truth there was in Pastorius' and Jawert's accounts cannot now be determined. Lloyd never wrote any defense of his conduct in the case that has survived the ravages of time. There was enough truth in the charges against him, however, to put him in an unfavorable light among many of his contemporaries. He was a hard man to deal with in a courtroom.

There were colonists who disliked Lloyd for the manner in which he had acquired some of his landed wealth, particularly "The Green" at Chester which he had purchased from the Swedish church wardens in 1693. Although Lloyd had long ago had his title to the land confirmed by the Provincial Council, some colonists refused to believe that he had acquired it by any but lawless means. An Anglican minister is said to have written in 1714: "The Glebe lands was [sic] irreligiously sold by some Swedes under the name of church wardens, to a powerful Quaker [Lloyd], who now plows and sows it, and disposes of it at his pleasure, but 'tis hoped his precarious title will be one day inquired into, and the Church restored to her rights again. "[12]

By 1714, however, Lloyd's political star was rising once more, Even his political opponents had recognized his talents as a lawmaker in preparing and enacting the judiciary act of 1711 which included Lloyd's concept of a supreme court with only appellate jurisdictions in law and equity. The Attorney General of England, however, had recommended the repeal of the judiciary act of 1711, and the Board of Trade, early in 1714, forwarded a copy of the Attorney General's analysis and recommendations to the government of Pennsylvania. At the Assembly's request Lloyd examined and signed the document and learned from it that his supreme court idea was not understood by English lawyers and that the Attorney General thought unusual the powers given the county justices of the peace by the act. [13]

Not long after Lloyd had read the Attorney General's analysis, word arrived that the Queen-in-Council had repealed the judiciary act of 1711, and on July 20, 1714, Deputy Governor Gookin published an ordinance for the establishment of the courts--an ordinance which contained much the same provisions as had the ordinance issued by Evans seven years earlier. [14] Pennsylvania jurisprudence was right back where it had started seven years before.

Another factor which resulted in Lloyd's political revival was the burgeoning popularity of legislative supremacy in 1714. Penn suffered an apoplectic stroke early in the year, and his family made an agreement with the Queen-in-Council at the Treasury Chambers, Whitehall, for the surrender of the Pennsylvania government to the Crown for £12,000 payable within four years. Because of Penn's incapacity, the Privy Council recommended that the agreement be perfected by an act of Parliament; consequently the surrender was not immediately consummated. [15] Again facing the prospect of a change in the provincial government, the colonists looked to Lloyd, the leading advocate of legislative supremacy in Pennsylvania, for political leadership. In August the Assembly seized one of the Proprietor's prerogatives by appointing a new Provincial Treasurer, theretofore an officer commissioned by the Proprietor, to replace Samuel Carpenter, who had passed away. [16] In October Lloyd was returned to the Assembly by the freemen of Chester County, and the convened assembly-men restored him to the Speakership he had lost four years before.

# 18. The Power of the Purse

Lloyd was fully conscious of Gookin's most glaring weakness as a Deputy Governor. Gookin had come to Pennsylvania expecting a regular salary and large financial rewards. He had been disappointed. Penn had given Logan £1, 000 for past services, £10 per annum for the rent of the office used for proprietary business, and £50 per annum for collecting rents, furnishing rent rolls, and other services.[1] He had made no provision for Gookin, however, and Gookin had turned hopefully to the Assembly. The Assembly had given him a small compensation, but he had been disappointed.[2]

Lloyd saw in Gookin's yearning for financial reward an opportunity to pass judiciary legislation that might otherwise have been thwarted by a Deputy Governor loyal to the Proprietor and to the Crown. He did not attempt, as he had in 1706, to write a single-package bill governing the organization, regulation, and procedures of the entire judiciary of the province and Lower Counties. The fault with such a single-package bill was that, when it was repealed, it threw the entire judiciary into confusion and resulted in its reorganization by executive ordinance. With the assistance of the Assembly, Lloyd, early in 1715, prepared separate legislative bills empowering justices to recover fines and forfeitures, governing the practice of the courts, establishing county courts of common pleas, establishing and regulating judicial fees, and erecting a supreme court of law and equity with exclusive appellate jurisdiction. Gookin at first resisted passage of the bills, but

his objections wilted rapidly as Lloyd dangled tantalizingly
before him the promise of a salary.

Lloyd procured from the Assembly an impost bill, increasing or continuing existing duties on the importation of wine,
Negro slaves, hops, cider, and rum, in order to raise money
for Gookin's salary. [3] He wanted the Philadelphia merchants,
rather than the farmers and artisans, to pay Gookin's salary,
and the merchants were quick to understand the significance
of the impost bill. They threatened to refuse payment of the
duties and to persuade the Crown to repeal the bill if it were
enacted. Gookin was pessimistic that the impost bill would
"Raise anything," but Lloyd explained that it was the only
provision the Assembly could make, "For the Circumstances
of the Country will at present Admitt of no other." Gookin replied that he could not "be persuaded but that it is as much
a part of the Assembly's business to provide for a support for
the Gov[erno]r as for any other Exigence of the Country" and
added that his concurrence in other legislation would depend
on the provision the Assembly made for his salary. Lloyd
yielded the point, and the Assembly subsequently added a land-
tax bill to the impost bill. Gookin passed both tax bills and
all of the judiciary bills. [4]

Thus Lloyd and the Assembly, over which he presided, exercised the power of the purse to obtain the passage of legislation which the Deputy Governor might otherwise have blocked.
The result was not only the Assembly's control of the Deputy
Governor by paying him his salary but also its control of the
judiciary by prescribing rules of practice and by regulating
salaries and fees.

The judiciary acts of 1715 and control of the Deputy Governor by the power of the purse were the fruits of Lloyd's return to the Assembly. The colonists' need for his leadership
disappeared, however, as the Crown evinced a lack of interest
in buying out the government of Pennsylvania. [5] After 1715 the
Speakership of the Assembly passed to other hands, notably
Joseph Growdon's. Lloyd remained in the Assembly, and succeeding Speakers drew upon his talents as a lawmaker. [6] The
Assembly's power of the purse became an accepted institution in the provincial government, and the policy of legislative supremacy, which Philadelphia merchants had vigorously

opposed not so many years earlier, was now followed even by such conservative Speakers as Richard Hill, a Philadelphia merchant.

By 1717, however, changing circumstances again brought Lloyd to the forefront of Pennsylvania politics. The growing non-Quaker population in Pennsylvania challenged Quaker principles of justice and the Quaker practice of substituting the affirmation for the oath. Crime increased as Philadelphia expanded into one of the most populous ports in the continental colonies. German immigrants from the Palatinate were pouring into the colony, and they rapidly took up western lands without legal provision for their property rights. Many feared that the appearance in the colony of so many foreigners without proper registration might encourage pirates and other lawless elements to use Pennsylvania as a haven. A financial depression, moreover, threatened the economic well-being of the province. An act of Parliament prescribed a uniform rate of exchange for foreign coin in the colonies in order to prevent each colony from tampering with the value of such coin to the detriment of other colonies. Pennsylvania had reduced the value of her foreign coin in conformity with the act, but other colonies, disregarding the law, had retained their old valuation. The effect was to drain currency out of Pennsylvania. Farmers resorted to the employment of country produce as a medium of exchange, but city creditors rejected it. Trade was nearly at a standstill. Colonists warned the Assembly that "the whole Government in General is depriv'd of the Sinews and Life of Trade without which no Countrey can Expect to flourish & prosper."[7] As had happened before, Lloyd ascended to political leadership when an emergency existed.

The appearance of Sir William Keith in 1717 as the Deputy Governor succeeding Gookin, who had aroused the hostility of the Penn family by impugning Logan's loyalty to George I, set the stage for Lloyd's return to power.[8] Lloyd and his old friend Joseph Wilcox dominated the Assembly which Keith addressed in October, 1717,[9] urging that its members strengthen his hand in the government of the colony. ". . . Unanimity," he said, "is the Life of Business. . . ."[10] But he said other things, too, which caused Lloyd to believe that he would be an ally, and not an enemy.

In January, 1717/18, Lloyd and Wilcox wrote a flattering Assembly message to Keith, declaring that they saw in him a man "who has given us an Assurance of making Law the Rule of his Administration."[11] Keith replied that he considered himself, as a colonial governor, entrusted with the King's prerogative but promised that he would respect the laws of the province. He urged the Assembly, however, to base its laws on the English Constitution so that they would be less repugnant to the laws of the homeland. When Lloyd and two other assemblymen asked Keith to cooperate with the Assembly in all matters of state, Keith agreed.[12]

Keith's cooperation was guaranteed when the Assembly appropriated £500 for his salary. Responding readily to the Assembly's power of the purse, Keith approved legislative bills so rapidly that several of the councilmen, whom he ignored, were offended. Finally, on February 22, Logan, Norris, Hill, and Jonathan Dickinson angrily walked out of the Council room and remonstrated against Keith for his failure to seek their advice before passing laws.[13]

Lloyd's amicable relations with Keith enabled him to achieve control of the provincial judiciary at a time when it was under severe attack by Anglicans. Keith gave Lloyd a commission as Chief Justice of the Pennsylvania Supreme Court,[14] and Lloyd was able thereafter to defend the Quaker principles of justice which were the chief object of Anglican attack. Anglican critics accused Quaker courts of being too mild in their punishment of crime and too sparing in their imposition of the death penalty and charged Quakers with meting out justice in a manner repugnant to the laws of England. The county courts of quarter sessions tended to yield to the pressure of such criticism.

Lloyd indicated, shortly after he ascended to the Supreme Court bench, that he intended to resist the trend toward more severe penalties for criminal violations. One of the first cases he reviewed was an appeal from one of the county courts of quarter sessions by a single woman who had received jury trial and had been sentenced to death for murdering her bastard child. Lloyd approved the death sentence, but he represented the convicted woman to Deputy Governor Keith as an object of compassion, and at his request Keith commuted her sentence to life imprisonment.[15]

Lloyd, however, did not oppose capital punishment in all cases. He discriminated carefully between convicted persons who were obviously victims of unusual circumstances and were, therefore, fit objects of compassion and those who were hardened criminals and deserved no sympathy. Lawlessness in growing Philadelphia was becoming a major problem as it was in the other major continental colonial cities, [16] and Lloyd approved of severe penalties to discourage any further expansion of the crime wave. Law enforcement, however, was somewhat hampered by Anglican prejudice against the Quaker practice of substituting the affirmation for the oath-- a prejudice which criminals attempted to employ to their advantage.

Philadelphia had for some years been terrorized by two allegedly hardened criminals and gangleaders, who had finally been brought to justice for murder and had been sentenced to death by a Quaker judge and jury. During the spring of 1718 the convicted murderers, whose names are not recorded in the records of the time, petitioned Keith and his Council and appealed directly to the throne, contending that they had been illegally convicted by a jury which had not been qualified by oath. Philadelphia Anglicans, who sympathized with the criminals, sent a representation to the English government, complaining that the verdict had been given by a jury which had declared solemn affirmation in place of "corporal Oaths."[17] The convicted criminals did not plead innocence but based their entire case on an attack on the Quaker abhorrence of swearing oaths.

Lloyd, at Keith's request, attended a meeting of the Council which Keith had called to discuss the petition from the convicted murderers, and the Chief Justice joined the majority of the Council in declaring that the criminals had been fairly tried and deserved execution. Lloyd believed that the constitution of the province would have to be supported and that it would be unwise to delay the execution of the murderers. Keith subsequently assured Lloyd and the Assembly that he had taken steps to quash the representation which Philadelphia Anglicans had sent to the English government on behalf of the criminals.[18]

Anglican criticism failed to save the convicted murderers from execution, but it pointed up the necessity of bringing

Pennsylvania criminal law more into conformity with English statutes, although within the framework of the Quaker ethos. Lloyd prepared a legislative bill, entitled "An Act for the Advancement of Justice, and more certain Administration thereof," which translated into Pennsylvania law certain English statutes governing judicial practice, including the extension of capital punishment to such relatively minor offenses as burglary and arson. The bill became law, and Keith, persuaded by Wilcox and another assemblyman, addressed a representation to the King urging that he permit the affirmation to pass as an oath universally in Pennsylvania. [19] Another six years were to pass before the King would grant Keith's request, but Keith's action showed how effectively Lloyd and Wilcox used the Assembly's power of the purse to insure continued Quaker control of the Pennsylvania judiciary.

Lloyd, early in 1718, also prepared legislation which confirmed the property rights of foreigners and which confirmed all sales made theretofore by them. At the request of Philadelphia cordwainers, he wrote a bill prohibiting the exportation of tanned leather and raw hides. Exercising the Assembly's power of the purse, he secured Keith's approval of these and other legislative bills, in spite of the opposition of the Provincial Council. [20]

Lloyd's membership in the Assembly, concurrent with his commission as Chief Justice of the Pennsylvania Supreme Court, enabled him to extend the Assembly's power of the purse as a means of controlling the provincial government and judiciary by securing for himself an annual salary of £150. The Assembly also granted the Attorney General of Pennsylvania an annual salary of £60 and thereby extended the power of the purse to that important office. [21]

News of Penn's death on July 30, 1718, reached Pennsylvania in December, and Lloyd and three other assemblymen prepared an address to Keith expressing their sorrow over the Proprietor's death, as well as satisfaction that Keith would continue as Deputy Governor of Pennsylvania. [22] Lloyd and the Assembly, however, had already prepared for Penn's expected demise by passing "An Act for the better securing the Administration of the Government," which contained a provision that in the event of a hiatus in the proprietary the Deputy Governor should possess the same powers as he had when Penn was alive. [23] This act was now in effect, and it strengthened the Assembly's control of the provincial government, even though it was challenged by some conservative colonists who circulated a report that Penn's death left Keith without authority to join the Assembly in passing laws. The proprietorship was being adjudicated in England, and Keith, as a Deputy Governor, was for the time being without a principal. [24]

William Penn, Jr., claimed the proprietorship of Pennsylvania, and his claim was resolutely opposed by Lloyd and other assemblymen. Penn had left two conflicting wills, and a suit at chancery for the Penn estate was under way in England, but Penn, Jr., believing himself the rightful heir, sent a commission for Deputy Governor to Keith and instructed him not to perform any act of government without the advice and consent of the Council. Lloyd, as chairman of a committee of three assemblymen, urged Keith not to publish the commission until the outcome of the suit at chancery was known and to govern in accordance with Pennsylvania law. Keith concurred by issuing a proclamation continuing his governorship in both Pennsylvania and the Lower Counties in accordance with the laws of both sections. [25]

Keith's willingness to accede to their wishes was fortunate for Lloyd and his fellow assemblymen and Quakers. The King-in-Council repealed the judiciary laws of 1715 in July, 1719, and a Deputy Governor, unfriendly to the Quakers and to the supremacy of the Assembly, could have seized the opportunity to administer the courts by executive ordinance. Keith, on the contrary, sought Lloyd's advice, and, at his request, Lloyd attended a meeting of the Council at which the order of the King-in-Council was read. Lloyd's influence on Keith resulted in the issue of commissions which continued the judicial system as it was described in the repealed laws. Lloyd prepared the forms for the commissions, and they were issued by Keith. [26] The commissions remained the only legal basis for Pennsylvania judicial process during the next three years.

With the issue of the judges' commissions the judicial crisis in Pennsylvania was past, and Lloyd withdrew from the Assembly. The Assembly exercised more power in the government than it ever had before, and the Assembly's power of the purse had made Keith a friendly, almost fawning, Deputy Governor. [27] To be sure, the Assembly granted Keith powers it had denied his predecessors, in exchange for his cooperation in securing the Assembly's objectives. In 1720 the Assembly permitted Keith to hold a court of equity with the advice of the Council as a reward for his aid in securing the King's approval of Lloyd's "An Act for the Advancement of Justice, " passed in 1718. [28] Lloyd, however, was in a position to control Keith's exercise of his equity powers.

During the five years following 1719 Lloyd devoted his time and labor to his duties as Chief Justice of the Pennsylvania Supreme Court, to his religious responsibilities as a Quaker, and to the augmentation of his landed wealth.

# 19. A Country Gentleman

After 1718 Lloyd was the most powerful and one of the wealthiest men in Pennsylvania. The financial stringency which distressed many colonists had little or no effect on him. He had chosen wisely in building his private wealth on the basis of land, rather than on the changing fortunes of commerce. His knowledge of the laws of property was widely recognized, and the Philadelphia merchants, who disliked his politics, sought his advice in litigation involving the ownership of land. After Lloyd became the Chief Justice of the Pennsylvania Supreme Court, two Philadelphia merchants, who needed Lloyd's advice in such litigation, presumed that "it may not be proper to apply to David Lloyd Considering his Station."[1] Nevertheless, they found it difficult not to avail themselves of Lloyd's knowledge of the laws of property and Lloyd did not hesitate to give them the advice they sought.[2]

Litigation over land titles had become a persistent problem.[3] Vacant land in the settled counties, at first plentiful, became scarce as continued immigration, especially of German Palatines, increased the population. As land became scarce, prices rose, and immigrant Germans pushed westward in search of cheaper or free lands. There appears also to have been chicanery involved on the part of interested persons who sought to profit by the increase in land prices. Lloyd in 1719 was said to have stated publicly that surveyors in Chester County were marking off great tracts of unclaimed land for themselves, thereby forcing colonists who possessed old rights to look farther west for lands. Since the lands farther west commanded lower prices than those allegedly marked off by the surveyors, Lloyd felt that possessors of old rights, including himself, were being swindled. He made public aspersions against Jacob Taylor, the Surveyor General of Pennsylvania; Isaac Taylor, the surveyor of Chester County; and James Steel, who was probably also a surveyor. Steel wrote to Isaac Taylor of Lloyd's public accusations and advised him to treat the outspoken Welshman kindly. [4]

After 1719 Lloyd tended to sell off his land holdings in eastern Chester County, where prices were high, and to take up lands farther west, where population was moving. In 1720 he sold a portion of a 1, 600-acre tract at French Creek, which he had purchased in two installments eight and nine years earlier. During the same year he procured the 1, 250 acres of land which Penn had originally granted to George Fox and located them near Uwchland in the western area of Chester County (now Lancaster County). Thomas Lower had bought out the full estate from his brothers-in-law four years earlier, but he was an old man who had neither the will nor the means to venture the long journey to America. He had given the estate to his grandsons, but the latter had preferred to remain in England, and the estate finally fell into Lloyd's hands. Lloyd added 800 acres to the estate in April, 1720, and the whole acquisition greatly augmented the land he already possessed at Uwchland--ninety-five acres on a hill which he called "the Mountain" and 290 acres in the upper part of Uwchland.

Lloyd improved his Uwchland holdings, erected houses, grouped together in small settlements, and rented them out to immigrants who could not pay the high prices asked for eastern land and who did not care to move farther west into the wild backwoods. His tenants appear to have used his acreage on "the Mountain" for agricultural purposes and moved regularly between it and the settlements. Unfortunately, Lloyd did not have clear title to a strip of land which lay between the settlements and the hill, and the owner of a neighboring tract claimed it for himself. Lloyd complained to the Chester County surveyor that if the claimant obtained possession of the strip of land his tenants' freedom of movement between their settlements and the hill would be obstructed. He therefore requested that the surveyor survey his lands on the edge of a nearby lake so that an amount of land in that location equal to the strip of land adjoining the hill might be exchanged, thereby saving to his tenants their right of way to the hill. [5] Existing records do not indicate if the request was granted or not.

In Chester Lloyd lived luxuriously and enjoyed the respect and friendship of his neighbors. He was the recorder of Chester County and employed a young English understudy who was one day to succeed him in that office. [6] His leadership extended into the Chester Monthly Meeting, where many religious duties devolved upon him. He was among the select few entrusted with the revision of the Book of Discipline, and he represented Chester Quakers in the Philadelphia Yearly Meeting. He served on Quaker arbitration committees, and at one time he helped to settle a dispute which existed among the members of the Middletown Monthly Meeting. He also performed disciplinary duties for the Chester Monthly Meeting, on one occasion "labouring" with one of the members for abusing his servants and on another occasion disciplining a Quaker for dancing and telling a falsehood. In January, 1720/21, Lloyd became the overseer of his meeting in Chester. [7]

Lloyd was diligent in attending religious meetings and sometimes visited meetings in other communities. One Sunday in 1719 or 1720 he and Grace attended a Quaker meeting at Haverford, and they were greatly attracted by a young woman who sat near them. The young woman was a stranger to them. Yet it seemed to them that she was meant to be a preacher, and they determined to take her under their care and to prepare her for religious service. [8] The young woman was Jane Fenn, an English schoolmistress whose highly mystical and religious memoir contains the most intimate portrayal of David Lloyd's private life extant.

Jane Fenn was born in London on March 3, 1693/94, the daughter of non-Quaker parents. A frail child, she nearly died of an illness at the age of sixteen. She appears to have been under Quaker influence at that time, for in her memoir she recalled that she had believed God had spared her for His ministry in Pennsylvania. Her father, who resisted her attraction to Quakerism, at first refused to let her go to Pennsylvania. She nevertheless persisted and arrived in Philadelphia on May 16, 1712, at the age of nineteen. Apparently she had no clear idea of what she intended to do in Pennsylvania; it was not her purpose to become a Quaker. According to her memoir, she believed that she was obeying a divine command. Perhaps she thought that God would let her know in time what He intended her to do. She was perfectly willing to follow wherever He led, or wherever she thought He led. A Welshman, Robert Davis, paid her passage, and when she arrived in Philadelphia he insisted that she sign indentures, binding herself as his servant for four years. She balked. Surely the Lord did not intend her to be an indentured servant. Even when Davis had her arrested and placed in confinement, she adamantly refused to sign the indentures. Her case came to the attention of several Philadelphia Quaker families who paid off Jane's debt to Davis and employed her as a schoolmistress for their children. Through the influence of these families Jane entered the Society of Friends. The decision to become a Quaker, like every other important decision in her life, seemed to her directed by the voice of God. At a meeting of Quakers she felt that God willed her to speak, and she spoke. From that day forward she was highly regarded by Quakers as a minister.

As Jane Fenn sat in the Haverford meeting house on the Sunday morning that Lloyd and his wife first saw her, she became aware of the two strangers who were looking at her so intently, and it seemed to her that a voice had spoken, "These are the people with whom thou must go and settle." But she observed that the Lloyds were persons of distinction, and she asked herself, "Lord, how can such an one as I get acquaintance with people who appear so much above the common rank?"[9]

After the meeting was over, David and Grace Lloyd approached Jane and proposed that she live with them. Jane, however, was hesitant and seemed uncertain of herself. She nevertheless moved to Chester to be nearer them and accepted employment as a maid in the home of Benjamin Head, a Chester Quaker. At the Heads' Jane became dangerously ill, and Quaker neighbors nursed her back to health. Once more Grace Lloyd tried to get Jane into her home, but the Heads were unwilling to part with her. Jane met Grace Lloyd again at a Quaker meeting soon after her recovery, and this time Grace successfully persuaded her to go home with her.

When Jane and Grace entered the parlor of the Edgmont Avenue house, David Lloyd was entertaining a large company of Quaker gentlemen. One of Lloyd's guests, an English Quaker, advised David and Grace to make Jane their adopted child. Jane, however, was too independent a person to accept charity, even when it was disguised as adoption, and she expressed her determination to enter the Lloyd household as a servant that she might earn her keep. Lloyd thereafter gave her full responsibility over the servants, furnishings, and valuables in his home. "I entered into David Lloyd's family as upper servant," Jane reminisced later, "such as we call in England, housekeepers, having all the keys, plate, linen, &c., delivered to me. They had a great family, and everything passed through my hands. . . ."[10]

The house in which Lloyd was living, when Jane Fenn entered his household, was, for the time, an imposing two-story structure with a large front porch and a pent roof over the second-story window. A door on the eastern side of the house led into a parlor, and behind the parlor was a dining room. Another door on the western side of the house led into a hallway which was of the same size as the parlor. From the hallway a staircase ascended to the upstairs rooms. Behind the hallway was a sitting room. In the hallway and parlor were fireplaces and hearths laid in blue tiles, illuminated with scenes from Bible history. In the upstairs chambers were large closets on each side of the fireplace chimney.[11] It was one of the most luxurious homes in Chester.

In 1721 Lloyd, his wife, Jane Fenn, and the entire household moved into an even more sumptuous, massively constructed stone mansion on the bank of the Delaware River in Chester.[12] Jane remained with the Lloyds in their new home, and David Lloyd, as she later wrote, treated her as "a father, and a sure friend." She thought him kind and generous to his servants and neighbors and wrote that he chose "rather to be loved than feared."[13] Lloyd, whose severity as a lawyer, politician, and businessman sometimes made enemies, was loved by those who were nearest to him and knew him best. As Jane Fenn's memoir testifies, Lloyd's love for her was genuine; she inherited all the paternal affection that Lloyd might have

lavished upon his own child, who had been dead twenty years.
When Jane expressed her desire to travel, Lloyd supplied her
needs, and in 1722 she began an eight-year journey as a Quaker missionary in the continental colonies, Barbados, England,
and Ireland. She returned to the Lloyds for a brief visit in
March, 1723, when she witnessed a real estate bond for Lloyd,
but Lloyd saw little of her until the last year of his life. [14]

# 20. Paper Money

Lloyd began his new life in the stone mansion and Jane Fenn began her journeys as a Quaker missionary at a time when Pennsylvania was beginning to feel the economic effects of the bursting of the South Sea Bubble. Already in 1722 the province was in the throes of a severe economic depression. Both merchants and farmers were short of money, and Philadelphians petitioned the Assembly to lower the interest rate to 6 per cent and to designate hemp and flax as media of exchange.[1] Only gold and silver were legal tender, but silver was dropping in value,[2] and gold was so scarce that, as one colonist subsequently wrote, "little but Cut Pieces, and some Scraps Passed. . . ."[3]

Barter, although unsanctioned by Pennsylvania law, became the general practice. Farmers, lacking gold and silver, used their produce to buy goods from the retail shops, and shopkeepers also used the produce as a medium of exchange when they bought wholesale goods from the merchants. The population of Pennsylvania, more than 40,000 in 1722, was not large enough, however, to consume all the wheat, barley, Indian corn, rye, beef, pork, hemp, and flax which were produced in the country, and the value of the surplus produce declined. Ordinarily, the farmers stored their surplus products in country mills and brought them to town in carts or river shallops to be sold to the merchants on the wharves, but in 1722 the merchants had no money to give to the farmers. Shipping declined,[4] and shipbuilding was at a standstill.

". . . The shipbuilder and carpenter starve for want of employment, " Deputy Governor Keith reported to the Board of Trade, "and we sensibly feel that our usual export decreases apace, the interest of money is high, and the usurer grinds the face of the poor so that law suits multiply. . . ."[5]

Some of the wealthier Philadelphia merchants believed that the depression was caused chiefly by the "luxury, idleness, and folly" of the poor and advised the Assembly to take steps to make the rich richer and to create a *nouveau riche* as the best means of improving economic conditions for all.[6] Others believed that the importation of rum from the West Indies served to drain gold and silver out of Pennsylvania because the West Indies had become a poor market for Pennsylvania wheat and flour. They advocated the manufacture of rum in Pennsylvania and a high duty on West Indies rum to discourage its importation.[7]

Francis Rawle, one of Lloyd's old partisans in the hectic days of the Evans administration, quickly became the chief propagandist for the issue of paper money by the provincial government, and the remedies he proposed were accepted by the Assembly and by most colonists.[8] The paper money experiment had been tried, not too successfully, in other colonies, but economic conditions were so bad that Pennsylvanians, as a rule, were in favor of adopting it. The Assembly opposed the use of farm produce as a medium of exchange, and the issue of paper money seemed the only course left open to it. Keith favored the introduction of the paper money experiment in Pennsylvania, and he so informed the Board of Trade.[9] Lloyd did not express his opinion of paper money, at least not in writing, until 1723, although he assisted the Assembly in legislative matters, particularly those pertaining to the judiciary.[10]

Lloyd took a positive stand on the side of the paper money advocates after the Assembly, in May, 1723, overrode the objections of the Board of Trade and a few of the wealthier Philadelphia merchants by passing an act for the issue of bills of credit at a face value totaling £15,000. The bills of credit were based on land and silver plate as collateral, and a General Loan Office was set up as a kind of provincial bank for the administration of the act. The bills were to be used to pay off debts, to stimulate trade and were to be destroyed by the trustees of the General Loan Office as they were repaid by the borrowers. In other words, they were to be self-liquidating as improving trade conditions brought hard money into the province. The paper currency act improved economic conditions, and trade promptly revived. James Logan and the conservative merchants, however, campaigned actively against the act, and Keith called for the election of assemblymen on October 1, 1723, who would support paper money and the needs of the debtor classes. Lloyd, who suffered little from the depression, was one of those who responded to Keith's call, and the paper money men at once rallied to his leadership. Lloyd was returned to the Assembly by the freemen of Chester County, and on October 14 the Assembly elected him its Speaker.[11] Once again the country gentleman from Chester ascended to popular leadership in a time of emergency.

Lloyd saw in the paper money experiment an opportunity to finance the provincial government and counties and to initiate a public works program in Philadelphia to employ idle workmen and artisans. The colonists were clamoring for another issue of bills of credit to supplement the act of May, 1723, and Lloyd responded to their wishes by preparing, early in November, a paper currency act which became the law of the province on December 12, 1723. Lloyd's act provided for the issue of bills of credit with a total face value of £30,000, subject to conditions similar to those in the act passed earlier, except that it granted more liberal terms to borrowers from the General Loan Office. It set aside £2,600 to defray the charges of the provincial government and counties and specified a loan of £300, repayable with interest, to the City Corporation of Philadelphia, and an additional loan of £300 to Philadelphia for the repair of public wharves and bridges.[12]

Conservative Philadelphia merchants reacted bitterly against Lloyd's paper money act. One group petitioned the Assembly against the act, urging that debts to the King, the Penn family, creditors in England, orphans, and minors be paid in sterling, rather than in bills of credit.[13] Others continued to argue as they had in the past, that paper money would inevitably depreciate in value, and that depreciated currency would help the poor, the debtors, and cheat the rich, the creditors.[14]

Logan, who believed that in economic crises poor men turn
to radicalism and agitation because they lack consideration,
wisdom, prudence, and knowledge, went to England to report
personally to the Penn family.[15] Keith, in a clash with Logan
during a Council meeting, had already deposed the Irishman
from the Council and from the office of Provincial Secretary,
and Logan's anger was directed against Keith rather than
against Lloyd.

Lloyd ignored the objections of the Philadelphia merchants to
the new paper money act. He joined the Deputy Governor,
Council, and Assembly in signing an address to the King, declaring their abhorrence of a plot against his life which had
recently been thwarted.[16] He wrote the bulk of the Assembly's
legislation, including an act prescribing the forms of the declarations to be used in lieu of oaths, which followed the King's
approval of the act substituting universally the solemn affirmation for the oath in Pennsylvania. When the Attorney General,
Andrew Hamilton,[17] resigned because he believed his salary
insufficient, Lloyd and the Assembly, at Keith's request, appointed a new Attorney General. Lloyd exercised complete
control of the General Loan Office, from which all official
salaries and fees were paid, and the trustees of that office
were men of his own political hue. Lloyd contributed his own
bit to the success of the paper money experiment by reducing
his salary as Chief Justice of the Pennsylvania Supreme Court
to £100 per annum.[18]

In August, 1724, Lloyd appointed a committee of five, including Francis Rawle, to inspect the accounts of the General
Loan Office--a privilege which he had provided for himself in
his paper money act. The inspection revealed that the paper
money experiment was working remarkably well. The sum of
£10, 923 had been loaned on mortgages. The first year's payments on these mortgages had been £1, 280 7s. 6d., and that
amount had been sunk and destroyed. Of the total interest due
the province for the first year's loan--£546 3s--£512 3s had
been collected by the General Loan Office. Everybody seemed
to be cooperating to make the experiment a success, and economic conditions were on the upturn. Trade was improving,
wheat prices were rising, and business throughout the province was greatly stimulated. Shipping from the British Isles,

which had formerly been detained at Philadelphia for months while awaiting payment of debts before loading, was now dispatched more rapidly. The lower interest rate attracted immigrants from other colonies, thereby increasing the population. Philadelphia shipbuilders again undertook a shipbuilding program in anticipation of a revived trade. [19]

The paper money experiment was so successful that Lloyd, with Keith's approval, prepared an act which continued in circulation the paper currency already issued and reduced the annual payments into the General Loan Office, thereby extending the circulation of bills of credit as the life blood of trade over a longer period of time. The Assembly maintained in London a colonial agent, originally appointed by Keith, to negotiate the royal allowance of the provincial laws, thereby forestalling any immediate action by the King-in-Council which might have an adverse effect on the paper money experiment. [20]

The principal opposition to the paper money experiment came from the Penn family, however, rather than from the Crown. William Penn, Jr., had died; the suit at chancery had ended with the decision that the proprietary belonged to the Penn family as a whole; and Hannah, who vigorously opposed paper currency, now conducted the business of the proprietary herself. In September, 1724, Logan returned from England with a letter from Hannah Penn, instructing Keith not to make any speech, write any message to the Assembly, return any legislative bills, or pass any laws without the consent of the majority of the Council. Hannah informed Keith that "the Dependance of the Proprietary and his Family has been chiefly on their Friends in the Council" and stipulated that at least one half of the Council was to be Quaker and that the Council was to consist of not more than twelve or less than eight members at any one meeting, thereby preventing Keith from convening a Council of two or three of his select friends. [21] She further instructed Keith to reinstate Logan as a member of the Council and as the Provincial Secretary. Warning that London merchants regarded the paper currency acts with great disfavor, she enjoined Keith not to allow any more issues of bills of credit, although she was resigned to the paper currency acts which had already been passed. She deferred Keith's dismissal as Deputy Governor only because she wanted to avoid any disturbance which might have an adverse effect upon a prospective settlement with the Crown for the sale of the Pennsylvania government. [22] Logan also brought with him a letter from Henry Gouldney and Joshua Gee, London mortgagers of the province, warning Keith that it would be well for him to obey Hannah even though powers of government were not directly lodged in her by Penn's will. [23]

Lloyd did not immediately challenge Hannah Penn's letter of instructions, although Keith denounced the latter publicly as an invasion of popular rights and wrote a letter to Hannah Penn, denying that the Council had any voting power in legislative matters such as she wanted it to have. [24] Lloyd withdrew from the Assembly in the election of October 1, 1724, and relinquished the leadership of that body to younger hands. [25] He continued to exert a powerful influence on Keith, but he avoided entering upon a controversy with Hannah Penn and her agents while occupying the office of Speaker of the Pennsylvania Assembly.

# 21. The Constitutional Debate

Lloyd remained silent in the controversy between Keith and Hannah Penn during the autumn and winter of 1724-25, but in March, 1725, he entered a pamphlet war with James Logan which took the form of a debate over the nature and content of Pennsylvania's constitution and over Pennsylvania's place in the developing British Empire. The debate followed an address to the Assembly by Deputy Governor Keith in January, 1724/25, who bitterly criticized Hannah Penn's instructions. Logan, taking up the quarrel on behalf of Hannah Penn, prepared "A MEMORIAL from JAMES LOGAN, in behalf of the Proprietary's Family, and of himself, Servant to the said Family, " which was published on February 2, 1724/25, and was subsequently entered in the journal of the Assembly, although Logan said later that he had not intended it to be published. [1] Keith replied with "The Governor's *Defence* of the Constitution of the Province of Pennsylvania, and the late honourable Proprietary's Character, in Answer to James Logan's Memorial, &c., " which was also entered in the journal of the Assembly. [2] Lloyd, unsatisfied with Keith's *Defence,* wrote *A Vindication of the Legislative Power,* which the Assembly published in March, 1725, for the public consumption. [3] On September 25, 1725, Logan published *The Antidote,* a reply to Lloyd's *Vindication,* and Keith immediately responded with a pamphlet, *William Keith to James Logan on Occasion of Mr. Logan's having sent to Sir William a Copy of his Printed Paper called the Antidote,* which was printed and sold by Andrew Bradford in Philadelphia.[4] Lloyd's reply to *The Antidote* did not appear until March 4, 1725/26, when he published *A Further Vindication of the Rights and priviledges of the People of this Province of Pensilvania.*[5]

The pamphlet war concerned two principal subjects: the functions and powers of the Provincial Council, and the powers of a Deputy Governor. Keith had placed several of his personal friends on the Council, and his tendency was to hold meetings of the Council when most of the councilmen, especially friends of the Penn family, were absent. During his administration the Council had become little more than an executive cabinet, entirely dependent on the Deputy Governor and without responsibility for the making of laws and administration of government apart from its advisory capacity as the Deputy Governor's cabinet--a fact which has not been hitherto noted by historians. Keith thought of the Council as "a Council of State, to advise, and be present, as solemn Witnesses of the Governor's Actions."[6] Logan, however, argued that the Council was necessarily a responsible body in the making of laws because its members were men of wealth and large landed interest in the province.[7] Lloyd, agreeing with Keith, took the position that the constitution of the province gave the Council no share in the legislative power, but he did not object to the Deputy Governor's seeking the advice and opinion in legislative matters of the councilmen who, he said, were "Men embark'd in the same Interest with the People, and for the most part aim at the publick Good."[8]

Logan cited Penn's letters patent of October 28, 1701, by which the late Proprietor had established the Council "To consult and assist the Proprietary himself, or his Lieutenants or Deputies, with the best of their Advice and Counsel, in all publick Affairs and Matters relating to the Government." Logan further cited Penn's instructions to his deputy governors to act with the advice and consent of the Council in all matters of public importance. He construed Penn's instructions as meaning that the Council had a voting power in legislation and that the Deputy Governor could not legally pass laws without the Council's approval.[9] His interpretation indicated that he considered the Council the upper house of a bicameral legislature, analogous to the House of Lords in England.

Lloyd, however, did not consider Penn's instructions to his deputy governors a part of the constitution of Pennsylvania. He recognized only Penn's charter, granted by Charles II in 1680/81, the Frame of 1701, and the act to ascertain the number of assemblymen, passed in 1705/6, as the legal basis for the constitution of the Pennsylvania legislature. Penn's charter gave the Penn family or their deputy the power to make laws with the concurrence of the freemen or their duly elected representatives. The Frame of 1701 and the act of Assembly regulating the number of assemblymen established the Assembly as a unicameral legislature and laid down the rules by which it was organized and according to which it conducted its business. Lloyd believed that proprietary instructions which altered or ignored the provisions of the Frame of 1701 and its accompanying act of Assembly were null and void, unless they met the approval of the freemen of the province through the Assembly. At the same time he had no objection to the existence of a Council. ". . . I have met none so senceless as to say," he wrote, "that the Governour is thereby concluded [i. e., precluded] of having a Council to advise and assist in Legislation and other matter relating to the State, and I have known divers of the Members of that Board very serviceable in that Station. . . ."[10] He insisted only that the Council had no voting power in legislation and was not the upper house of a bicameral legislature, as councils were in other colonies.

Hannah Penn's instructions to Keith that he act in legislation only with the advice and consent of the Council also raised a very tricky and difficult question of whether or not the proprietary family had any control over the Deputy Governor. Keith insisted that Hannah Penn's instructions were a breach of the Frame of 1701.[11] Logan argued, on the contrary, that the charter Penn had received from Charles II did not prevent his heirs from laying deputy governors under restrictions in legislation. He pointed out that Penn, by giving private instructions to every Deputy Governor, had effectively restricted the powers and functions of his deputies. By enjoining deputy governors to obtain the advice and assistance of the Council in legislation, Logan wrote, Penn had, in effect, exercised a veto power in legislation, because in practice the Council, representing Penn's interests, had often greatly influenced deputy governors' decisions in the passage and veto of legislative bills.[12]

Lloyd was chiefly interested in the point Logan raised, that the proprietary family had the legal right to restrict the law-making powers of the Deputy Governor of Pennsylvania, and he devoted the bulk of his *Vindication* to a refutation of Logan's argument. He began with the assumption that the charter Penn had received from Charles II in 1680/81 was the fundamental law of Pennsylvania and buttressed his thesis with reference to English case law. Penn's charter, he wrote, specifically invested the legislative authority in the Proprietor, his heirs, deputies, and lieutenants, on the one hand, and the freemen of the province or their representatives, on the other. Although Penn's charter authorized the Proprietor to appoint deputies, Lloyd pointed out, it did not specify what the powers of the deputies should be. The powers of the Proprietor's deputies, he wrote, were established by English law which gave a deputy "full Power to do any act or thing which his Principal may do." This power, he continued, "is so essentially incident to a Deputy, that a Man cannot be a Deputy to any single act or thing, nor can a Deputy have less Power than his Principal, and if his Principal make him *Covenant, That he will not do any particular thing which the Principal may do,* the Covenant is void and repugnant. . . ." He cited the judgment of the Court of King's Bench in *Parker* v. *Kett* (13 William III) that a covenant, precluding an undersheriff from executing any process for more than £20 without a special warrant from the high sheriff, was void, "because the Under-Sheriff is his Deputy, and the Power of the Deputy cannot be restrained to be less than that of his Principal, save only that he cannot make a Deputy, because it implies an Assignment of his whole Power. . . ."[13] Thus Lloyd, employing the analogy of the sheriff and the undersheriff in English case law, concluded that the powers of a deputy were equal to those of his principal, except that a deputy could not assign his powers to another deputy. He recalled that the undersheriff analogy had governed the opinion of the Council in 1704 that the clause in Deputy Governor John Evans' commission reserving to the Proprietor a veto power in legislation was null and void, and he marveled that Logan, who had concurred in that opinion, now insisted on the contrary that the principal could place restrictions on his deputy by covenant.[14]

Lloyd, in employing the undersheriff analogy, assumed that the judgment of the Court of King's Bench in *Parker* v. *Kett* held for all deputies without distinction as to the office and function of the deputy concerned. Logan seized upon this apparent weakness in Lloyd's argument in his pamphlet, *The Antidote*. He accused Lloyd of a play on words and insisted that the word "deputy" did not always mean the same thing and the particular kind of deputy, his duties and functions, should have been taken into account. He argued that the undersheriff analogy did not hold, because it involved a deputy whose duties and powers differed greatly from those of the colonial deputy governor. He insisted, moreover, that the authority of the Proprietor and his deputies was to be found in Penn's charter and the proprietary grants, not in English case law.[15]

Lloyd replied, in his *Further Vindication*, that he based his interpretation of the unrestricted powers of a deputy on English common law and that the judicial decision in *Parker* v. *Kett* had been based on common law, not on acts of Parliament. He explained that, wherever the authority of deputies in England was limited, it was limited by statute, not by common law, and that when there were no statutory limitations to their powers deputies were free to do anything that their principals might do. In support of this argument, he cited *Leak* v. *Michel*, reported in Sir Edward Coke's *Institutes*. Lloyd concluded that, because English common law precluded the principal from placing any restrictions on his deputy, unless allowed to do so by statutory law, the Deputy Governor of Pennsylvania had the same freedom of action as any deputy in the homeland. He believed, therefore, that so much of Hannah Penn's instructions to Keith as forbade the Deputy Governor to make any speech or to send any written message to the Assembly and to amend and return legislative bills to the Assembly without the approval of the Council was legally void. No more legally valid, in Lloyd's opinion, was Hannah Penn's denial of the Deputy Governor's right to commission a Provincial Secretary and clerk of the Council of his own choosing. The Deputy Governor, lawfully commissioned by the Proprietor and approved by the King, had full power, Lloyd believed, to do anything that the Proprietor could do. There was, he said, no statute, English or Pennsylvanian, stipulating that the powers of the Deputy Governor were less than the powers of the Proprietor. Hence, he argued, the proprietary family had no legal right to restrict the powers of the Deputy Governor by instructions. He declared further that a deputy's office must be granted entirely; it cannot be granted in parcels. The proprietary family might remove the Deputy Governor, but it could not legally abridge his powers. [16]

The question remained, if the full powers of a principal were delegated to his deputy in accordance with English common law, could the deputy legally delegate those powers to still another deputy? The question was important, because Hannah Penn's instructions indicated that Keith was to delegate his veto power in legislation to the Council. Lloyd contended that the powers of a deputy were not transferable to another, and he quoted a justice at the Court of King's Bench as having once said that "a Deputy is but a p[er]son authorized who cannot authorize another. . . . "[17] To Lloyd this precedent in English case law meant that the legislative authority in the executive branch of the provincial government resided entirely in the Deputy Governor and that no part of it, including the veto power, could be delegated to the Council.

Lloyd's thesis was that the Deputy Governor was empowered by English common law to perform any act of state that the Penn family might perform if it were physically present in Pennsylvania. Lloyd made it clear, however, that the Deputy Governor's powers were limited by the Crown through the charter which Charles II had given Penn in 1680/81. The charter, he wrote, defined the powers which the King had granted to Penn, his heirs, and his deputies, and it prescribed limitations upon those powers. It forbade the Proprietor and his deputy "to part from the Faith and Allegeance due to the King, or to maintain Correspondence with his Enemies, or to commit Hostility against such as are in League with him, or Transgress against the Laws of Trade and Navigation, or for discharging of his Trust and Duty in the Administration of the Government according to the purport of the said Royal Grant and the Laws and Constitutions of this Province. . . . "[18] Lloyd added that the charter authorized the Deputy Governor to make ordinances in emergencies when the Assembly was in adjournment but precluded him from extending such ordinances "to

bind change or take away the Right or Interest of any Person
or Persons for or in their Life, Members, Free-hold, Goods
or Chattels. "[19] The King not only gave the Proprietor and his
deputy powers of government but placed limitations upon them
for the protection of the colonists.

For Lloyd, the King was the "Fountain of Justice" from whom
flowed the popular liberties and privileges. The King, Lloyd
wrote in the *Vindication,* had made the colonists "Sharers
with the Proprietary in the greatest Rights, Liberties and
Privileges" granted in the royal charter of 1680/81. Lloyd
referred to the King as "the first Founder of this Province"
and asserted that "the King was very well apprized, and so
was the Draughts-Man of that Excellent Charter, [20] That this
part of the *English* Empire could not be Enlarged, nor the
true Design of the *Grant* answered, without due Encouragement to the Adventurers. . . . "[21] Lloyd was fully aware of
the importance of individual incentive in empire building, and
his argument was that the incentives given the colonists by
the King--their privileges in government and their property
rights--tended to encourage imperial expansion. He denied
that the colonists had ever demanded privileges "in Dimin[u]-
tion of any Rights, Royalties or Powers of any kind really and
truly belonging to or reserved by the Proprietor. . . . " The
colonists, Lloyd believed, insisted only that the liberties given
them by the King be untrammeled by the proprietary family. [22]

Lloyd asserted, moreover, that the legislative authority, exercised by the freemen of the province through their elected
representatives in the Assembly, was not a proprietary grant,
but the gift of the King of England to his people. The power
of legislation, he wrote, was expressed so clearly in the royal
charter of 1680/81 that he was "induced to conclude, that, by
Virtue of this Grant, there was such a Right originally vested
and become inherent in every Free-man of this Province as
wanted not the help of any Grant or Charter from the Proprietary to confirm it. "[23] Penn's frames of government "prescribed
the form of Assembling the Free-men to act in Legislation, "
Lloyd added, but the colonists already possessed "the Right
of Meeting together to make Laws" by virtue of the royal grant,
and the form could be prescribed by an act of Assembly as well
as by a frame granted by the Proprietor.[24]

Although Lloyd believed that the colonists' privileges in government came from the King rather than from the Proprietor
and that the royal charter of 1680/81 was the fundamental law
of Pennsylvania, he considered the Frame of 1701 the constitution of the Pennsylvania government. Logan, in his memorial
and other papers, had eulogized the English constitution and
had supposed that the colonial governments were modeled upon
the English King, Lords, and Commons, [25] but Lloyd denied
that the government of Pennsylvania was an imitation of the
English constitution. The Frame of 1701, Lloyd pointed out,
was a departure from the English constitution in that it "Lodged
the Powers of Legislation in the Governour and Representatives of all the Freemen of this Province in General Assembly. . . ."[26] King and Commons, yes; but the Lords were excluded. The Council, in other colonies, was the upper house
of a bicameral legislature and was therefore a colonial imitation of the House of Lords in England; Lloyd, however, regarded the Pennsylvania Council as a kind of privy council or
executive cabinet which could advise the Deputy Governor but
which had no legislative authority. Even the Privy Council in
England had more powers in legislation than Lloyd conceded
the Pennsylvania Council. The Privy Council, with the King,
could veto laws; Lloyd denied the Pennsylvania Council even
that right. In Lloyd's political thought the colonists derived
their lawmaking powers directly from the King and rightfully
used those powers to establish a form of government which
differed significantly from the English constitution and from
the constitution of every other English colonial government
of the time.

One of the arguments Logan advanced in favor of the Council's functioning as the upper house of a bicameral legislature
was that its members "have . . . as large an Interest in it
[the province], generally speaking, as the like Number of any
other whatsoever. . . ."[27] Lloyd, expressing an inability to
understand the merit of Logan's argument, replied that "according to my Experience, a mean [i. e., a common] Man, of
small Interest, devoted to the faithful discharge of his Trust
and Duty to the Government, may do more good to the State,
than a Richer or more Learned Man, who by his ill Temper
and aspiring Mind becomes an opposer of the Constitution by

which he should act."[28] Farmers and artisans, Lloyd believed, were as capable of governing as wealthy merchants and landed aristocrats. He added, however, that, "since an Interest in the Colony is pointed out as a Qualification to act for the good of the Publick," the members of the Assembly should be considered in that light. The Assembly, he wrote, consisted "of some Ancient Settlers, who have a good Competency, and others, who are descended from such as brought considerable Estates into the Province, and went through great Difficulties in the first Settlement of this Wilderness. . . ." Those first settlers, Lloyd added, had "spent their Strength and Substance in Emproving the Country, and by their indefatigable Industry upon the Land, which . . . would have been of little worth to the Proprietary or any Body else, if Divine Providence had not blessed the Labours of the first Settlers and succeeding Inhabitants. . . ." The first settlers and those who followed them, Lloyd pointed out, had made Pennsylvania "of value to the Proprietary and his Family," and, because their lives and fortunes were bound to Pennsylvania and to "Peace and Plenty under a mild Administration," they had "great reason to lay the good of the Publick and it's true Interest as close to Heart as any others."[29] In Lloyd's opinion the first settlers and their sons, who had cleared the wilderness and had built the colony, were the most deserving of all to participate in the government of Pennsylvania.

Lloyd's pamphlets in the constitutional debate of 1724-26 contain the most complete statement of his political thought extant. To be sure, it was not a well-rounded political philosophy; Lloyd was not a Locke, Hobbes, or Harrington. He was too much of a controversialist, too subjective and passionate in his manner of presentation, to have attempted a *Leviathan* or *Oceana*. He emphasized his arguments with invective, and he drove his points home with biting sarcasm. His purpose was to defeat an opponent, not only by a learned recitation of the law and by a reasoned exposition of his thesis, but by portraying his opponent in the worst possible light and by holding him up to public ridicule--as he had held up the King's and Queen's effigies to public ridicule in the Philadelphia County Court of Quarter Sessions in 1698. In his *A Vindication of the Legislative Power*, Lloyd insinuated that Logan's real purpose was to

effect a political change in Pennsylvania "from a State of Freedom . . . into an Arbitrary Government, subjected to the Power of one Person. . . ." "I am apt to think, " Lloyd added, "by
what I gather from this Memorial and some more of these
Printed Papers, that the ready way to bring us under this
Change must be by . . . [getting] a new Council . . . who must
be such as will assent to all the Secretary proposes, and when
a Council Board is thus furnished, any Body (without much
Penetration) may guess who that *one Person* must be. "[30] A
passage in *A Further Vindication* also illustrates Lloyd's employment of invective and sarcasm as weapons on the field of
controversy. Lloyd, in that passage, accused Logan of being,
not only "an evil Minister and ungrateful Servant, " but disloyal to the English common law. Lloyd warned that it was

> . . . a thing utterly unlawfull for any Subject to Speak or write against
> that Law under which he Liveth--and it is a Known rule That to Slander
> and Disgrace the Law and Government is with out excuse It being a
> Simple act of a Malignant will, not induced nor excited by any outward
> provocacon, The Law carrying an equal and Constant respect to all,
> and to be reverenced by all. [31]

Aside from his use of invective, sarcasm, and unjust accusations, which were customary, to be sure, in the literature of
political controversy, [32] Lloyd's pamphlets were a revealing exposition of the political thought of early eighteenth-century
Pennsylvania's foremost advocate of legislative supremacy.
Lloyd's political pamphleteering in 1725 and 1726 did not
save Keith from being discharged from his post by the Penn
family, but it resulted in Lloyd's being returned to the Speakership of the Assembly in October, 1725. In December Lloyd
and his fellow assemblymen sent an address to the Penn family
defending Keith and the paper money acts. Because of the
paper money acts, they wrote:

> The Administration of Government [is] well Supported without Clog-
> ging the Importations, our Ports Clear, Trade revived and the Honest
> Debtors rescued from the oppression of their Creditors, The Value of
> our Country product advanced, and the Ship-Wrights . . . are . . .
> come into full Imployment at their Trade so that many Stately Vessells
> have been built and more upon the Stocks, and Several Iron-works are
> carryed on. . . . [33]

The Board of Trade's legal adviser, however, had already advised the King-in-Council to veto the Pennsylvania paper money acts. Moreover, the Penn family, in 1726, removed Keith from the office of Deputy Governor and replaced him with Patrick Gordon, who assumed office on June 22, 1726. [34]

# 22. The Grand Inquisitors

Lloyd found Gordon as easy to get along with as Keith had been, although Gordon was a more brusque, businesslike, and ruggedly honest man than his predecessor. Gordon evinced none of the cloying flattery which had characterized Keith in his messages to the Assembly, but the new Deputy Governor was friendly to the Assembly and approved of the paper money experiment. Lloyd and Gordon were favorably impressed with each other, and, in September, 1726, just two weeks before the election, Gordon gave Lloyd a new commission as Chief Justice of the Pennsylvania Supreme Court. Satisfied with the new administration, Lloyd expressed a desire to forget the quarrels of the past and to heal the old wounds which had been reopened by Hannah Penn's letter of instructions to Keith. Logan was surprised to find that Lloyd, as he wrote to a friend, "now professes a Reconciliation w[i]th me, a just Regard to the Prop[rieto]rs family & a great fr[ien]dship for the present Gov[erno]r whom he believes (he Sayes) to be a real honest man. "[1]

Lloyd and Keith, however, came to the parting of the ways. Their political alliance had served their individual purposes up to the day that Keith had ceased to be the Deputy Governor of Pennsylvania. They had agreed in some respects on the nature of the Pennsylvania constitution. Keith accepted Lloyd's interpretation of the Frame of 1701, that the government of Pennsylvania consisted of the Deputy Governor and the Assembly, the Council being a mere advisory adjunct of the Deputy

Governor. Like Lloyd, he denied that the Pennsylvania government was a copy of the English King, Lords, and Commons.[2] So far as Pennsylvania's place in the British Empire was concerned, however, Lloyd and Keith were fundamentally at variance. Lloyd believed that the Pennsylvania Assembly was a colonial version of the House of Commons and that it possessed all the parliamentary privileges of the House of Commons in England. He believed, moreover, that Pennsylvania was legislatively autonomous. As his entire career as a lawmaker testifies, he considered acts of Assembly in Pennsylvania superior to acts of Parliament; acts of Parliament were rendered effective in Pennsylvania by acts of Assembly and were often amended and altered by their translation into acts of Assembly.[3] Keith, on the other hand, denied that the English constitution was imitated in any respect by the colonies.[4] He considered the colonies "so many Corporations at a distance invested with ability to make Temporary By Laws for themselves agreeable to their Respective Situations & Clymates but no ways interfering with the Legal Prerogatives of the Crown or the true Legislative Power of the Mother State."[5] For Keith, Parliament was the only true legislature in the British Empire.[6]

Keith had agreed with Lloyd's interpretation of the powers of a Deputy Governor,[7] but for very different reasons. He had economic ambitions in Pennsylvania,[8] and he hoped to secure sole political control of that colony, after he had first succeeded in converting it into a royal province. He organized political clubs in Philadelphia, and, as two of his adherents later testified, he intended to organize a party in the Assembly which would so conduct itself as to force the Penn family "to throw up the Government into the hands of the Crown."[9] In the election of October 1, 1726, he ran for election to both the Pennsylvania and Lower Counties Assemblies in Philadelphia and New Castle. With the help of his political clubs, "The Gentlemen" and "The Tiff Club," he won a seat in the provincial Assembly, but was defeated in New Castle.

Lloyd, returned to the Assembly by the freemen of Chester, opposed Keith's bid for power when the Assembly convened in Philadelphia on October 14. Keith rode into the city at the head of eighty horsemen and, amid the firing of guns, pre-

The Stokes view of Philadelphia, 1731

sented himself as a candidate for Speaker. The assemblymen, however, rallied to Lloyd. Someone entered Lloyd's name in opposition to Keith, and in the voting which followed, Lloyd, as Logan subsequently reported, received every vote but three.[10] Keith made no further effort to challenge Lloyd's leadership of the Assembly during the session of 1726-27.

Lloyd and his fellow assemblymen continued their policy of controlling the Deputy Governor by exercising their power of the purse. They paid Gordon £400 to defray the cost of his voyage to Pennsylvania and rewarded his friendliness to the Assembly by permitting him to continue establishment of the Court of Equity in himself and his Council. In February, 1726/27, Gordon appointed Lloyd to draw up the rules for the regulation of the Court of Equity, and Lloyd secured Gordon's approval of an act which removed from the Supreme Court the power to issue original writs, thereby making the Supreme Court a purely appellate court as Lloyd had long intended it to be.[11]

Keith did not give up hope of supplanting Lloyd as the most powerful political figure in Pennsylvania. He continued to build his political strength in Philadelphia and won a considerable following among the artisans, particularly those of the Anglican faith. On October 1, 1727, the freemen of Philadelphia County re-elected him to the Assembly, and eight of his followers also won seats in the Assembly as representatives of Philadelphia County. Lloyd, however, retained a powerful following in Bucks and Chester counties, and he successfully defeated Keith's second bid for the Speakership of the Assembly. This defeat probably dampened for all time Keith's hopes of achieving political leadership in Pennsylvania. One dark night in March, 1728, Keith sneaked aboard ship at New Castle and sailed for England, ostensibly for business reasons.[12]

Even while at sea, however, Keith influenced his followers in Philadelphia to attack Lloyd's leadership of the Assembly. Economic conditions in Pennsylvania gave him the opportunity. The prosperity, which had followed the emission of £45,000 in paper currency in 1723, had come to an end. The population had grown rapidly because of the increased immigration of German Palatines,[13] and money was again in short supply. The price of wheat had fallen, trade had declined, and poverty had

increased.[14] Keith, writing from shipboard, advised his followers in Philadelphia that if the Assembly were "rightly informed
by the Merchants & other Men of Business Concerning the Increase or Decay of any Material Branches of trade, as the
members of that house are most certainly the proper Judges
of Peoples Necessities they will doubtless prepare and apply
Suitable Remedies for all publick Wants or Grievances. . . ."[15]
Keith's insinuation was that Lloyd and his following in the Assembly did not understand the economic plight of the colonists
and would have to be prodded into passing another paper money
act. Encouraged by Keith's letter, the Keithian clubs in Philadelphia agitated for another issue of paper currency and created
a stir which troubled both Lloyd and the Philadelphia merchants. One Philadelphia merchant observed that Pennsylvania
"should be very quiet, if th[a]t Spirit raised among the people
for paper money by S[i]r Will[ia]m did not constantly perplex
us. . . ."[16]

Lloyd was somewhat hesitant to prepare further paper money
legislation. He appeared anxious to avoid another controversy
with the Penn family and took no action during 1728 to re-
plenish the diminishing supply of paper money. He refused,
moreover, to issue a writ ordering the election of a new assemblyman from Philadelphia to fill the seat left vacant by
Keith's departure. Lloyd could easily have followed the same
procedure as he had a year earlier when he had issued, ex
officio, an order to the Provincial Secretary [17] for a writ of
election to fill an Assembly seat left vacant by the death of
Francis Rawle. Lloyd and his fellow assemblymen took the
position, however, that Keith was only absent from his seat
and, therefore, could not legally be replaced by another until
the next regular election.[18] To the Keithian clubmen in Philadelphia, however, Lloyd's refusal to act was motivated chiefly
by a desire to keep the Keithian representation in the Assembly
at a minimum and thereby to frustrate the popular agitation for
a new paper money act.

The eight Keithian assemblymen from Philadelphia County
and the City Corporation of Philadelphia struck back at Lloyd
by deliberately absenting themselves from the Assembly--an
action which effectively interrupted the session of that body
for want of a quorum. Lloyd and the rest of the assemblymen,

who were mostly Quakers, submitted a representation to Deputy
Governor Gordon complaining of the conduct of the eight Keithians, and a bitter controversy ensued. The Keithian clubmen
attacked Lloyd publicly, and Lloyd's followers published a
broadside defending his Speakership. They condemned the attacks on Lloyd as unjust, because Lloyd, as the Speaker of
the Assembly, was responsible to the entire membership of
that body. The Speaker, they wrote, "is the Mouth of the House,
and is to speak or not only as they shall direct him, he is constantly under an Obligation to execute the Orders." So far as
the procedures followed by the Assembly were concerned, they
explained, "Tis well known, that the Assemblies in these *English*-Plantations are formed on the Plan of an *English* Parliament: And as the Method of Proceedings in *Westminster-Hall*
are made a Rule to us, in our Courts of Justice, so our Assemblies in like Manner take their Rules from the House of Commons there."[19]

The eight Keithians, in a broadside of their own, replied
that colonial courts and assemblies were not necessarily guided
by the rules of the great common law courts at Westminster
Hall and the English House of Commons and that they made
their own rules to govern themselves. They thought the com-
parison between the Pennsylvania Assembly and the English
House of Commons an invidious one. The Pennsylvania Assembly, they pointed out, derived its rules from the charter which
Charles II had given William Penn in 1680/81, but the English
House of Commons derived its rules from immemorial usage.
They contended that the Frame of 1701 empowered Lloyd, as
the Assembly's Speaker, to order the election of a representative to replace Keith without the consent of the Assembly
and that the majority of the Assembly had infringed the Frame
of 1701 by forbidding Lloyd to issue such an order, as Lloyd's
followers in the Assembly claimed they had done.[20]

Lloyd answered the Keithian broadside by reinterpreting
the Frame of 1701 in such a manner as to exclude the eight
Philadelphia Keithians permanently from the Assembly. When,
at Gordon's request, Lloyd and sixteen other Assemblymen
met in Philadelphia on May 14, 1728, they voted themselves
a bona fide Assembly with lawmaking powers.

The Philadelphia Keithians immediately challenged the con-

stitutionality of Lloyd's action. In a printed attack they used
the very same arguments that Lloyd had employed in *A Vindication of the Legislative Power,* specifically citing that pamphlet, in order to prove that the Assembly then in session did
not have a quorum and had no legislative powers. They pointed
out further that the Frame of 1701 could not be legally amended
except by the Proprietor or his deputy with the concurrence of
six-sevenths of the Assembly. They reminded Lloyd that he
had recently ordered an election in Chester County to fill a
vacancy in the Assembly and that he had accepted the new assemblymen so elected on May 14; and they asked why, if Lloyd
ordered an election in Chester to fill a vacant seat in the Assembly, did he not order an election in Philadelphia to fill the
vacancy caused by Keith's departure?[21]

The Keithians' arguments were sound, but Lloyd, encouraged
by Deputy Governor Gordon, obtained from the rump Assembly
a resolution that the absent Philadelphia assemblymen were in
contempt of the legislature and that their proceedings tended to
stir up public disorders and riots. Lloyd and his followers, as
the resolution indicates, were vexed, and they endeavored to
paint the eight Keithians as black as they could. At an earlier
session of the Assembly, they said, the eight Philadelphia assemblymen had voted against an appropriation to defray the cost
of making treaties with the Indians, and they accused them,
therefore, of having exposed the province to the danger of
Indian hostility. As if to stress the Keithians' alleged lack of
patriotism, they passed an appropriation of £100 for the making
of Indian treaties. [22]

The Keithians retorted that the Assembly had no such powers
as Lloyd claimed for it. They reminded Lloyd and his followers
that "the only Military Authority in this Colony, is lodged at
present solely in the Governour, as Capt[ain] General, by
Virtue of his *Commission;* who may undoubtedly exercise that
Authority, upon sudden Emergencies, without the Assistance
of the Assembly."[23] Moreover, they accused Lloyd of exceeding
his authority by appointing committees to inspect the accounts
of the General Loan Office and by adjourning the Assembly for
long periods of time. Penn's charter from Charles II, they
insisted, did "not impower the Assembly to *meet upon their
own Adjournments,* otherwise than *de die in diem* . . . and

for any longer Time, it must be adjourned or prorogued by
the Proprietor, his Heirs, or Assigns."[24] They believed that
the powers Lloyd claimed for the Assembly were a dangerous
thing, and that they transcended the assemblymen's legitimate
authority as the representatives of the people. "The Estate
goes before the Steward," they wrote, "the Foundation before
the House, People before their Representatives, and the Creator before the Creature: The Steward lives by preserving the
Estate, the House stands by Reason of it's Foundation; the
Representative depends upon the People, as the Creature sub-
sists by the Power of it's Creator." For the Keithians a free
people was the foundation of a representative legislature, and
a legislature which transcended its authority subverted the
very foundation of its authority--popular freedom.[25]

Lloyd, in his *A Vindication of the Legislative Power*, had
argued that a deputy has full power to do anything that his
principal may do. Although he had applied his argument specifically to the relationship between the Proprietor and Deputy
Governor of Pennsylvania, the same principle was also applicable to the relationship between the assemblymen, as deputies, and the voters, as principals. The question was, did
election constitute a delegation of absolute authority by the
people to their representatives in the Assembly? "What Spring
ever rose higher than it's Head?" asked the Keithians. "The
Representative is at best but a true Copy, an Exemplification;
the free People are the Original, not Cancellable by a Tran-
script. . . ." They defined the assemblyman as a "Creature
of the People, because the People make them, and to them
they owe their Being." The lawmaking power of the people,
they said, granted by the fundamental law of Pennsylvania,
did not become the exclusive property of the assemblymen upon
election; assemblymen were responsible to the people in whom
the lawmaking power fundamentally resided. "Here is no *Trans-
essentiating* or *Transubstantiating* of Being, from People to
Representative," they asserted, "no more than there is an
absolute Transferring of a Title in a Letter of Attorney."[26]

As the Keithians pointed out, Lloyd and his Quaker followers in the Assembly, by constituting themselves as a legal
assembly even though they lacked the quorum required by provincial law, had violated both the Frame of 1701 and the act

of Assembly passed in 1705 which regulated the election of assemblymen.[27] Lloyd had, in fact, organized an oligarchy in order to exclude the Keithians from the Assembly and to guarantee the continuance of Quaker supremacy in the government.

Lloyd did not write a defense of his reinterpretation of the Frame of 1701, but during the summer of 1728 he and his followers obtained depositions from two disaffected Keithians which gave them a more effective issue than any the Keithians had raised. The depositions, which Lloyd had published as a broadside for popular distribution, indicated that the partisans of Sir William Keith were chiefly motivated by a desire to create political disturbances which might result in the conversion of Pennsylvania into a royal province.[28] Publication of the depositions constituted a warning to the Quaker freemen that a Keithian victory in the Assembly would put an end to Quaker political power in Pennsylvania, and the Quakers of Chester and Bucks counties rallied to insure the continued control of the Assembly by Lloyd and his followers in the election of October 1, 1728.[29]

Lloyd, however, was tired of the political wars. He had been in public service almost continuously during his forty-two years in Pennsylvania. He was getting old, and his old political passions had cooled. He was not the aggressive politician he had once been; changing conditions compelled him to adopt an entirely defensive position. He accepted re-election to the Assembly, but he was reluctant to assume once more the Speakership, which the Quaker majority in the Assembly accorded him on October 14. It had long been a meaningless custom for a newly elected Speaker to plead unfitness to hold such an office, but Lloyd now sincerely begged to be replaced. Deputy Governor Gordon, however, ignored his pleas.[30]

Lloyd disliked holding the Assembly's sessions in Philadelphia. The "City of Brotherly Love" had become riotous, torn by political dissension, and inimical to Quakerism. Depressed economic conditions, the continued immigration of indigent people into the city, and the popular clamor for more paper money led to violence on the part of the city's poor. The impoverished Anglican workmen of Philadelphia made little distinction between the Quaker assemblymen and the

Quaker merchants. Propagandists assailed the Quaker merchants as "the most tyrannical Aristocracy in the World"
and charged that they were led by a triumvirate, probably the
Commissioners of Property, who deliberately hoarded the
existing supply of paper money in order to deprive debtors
of their lands. [31] Many Philadelphia workmen supposed that
Lloyd and his followers were in league with the Quaker merchants and treated them with little respect. Men, who were
total strangers to the assemblymen, laid brutal hands upon
them and so belabored them that the Quakers lost all desire
to remain in the city for the balance of the session. [32]

Lloyd complained to the Deputy Governor of the violence
to which the assemblymen were subjected in Philadelphia and
asked that the Assembly be removed to a safer place. Without
waiting for a reply, the Assembly adjourned until December,
and Lloyd and his fellows, presumably, hastened to their quiet-
er abodes in the country to nurse their bodily aches and pains,
as well as their wounded feelings. When they met again in
December, Gordon agreed to remove the Assembly to Chester,
but he reminded them that "a Legislative Assembly, in Conformity to a British House of Commons, is invested with a very
great Authority." The members of the Assembly, he said,
should use that authority in their own defense. ". . . You . . .
are one part of the Legislature," he admonished them, "which
in every Government is the Supreme, & are the Grand Inquisitors of the whole Province. . . ." [33]

This recognition of the supremacy of the Assembly on the
part of the Deputy Governor, unusual because it was stated so
early in the eighteenth century, was all that Lloyd had ever
desired. Lloyd, however, did not exercise the powers of the
Assembly to punish the rioters in Philadelphia. Instead, he
yielded to the popular clamor by securing from the Assembly
an act providing for the issue of £30,000 more of paper currency and sent an address to the Penn family explaining the
necessity for the act. He and his followers were aware of the
prejudices against paper money but asserted that "it was
Necessity and the Want of other Species prevailed with . . .
Legislature to promote it." They added that "it is now manifest from indisputable Proof after Six Years Tryal of this
Currency amongst us That nothing has ever so much contributed

to advance Trade, Navigation, the price of Lands, and the general Interest of the whole Colony. . . ."[34]

Lloyd's concession to the popular outcry for more paper money failed, however, to relieve economic conditions. Trade failed to improve as expected, and the continued immigration of needy people aggravated both social and economic problems. At the end of the session of 1728-29 Lloyd departed from the Assembly, never to return, and Pennsylvania's economic problems passed to other hands. John Penn's hope that an Assembly more in the proprietary interest would be elected was realized, and Andrew Hamilton succeeded Lloyd to the office of Speaker.[35] Hamilton was a conservative lawyer who was more in sympathy with the Penn family and the Philadelphia merchants than with the poorer people. The indigent workmen of Philadelphia reacted as violently against Hamilton as they had against Lloyd and his followers and at one time threatened to carry out a physical assault upon the proprietary Assembly. Logan warned the Penns that Pennsylvania was "in all appearance in real danger of an Insurrection."[36] Hamilton, however, induced the Assembly to put in force an act of Parliament which made rioting punishable by death. This move discouraged the would-be assailants, and the threatened attack never took place.[37] Lloyd had never interpreted Gordon's admonition that assemblymen were "the Grand Inquisitors of the whole Province" in that fashion.

# 23. The Last Years

Lloyd tended to become less a man of action and more a man of thought and culture during the last years of his life. After 1725 he was the archivist of the Philadelphia Yearly Meeting and devoted a part of his time to the collection of historical records. He did not write a history of Pennsylvania, but the records he and others collected were many years later incorporated in Robert Proud's *History of Pennsylvania.*[1]

Lloyd's literary activity, not to mention his state papers and political pamphlets, was limited to editing and to promoting the publication in Pennsylvania of books published in Europe. He was one of six members of the Chester Monthly Meeting who collected an account of the religious services in America of Thomas Wilson, a Quaker missionary, which was later published in London as part of *A Brief Journal of the Life, Travels and Labours of Love, in the Work of the Ministry of . . . Thomas Wilson.*[2] Lloyd revised and corrected the English translation of a Welsh book, Ellis Pugh's *A Salutation to the Britains, to Call them From the Many Things, to the One Thing needful, for the Saving of their Souls*, which was printed by Samuel Keimer in 1727.[3] Lloyd also took up subscriptions in Quaker meetings and arranged for the republication in English of William Sewel's *The History of the Rise, Increase, and Progress of the Christian People called Quakers*, which was translated into English from the Dutch and printed in Philadelphia in 1728.[4] In 1728 Lloyd collected the second edition of

Pennsylvania laws then in force, and it was published by Andrew Bradford. [5]

Lloyd's encouragement of literary activity and book publishing was recognized by a Welsh Baptist minister, Abel Morgan, who dedicated his *Cyr-Gordiad Egwyddorawl o'r Scrythurau* to Lloyd. *The Cyr-Gordiad*, probably the first Welsh concordance of the Bible ever written, was published posthumously in 1730. [6]

Unfortunately, there is no list of the books which Lloyd might have kept in his own private library, if he had one. The only book which is known to have been his is a volume of sermons, *Several Sermons and Discourses of William Dell, Minister of the Gospel.* [7] Lloyd's references to English law books in his state papers and political pamphlets indicate that he had access to the literature of English law. The most extensive private libraries in Pennsylvania were those owned by James Logan and Henry Brooks, reputedly two of the most cultured men in the province. [8] Unless Lloyd used their libraries, he possessed a law library of his own. If he did, his library included copies of the English law reporters, Chief Justice John Holt's decisions, and Coke's *Institutes,* which he cited in his state papers and political pamphlets. [9]

Although Lloyd never returned to the Assembly after 1729, he remained in public service as the Chief Justice of the Supreme Court and as the Recorder of Chester County. More complex social conditions caused him to adopt a harsher attitude toward crime and punishment. Although as late as June, 1728, he had recommended lenience toward a colonist who had murdered an Indian, by 1730 he favored the death penalty for less serious offenses. On January 4, 1729/30, he wrote to the Provincial Secretary that a convicted burglar "justly deserves to die and it may be of ill Consequence to Spare him. "[10]

Lloyd's health declined throughout 1730. His old friend Thomas Chalkey, the Quaker missionary, visited him then and later wrote in his journal, "I visited my old friend David Lloyd, who, with his good spouse Grace, treated me with tender, Christian love; the Judge and I, being old acquaintance, and both of us in years, and he not well, we took leave, as if we were not to see one another any more, which happened accordingly, for he died before I returned. "[11] Jane Fenn returned from her travels late in 1730 and attended Lloyd

during his last, lingering illness. Throughout the winter of
1730-31 Lloyd hovered uncertainly between life and death,
and early in April, 1731, he breathed his last. He was buried
in Friends' Burial Ground at Chester. [12]

Lloyd died at a time when changing events were presaging
the rise and expansion of a new civilization from the primitive
conditions of the North American continent. Many of the issues
to which he had devoted years of his life in bitter controversies
were already passé. His old arguments with the Proprietor
over the colonists' property rights and the administration of
the Land Office were of little importance now, as German
Palatine and Scotch-Irish immigrants moved rapidly to the
western frontier and squatted on proprietary lands without
bothering to take up legal titles. [13] The westward movement
of population, stimulated largely by increased immigration
and by high land prices in the east, was well under way. Already it had reached the foothills of the Alleghanies and was
moving southward into the valleys of Maryland and Virginia
and into the Piedmont region of the Carolinas. Pennsylvania,
almost from the beginning a melting pot of European nationali-
ties, had become a distributing center of the growing, restless,
and dynamic population of the continental colonies. [14] As the
keystone colony, linking north and south, Pennsylvania sent
ideas and institutions with the southward moving population [15]
--ideas and institutions to which Lloyd had made his own unique
contributions.

Lloyd had lived during an era that had seen the development
of colonial assemblies into little parliaments, which imitated
the growing power of the House of Commons in England, and
the acquisition of a considerable measure of legislative supremacy and political autonomy by Pennsylvania, Connecticut,
and Rhode Island. Lloyd himself had been a kind of colonial
Robert Walpole, organizing the burgeoning power of the Pennsylvania Assembly as a colonial parliament and for some years
maintaining a tight control over his following in that body. The
results of his organizing and legislative genius remained long
after his passing. Pennsylvania retained until the American
Revolution the principal innovations he had introduced--the
unicameral legislature and the Supreme Court as an exclusively
appellate tribunal. [16] His had been an unusually inventive mind;

he had approached lawmaking with great imaginative power, so great that, during his career after 1700, of all the continental colonies, Pennsylvania had the largest percentage of laws disallowed by the King-in-Council. [17] He had shared with other Englishmen their admiration for the English constitution, and he had insisted on the reception of the English common law in Pennsylvania. Nevertheless, he had introduced departures from the English constitution, when he had felt that such departures were necessary to further the development of legislative supremacy.

Lloyd never had to face the problem of a conflict between his loyalty to the colonial assembly and that to the Crown; to him loyalty to the Crown (King, Lords, and Commons) and loyalty to the institutions of Pennsylvania were, for all practical purposes, the same. He could never have foreseen that the ultimate consequence of the rise of legislative supremacy in the continental colonies would be a clash between the colonial assemblies and the English Parliament and the disruption of the British Empire. Throughout most of his public service in Pennsylvania he had opposed the Proprietor and had endeavored to strip him of much of his prerogative in the government of the province, but he had never set himself against King and Parliament. He had considered the King the fountain from which flowed the liberties enjoyed by the colonists in Pennsylvania, and Parliament as the originator and exemplar of the privileges claimed by the Pennsylvania Assembly. If anything, he had claimed the protection of King and Parliament in his struggles with the Proprietor.

Lloyd, moreover, had never belonged to that race of backwoodsmen, the children of the forest, whom de Crèvecoeur was one day to call "that new man, the American."[18] He belonged rather to that generation of colonists which had rooted itself and its descendants to the settled areas adjacent to the most easily accessible outlets to the sea--a generation which was to contribute to the future United States some of the oldest names in the Social Register and in patriotic societies whose members claim descent from the colonists. Lloyd was a Pennsylvanian--a Welsh colonist, educated in England, who had so identified himself with Pennsylvania that he was, in fact, a provincial, not "that new man, the American." Nevertheless,

his contributions to the developing colonial institutions and
ideas, which were already evincing some divergences from
the institutions and ideas of the homeland, marked him as
having been, if not an American, at least an American in the
making.

# Notes

*Chapter 1*

1. Burton Alva Konkle, David Lloyd and the First Half Century of Pennsylvania, (MS, Friends Historical Library, Swarthmore, Pa.), p. 15, cited hereafter as Konkle, David Lloyd; William Henry Egle (ed.), *Old Rights, Proprietary Rights, Virginia Entries, and Soldiers Entitled to Donation Lands* (Pennsylvania Archives, 3rd ser.), III, 206, cited hereafter as Egle, *Old Rights.*

2. David Lloyd's notebook is preserved in the manuscripts section of the Historical Society of Pennsylvania under the catalogue title, Old Manuscript Book belonging to David Lloyd, cited hereafter as Notebook.

3. William Penn to the Provincial Council, 1686, "Letters of William Penn," *Pennsylvania Magazine of History and Biography,* XXXIII (1909), 306-7, cited hereafter as "Letters of William Penn."

4. Penn to the President and Provincial Council, Worminghurst, September 25, 1686, *ibid.,* p. 305. Any violation of the terms of the charter would have given the Crown an excuse to issue a writ.

5. Samuel Hazard (comp.), "Minutes of the Provincial Council of Pennsylvania, from the Organization to the Termination of the Proprietary Government," *Colonial Records of Pennsylvania* (Philadelphia: Jo. Severns and Co., 1852), I, 184, 188, cited hereafter as *Col. Rec.;* Penn to Thomas Lloyd, Secretary William Markham, and William Hampton, London, April 24, 1686, "Letters of William Penn," pp. 303-4.

6. Penn to Thomas Lloyd, Markham, and Hampton, London, April 24, 1686, "Letters of William Penn," pp. 303-4.

7. David Lloyd, Notebook.

8. Thomas Allen Glenn, the late Welsh genealogist, thought that David Lloyd was born in Meifod, rather than Manafon, but he offered no proof of it (Konkle, David Lloyd, p. 2). The present rectors of Manafon and Meifod could find no reference to David Lloyd in the records of their parishes (Bishop David St. Asaph to the author, St. Asaph, Flintshire, Wales, January 8, 1952; Rev. T. Meurig Morgan to the author, The Vicarage, Meifod, Montgomeryshire, Wales, December 1, 1953). The Registry of Arrivals at Philadelphia for 1686, however, contains the following entry: "David Lloyd borne in the year 1656 in the Parish of Manavan in the County of Mount Gomory in North Wales." (The man-

uscript Registry of Arrivals, which includes entries for the years 1682
to 1686, is preserved in the Historical Society of Pennsylvania.) "Manavan" was undoubtedly a misspelling of "Manafon" because there is no
"Manavan" in Wales.

9. Although the exact date of David Lloyd's birth is unknown, other
evidence supports the statement in the Registry of Arrivals that he was
born in 1656. The minutes of the Middletown Monthly Meeting show that
he was forty-one when he married Grace Growdon in 1697, and an inscription on Lloyd's tombstone shows that he was seventy-five at the
time of his death in 1731 (Konkle, David Lloyd, p. 163; William Wade
Hinshaw, *Encyclopedia of American Quaker Genealogy* [Ann Arbor,
Mich.: Edward Bros., 1936-50], II, 583; Allen Johnson and Dumas
Malone [eds.], *Dictionary of American Biography* [New York: Charles
Scribner's Sons, 1928-44], XI, 329-30, cited hereafter as *DAB)*.

10. For the relationship between David Lloyd and the Dolobran Lloyds
see *DAB*, XI, 329.

11. The Lloyd family was established in Montgomeryshire about 1300
by Celynin of Llwydiarth, and it founded Dolobran about one century
later. In 1476 Owen, the son of Ivan Teg "the Handsome," adopted the
name Lloyd, which he derived from "Llwydiarth," the ancient seat of
his ancestors (Charles P. Keith, *The Provincial Councillors of Pennsylvania Who Held Office between 1733 and 1776, and Those Earlier
Councillors who Were Some Time Chief Magistrates of the Province,
and Their Descendants,* [Philadelphia, 1883], p. 7; Sir John B. Burke,
*Burke's Genealogical and Heraldic History of the Landed Gentry, in-
cluding American Families with British Ancestry* [London:.Burke's
Peerage, 1939], p. 1167; Rachel J. Lowe, *Farm and Its Inhabitants,
with Some Account of the Lloyds of Dolobran* [Privately printed, 1883],
p. 203, cited hereafter as Lowe, *Farm)*.

12. Lowe, *Farm,* pp. 11-12.

13. Testimony from Friends & Brethren of the Quarterly Meeting,
Held at Dolobran, in Montgomeryshire, North Wales, the 30th of the
8th mo. 1711, Concerning Our Dear & worthy friend, Thomas Lloyd,
Deceased (MS preserved in the Library Company of Philadelphia [Ridge-
way]).

14. An account of a conference between the Right Reverend the B[ish-
o]p of S[ain]t Asaph & Mr. Charles Lloyd & Mr. Tho: Lloyd, Norris
of Fairhill MSS, Family Letters, I, 94-96, Historical Society of Pennsylvania (HSP).

15. For a record of land purchases by Charles and Thomas Lloyd,
see Egle, *Old Rights,* pp. 206-7.

16. Little is known of David Lloyd's parents aside from the fact that
his father was named Thomas and that the paternal grandfather, named
David Lloyd, lived in Meifod. Nothing at all is known of the mother
*(DAB,* XI, 329).

17. For an account of common-school education in seventeenth-cen-

tury Wales see John Rhys and David Brynmor-Jones, *The Welsh People: Chapters on Their Origin, History, Laws, Literature, and Characteristics* (New York: Macmillan Co., 1900), pp. 432, 433, 479.

18. James G. Wilson and John Fiske (eds.), *Appleton's Cyclopedia of American Biography* (New York: D. Appleton and Co., 1887-89, 1918-31), III, 748.

19. *DAB,* XI, 329; Registry of Arrivals, 1686, HSP. Sarah's maiden name and family background are unknown.

20. David Lloyd to [James] Hariss [Harrison], London, August 30, [16]86, Pemberton Papers, HSP. The date on the letter is puzzling. Lloyd arrived in Philadelphia on July 15 and could hardly have written a letter from London on August 30. The internal evidence of the letter, however, indicates that it was probably written in 1685, when Lloyd had no reason to expect that he was going to Pennsylvania.

21. Albright G. Zimmerman, "Daniel Coxe and the New Mediterranean Sea Company," *Pa. Mag. Hist. & Biog.,* LXXVI (1952), 86-87; John E. Pomfret, "The Proprietors of the Province of West New Jersey, 1674-1702," *ibid.,* LXXV (1951), 142. A portion of this tract appears to have been located in present-day East and West Vincent Townships, Chester County.

22. Grant by Wm. Penn of land for formation of a company, to be called the New Mediterranean Sea Co., June 7, 1686, in Zimmerman, "Daniel Coxe and the New Mediterranean Sea Company," p. 88.

*Chapter 2*

1. Robert Turner to Penn, August 3, 1685, in John F. Watson, *Annals of Philadelphia and Pennsylvania in Olden Times* (Philadelphia: J. M. Stoddart and Co., 1881), I, 22, cited hereafter as Watson, *Annals;* Daniel B. Shumway, "A Rare Dutch Document Concerning the Province of Pennsylvania in the Seventeenth Century," *Pa. Mag. Hist. & Biog.,* XLIX (1925), 116; William Penn, "A Further Account of the Province of Pennsylvania, 1685," in Albert C. Myers (ed.), *Narratives of Early Pennsylvania, West New Jersey and Delaware 1630-1707* (New York: Charles Scribner's Sons, 1912), p. 261, cited hereafter as Myers, *Narratives of Pa.*

2. William Penn, "A Further Account of the Province of Pennsylvania, 1685," pp. 268, 272, 273; Watson, *Annals,* I, 132; Edward P. Allinson and Boies Penrose, "The Early Government of Philadelphia and the Blue Anchor Tavern Landing," *Pa. Mag. Hist. & Biog.,* X (1886), 65-66.

3. William Penn, *A Letter from William Penn, Proprietary and Governour of Pennsylvania in America, to the Committee of the Free Society of Traders . . . To which is added, An Account of the City of Philadelphia Newly laid out* (London, 1683), p. 10, cited hereafter as

Penn, *Account of Philadelphia;* William Penn, "A Further Account of the Province of Pennsylvania, 1685," pp. 271-72.

4. To be sure, Philadelphia Quakers did not yet wear the uniform drab-colored dress that was later to become the custom, but they omitted superfluous ornaments, ribbons, laces, and unnecessary buttons from their attire. Quaker meetings also disapproved of the long, curly baroque periwigs, which were the fashion of the day, but some of the more affluent Quakers wore them nevertheless (Albert C. Applegarth, *Quakers in Pennsylvania* [Baltimore: Johns Hopkins Press, 1892], pp. 26-7; Frederick B. Tolles, *Meeting House and Counting House: The Quaker Merchants of Colonial Philadelphia, 1682-1763* [Chapel Hill: University of North Carolina Press, 1948], pp. 125-27, cited hereafter as Tolles, *Meeting House).* For a more complete account of Quaker customs and private life in the seventeenth century see William C. Braithwaite, *The Beginnings of Quakerism* (London: Macmillan and Co., 1912), chap. xix.

5. "Letter of Thomas Paschall, 1683," Myers, *Narratives of Pa.,* pp. 250-51.

6. James J. Levick, "The Early Welsh Quakers and Their Emigration to Pennsylvania," *Pa. Mag. Hist. & Biog.,* XVII (1893), 393. For a special study of the Irish in Pennsylvania see Albert C. Myers, *Immigration of the Irish Quakers into Pennsylvania, 1682-1750, with their Early History in Ireland* (Swarthmore, Pa.: The Author, 1902).

7. William Thomas Johnson, "Some Aspects of the Relations of the Government and German Settlers in Colonial Pennsylvania, 1683-1754," *Pennsylvania History,* XI (1944), 82; Edward R. Turner, "Slavery in Colonial Pennsylvania," *Pa. Mag. Hist. & Biog.,* XXXV (1911), 142; Albert S. Bolles, *Pennsylvania, Province and State, A History from 1609 to 1790* (Philadelphia: J. Wanamaker, 1899), I, 17.

8. Penn, *Account of Philadelphia,* p. 9; Penn, "A Further Account of the Province of Pennsylvania, 1685," pp. 261-62, 271-72; Cheesman A. Herrick, *White Servitude in Pennsylvania: Indentured and Redemption Labor in Colony and Commonwealth* (Philadelphia: J. J. McVey, 1926), pp. 33-36.

9. Penn, "A Further Account of the Province of Pennsylvania, 1685," pp. 261-62; Samuel W. Pennypacker, *Pennsylvania Colonial Cases: The Administration of Law in Pennsylvania prior to A. D. 1700 as shown in the cases decided and in the Court proceedings* (Philadelphia: George T. Bisel Co., 1892), pp. 71-73, cited hereafter as Pennypacker, *Pa. Col. Cases.*

10. Dr. Nicholas More to Penn, Green-spring, December 13, 1686, Myers, *Narratives of Pa.,* pp. 284-85. More denied the rumor which Penn had reported to him.

11. Extract of a letter from David Lloyd, October 2, [1686], quoted in a "Letter of Doctor Nicholas More, 1686," *ibid.,* p. 291.

12. *Ibid.;* Daniel B. Shumway, "A Rare Dutch Document Concerning the Province of Pennsylvania in the Seventeenth Century, " p. 116.

13. See note 11 above.

14. Staughton George, Benjamin M. Nead, and Thomas McCamant (eds. ), *Charter to William Penn, and Laws of the Province of Pennsylvania, Passed between the Years 1682 and 1700* (Harrisburg: L. S. Hart, State Printer, 1879), p. 145, cited hereafter as *Charter and Laws of Pa.*

15. Penn to the Council, 1686, "Letters of William Penn, " p. 308; Watson, *Annals,* I, 22.

16. *Col. Rec.,* I, 84-89.

17. Penn to the Council, 1686, "Letters of William Penn, " p. 308.

18. *Col. Rec.,* I, 23.

19. See note 11 above.

*Chapter 3*

1. *Col. Rec.,* I, 58, 188.

2. Penn to Harrison, 1686, quoted in Watson, *Annals,* I, 22.

3. Statement of William Penn's Agreement with Philip Ford, about 1705, Penn Papers, Ford vs. Penn, p. 7, HSP; Watson, *Annals,* I, 22; Penn to Thomas Lloyd, September, 1686, extract copy, Parrish Collection, HSP.

4. Penn to Harrison, Worminghurst, January 28, 1686/87, copy, Parrish Collection, HSP.

5. David Lloyd to Pemberton, Philadelphia, November 25, 1686, Etting Papers, Pemberton, HSP.

6. The details of Phineas Pemberton's life have been gleaned from Watson, *Annals,* II, 95; "A Penn Rarity, " *Quakeriana Notes,* No. 1 (1933), p. 3; Harold D. Eberlein and Cortlandt Van Dyke Hubbard, *Portrait of a Colonial City, Philadelphia, 1670-1838* (Philadelphia: J. B. Lippincott Co., 1939), pp. 76-77.

7. David Lloyd to Pemberton, Philadelphia, November 25, 1686, Etting Papers, Pemberton, HSP.

8. *Col. Rec.,* I, 59.

9. Gertrude MacKinney (ed. ), *Votes and Proceedings of the House of Representatives of the Province of Pennsylvania, December 4, 1682-June 11, 1707* (Pennsylvania Archives, 8th ser. ), I, 66, cited hereafter as MacKinney, *Votes.*

10. *Col. Rec.,* I, 137-38; MacKinney, *Votes,* I, 66-67.

11. *Col. Rec.,* I, 153; John Hill Martin, *Martin's Bench and Bar of Philadelphia* (Philadelphia: Rees Welsh and Co., 1883), pp. 18, 167, cited hereafter as *Martin's Bench and Bar.*

12. *Col. Rec.,* I, 190, 192; *Martin's Bench and Bar,* p. 25.

13. David Lloyd to Pemberton, Philadelphia, October 12, 1686, Pemberton Papers, II, 62, HSP.

14. "Letter of Doctor Nicholas More, 1686," Myers, *Narratives of Pa.*, p. 284.

15. William H. Egle (ed.), *Minutes of the Board of Property of the Province of Pennsylvania* (Pennsylvania Archives, 2nd ser.), XIX, 18, cited hereafter as Egle, *Minutes*.

16. *Col. Rec.*, I, 20.

17. *Ibid.*, p. 30.

18. See H. F. Russell Smith, *Harrington and His Oceana: A Study of a 17th Century Utopia and Its Influence in America* (Cambridge, Eng.: Cambridge University Press, 1914).

19. *Col. Rec.*, I, 42-47.

20. MacKinney, *Votes*, I, 15, 17, 46; *Col. Rec.*, I, 42-43, 183-84.

21. Penn to Harrison, Worminghurst, January 28, 1686/87, copy, Parrish Collection, HSP; Penn to the President and Council, Worminghurst, September 25, 1686, "Letters of William Penn," p. 305; Penn to Thomas Lloyd, More, Claypoole, Robert Turner, and John Eckley, Worminghurst, February 1, 1686/87, copy, Parrish Collection, HSP.

22. Penn to Harrison, Worminghurst, January 28, 1686/87, copy, Parrish Collection, HSP.

23. Penn to Thomas Lloyd, More, Claypoole, Turner, and Eckley, Worminghurst, February 1, 1686/87, copy, Parrish Collection, HSP.

24. Penn was fully aware of the Council's tendency to ignore his letters (Penn to Harrison, Worminghurst, January 28, 1686/87, copy, Parrish Collection, HSP).

25. W. L. Grant and James Munro (eds.), *Acts of the Privy Council of England, Colonial Series, 1613-1783* (Hereford, Eng.: Printed for H. M. Stationery Office, by Anthony Bros., 1908-12), II, 92.

26. Quoted in Tolles, *Meeting House*, pp. 12-13.

27. Pennypacker, *Pa. Col. Cases*, p. 112.

28. *Martin's Bench and Bar*, p. 73.

29. *Records of the Court of Chester County, Pennsylvania, 1681-1697* (Philadelphia: Colonial Society of Pennsylvania, 1910), pp. 134, 200-1, cited hereafter as *Chester Co. Ct. Rec*:

30. Works Progress Administration, *Inventory of the County Archives of Pennsylvania, Delaware County, No. 23* (Philadelphia: The Historical Records Survey, 1939), p. 7; F. R. Diffenderffer, "Early Local History as Revealed by an Old Document," *Historical Papers and Addresses of the Lancaster County Historical Society,* II (1897), 17.

31. *Records of the Courts of Quarter Sessions and Common Pleas of Bucks County, Pennsylvania, 1684-1700* (Meadville, Pa.: Colonial Society of Pennsylvania, 1943), p. 78, cited hereafter as *Bucks Co. Ct. Rec.*

Chapter 4

1. Coxe to David Lloyd, London, October 15, 1687, in Zimmerman, "Daniel Coxe and The New Mediterranean Sea Company," pp. 93-94.

2. Penn to Thomas Lloyd, London, March 28, 1688, copy, Parrish Collection, HSP.

3. According to a biographer of Captain John Blackwell, Penn appointed Blackwell at the instance of the latter's wife. Penn already knew Blackwell by reputation as having been a man of authoritative personality, ability, and character (Nicholas B. Wainwright, "Governor John Blackwell," *Pa. Mag. Hist. & Biog.*, LXXIV [1950], 457).

4. Quoted *ibid.*, p. 459.

5. John Blackwell to Thomas Lloyd, Boston, November 11, 1688, in Samuel Hazard ( ed. ), *Pennsylvania Archives, Selected and Arranged from Original Documents in the Office of the Secretary of the Commonwealth* (Pennsylvania Archives, 1st ser. ; Philadelphia: Jo Severns and Co., 1852-56), I, 106-7, cited hereafter as Hazard, *Pa. Arch.*, *1st ser.*

6. Blackwell to Penn, Philadelphia, January 25, 1688/89, Blackwell Papers, Am. 025, pp. 33-35, HSP.

7. *Col. Rec.*, I, 45, 236-37, 256-57; *Charter and Laws of Pa.*, pp. 496, 520, 522.

8. Wainwright, "Governor John Blackwell," pp. 457-72.

9. This correspondence is not extant, but it is mentioned in James Logan to John Penn, December 12, 1726, Logan Letter Books, HSP.

10. Penn to friends in Pennsylvania, Windsor, September 18, 1688, in Samuel Hazard (ed. ), *The Register of Pennsylvania, Devoted to the Preservation of Facts and Documents, and Every Other Kind of Useful Information Respecting the State of Pennsylvania* (Philadelphia: W. F. Geddes, 1828-36), IV, 104-5, cited hereafter as Hazard, *Register*.

11. Joseph Growdon to Nicholas Waln, Trevose, January 20, 1688/89, Provincial Council, Etting Papers, p. 14, HSP; *Col. Rec.*, I, 299.

12. *Col. Rec.*, I, 241-43.

13. *Ibid.*, pp. 244-45.

14. A copy of the commission with its seal is in *ibid.*, pp. 256-57.

15. *Ibid.*, pp. 256-58.

16. *Ibid.*, pp. 255, 257.

17. Blackwell to Penn, Philadelphia, January 13, 1689/90, Blackwell Papers, Am. 025, p. 8, HSP.

18. Penn to friends in Pennsylvania, Windsor, September 18, 1688, in Hazard, *Register*, IV, 104-5.

19. Penn to Blackwell, February 14, 1688/89, Blackwell Papers, Am. 025, p. 95, HSP.

20. *Col. Rec.*, I, 252.

21. The object of Quaker criminal law was to reform rather than to punish. A historian of colonial Pennsylvania law, however, has suggested that imprisonment in seventeenth-century Pennsylvania was rare because "the colony could ill afford to spare the labors of any individual, however depraved, and still less was it inclined to support him in idleness" (William H. Loyd, Jr., *The Early Courts of Pennsylvania*

[Boston: Boston Book Co., 1910], p. 56). Also see Auguste Jorns, *The Quakers as Pioneers in Social Work* (New York: Macmillan Co., 1931), chap. v.

22. *Col. Rec.*, I, 269, 270, 273, 282-83.

23. See p. 24 above.

24. Growdon, John Simcock, William Yardley, John Curtis, Samuel Carpenter, Bartholomew Coppock to Penn, Philadelphia, April 9, 1689, Penn Papers, Official Correspondence, I, 11, HSP.

25. Blackwell to Penn, Philadelphia, April 9, 1689, Gratz Collection, Governors of Pennsylvania, Case 2, Box 32, HSP.

26. *Col. Rec.*, I, 260-61.

27. *Ibid.*, p. 261; MacKinney, *Votes*, I, 94.

28. MacKinney, *Votes*, I, 99.

29. *Ibid.*, p. 108.

30. *Ibid.*, pp. 94-96, 105; Account of the Arrest of John White, May, 1689, Norris of Fairhill MSS, Family Letters, I, 123, HSP.

31. MacKinney, *Votes*, I, 109.

32. *Charter and Laws of Pa.*, p. 175; *Col. Rec.*, I, 291, 297.

33. Thomas Lloyd, *A Seasonable Advertisement to the Freemen of this Province etc.* (Philadelphia, 1689). A copy of this pamphlet is preserved in the Society Collection at the Historical Society of Pennsylvania.

34. *Ibid.*

35. Blackwell to Penn, June 24, 1689. Portions of this letter are quoted in Wainwright, "Governor John Blackwell," p. 469. Also see *Col. Rec.*, I, 299, 300, 306, 310.

36. Edward Blackfan to Pemberton, Deal, September 6, 1689, copy, Parrish Collection, HSP.

37. Blackwell to Penn, Philadelphia, January 13, 1689/90, Blackwell Papers, Am. 025, pp. 1, 5, 6, 14, HSP; *Col. Rec.*, I, 312-17.

*Chapter 5*

1. *Chester Co. Ct. Rec.*, p. 246.

2. Watson, *Annals*, I, 94; *Chester Co. Ct. Rec.*, pp. 213, 224, 226, 248, 254.

3. "The First Charter of the City of Philadelphia, 1691," *Pa. Mag. Hist. & Biog.*, XVIII (1894), 504-9; *Col. Rec.*, I, 276.

4. The petition may be found in Allinson and Penrose, "The Early Government of Philadelphia and the Blue Anchor Tavern Landing," pp. 65-66, and in Watson, *Annals*, I, 336.

5. Minutes of a meeting of the Council held at Philadelphia, August 3, 1691, quoted in Allinson and Penrose, "The Early Government of Philadelphia and the Blue Anchor Tavern Landing," p. 69.

6. Watson, *Annals*, I, 336.

7. Minutes of the meeting of the Commissioners of Property, Jan-

uary 19, 1691/92, in Allinson and Penrose, "The Early Government of Philadelphia and the Blue Anchor Tavern Landing," pp. 65-66; Watson, *Annals*, I, 337.

8. John Locke, *An Essay Concerning the True Original, Extent and End of Civil Government: Second Treatise* (London, 1690), V, 35, 40.

9. Levick, "The Early Welsh Quakers and Their Emigration to Pennsylvania," pp. 393, 410-11; *Chester Co. Ct. Rec.*, p. 239.

10. Richard S. Rodney, "Early Relations of Delaware and Pennsylvania," *Pa. Mag. Hist. & Biog.*, LIV (1930), 229; Robert Proud, *The History of Pennsylvania, in North America, from the Original Institution and Settlement of that Province, under the first Proprietor and Governor William Penn, in 1681, till after the Year 1742* (Philadelphia: Zachariah Poulson, Jr., 1797-98), I, 356, cited hereafter as Proud, *Pennsylvania.*

11. Assembly and Provincial Council to Penn, May 18, 1691, Penn MSS, Petitions, Beaver Skins, XII, 11, HSP.

12. Act of Assembly as to Three Lower Counties, August 17, 1691, Norris of Fairhill MSS, Family Letters, I, 102, HSP; *Martin's Bench and Bar*, p. 163.

13. Penn to Friends, September 11, 1691, quoted in Catherine Owens Peare, *William Penn: A Biography* (Philadelphia: J. B. Lippincott Co., 1957), pp. 323-24.

14. "Unpublished Minutes of the Provincial Council of Pennsylvania, 1692," *Pa. Mag. Hist. & Biog.*, XI (1887), 153, 505.

15. John Blackwell to Penn, Philadelphia, June 24, 1689, *Pa. Mag. Hist. & Biog.*, VI (1882), 363.

16. See entries for 1692 in Epistles of George Fox and others, preserved at Friends Bookstore, 302 Arch Street, Philadelphia, Pennsylvania.

17. William Sewel, *The History of the Rise, Increase, and Progress of the Christian People called Quakers* (Philadelphia, 1728), p. 348, cited hereafter as Sewel, *History of the Quakers;* Pennypacker, *Pa. Col. Cases*, p. 118.

18. Quoted in Sewel, *History of the Quakers*, p. 349.

19. Burlington Yearly Meeting to London Yearly Meeting, Burlington, West New Jersey, September 7, 1692, Epistles of George Fox and others.

20. Pennypacker, *Pa. Col. Cases*, pp. 118, 122, 126; Gabriel Thomas, quoted in Henry J. Cadbury, "John Hepburn and His Book Against Slavery, 1715," *Proceedings of the American Antiquarian Society*, LIX (1950), 111.

21. *Charter and Laws of Pa.*, pp. 114-15; George Keith's account, quoted in Pennypacker, *Pa. Col. Cases*, p. 127.

22. Pennypacker, *Pa. Col. Cases*, p. 127.

23. *Ibid.*, pp. 129-30.

24. Quoted in Herbert W. K. Fitzroy, "The Punishment of Crime

in Provincial Pennsylvania, *"Pa. Mag. Hist. & Biog.,* LX (1936), 248.
   25. *Martin's Bench and Bar,* p. 163.

## Chapter 6

1. Extract of a letter from Penn to a certain person in Philadelphia,
[1692], in E. B. O'Callaghan (ed.), *Documents Relative to the Colonial
History of the State of New York* (Albany, N.Y.: Weed, Parsons and
Co., 1853-87), IV, 34-35, cited hereafter as O'Callaghan, *Doc. Rel.
Col. Hist. N.Y.*
   2. *Ibid.,* pp. 856-60; *Col. Rec.,* I, 352-57.
   3. Penn to Benjamin Fletcher, London, December 5, 1692, O'Callaghan, *Doc. Rel. Col. Hist. N.Y.,* IV, 33-34.
   4. Most of Fletcher's appointees took oath, as no Quaker would have
done because of the Quaker testimony against swearing. Robert Turner,
the Provincial Treasurer, and Francis Rawle, a Philadelphia County judge, were Keithians *(Col. Rec.,* I, 365, 368-72 *passim; Martin's
Bench and Bar,* pp. 29, 170; Tolles, *Meeting House,* p. 141.
   5. MacKinney, *Votes,* I, 127.
   6. *Martin's Bench and Bar,* pp. 105, 169; Charles P. Keith, *Chronicles of Pennsylvania from the English Revolution to the Peace of Aix-
la-Chapelle, 1688-1748* (Philadelphia: Patterson and White Co., 1917),
I, 264.
   7. MacKinney, *Votes,* I, 133-35.
   8. Herbert L. Osgood, *The American Colonies in the Seventeenth
Century* (New York: Columbia University, 1904), II, 269; *Martin's Bench
and Bar,* p. 166; *Col. Rec.,* I, 43, 356.
   9. MacKinney, *Votes,* I, 138.
   10. *Col. Rec.,* I, 417.
   11. *Ibid.*
   12. *Ibid.,* pp. 419-21.
   13. *Ibid.*
   14. *Ibid.,* p. 421; MacKinney, *Votes,* I, 138-40.
   15. "An Early Petition of the freemen of Pennsylvania to the Assembly, December 3, 1692," *Pa. Mag. Hist. & Biog.,* XXXVIII (1914),
495-501.
   16. *Col. Rec.,* I, 427.
   17. *Ibid.*
   18. MacKinney, *Votes,* I, 152. This paper appears to be no longer
extant, and its contents are not known in specific detail.
   19. *Ibid.,* pp. 152-53; *Col. Rec.,* I, 428-31.
   20. MacKinney, *Votes,* I, 153-54.
   21. W. Noel Sainsbury (ed.), *Calendar of State Papers, America and
West Indies, 1693-96* (London: Eyre and Spottiswoode, 1893), p. 90,
cited hereafter as Sainsbury, *Cal. State Papers, Col.;* Instructions of
the Governor and Council of New York to Charles Lodowyck, June 13,

1693, *ibid.*, p. 119; Memorial of Charles Lodowyck to Lords of Trade and Plantations, September 15, 1693, *ibid.*, p. 160.

22. The date of this paper is unknown, but internal evidence indicates that it was written after Fletcher had assumed office on April 20, 1693, and Fletcher mentions it in a letter dated August 18, 1693 (Fletcher to the Secretary of State, New York, August 18, 1693, O'Callaghan, *Doc. Rel. Col. Hist. N. Y.*, IV, 52-53). The paper is preserved in the Norris of Fairhill MSS, Family Letters, I, 122, HSP.

23. "Some proposals what may be done. . . ," Norris of Fairhill MSS, Family Letters, I, 122, HSP.

24. Fletcher to the Secretary of State, New York, August 18, 1693, O'Callaghan, *Doc. Rel. Col. Hist. N. Y.*

25. *Ibid.*

26. George Keith, "An Exhortation & Caution to Friends concerning Buying or Keeping of Negroes," *Pa. Mag. Hist. & Biog.*, XIII (1889), 265-70.

27. *Col. Rec.*, I, 383, 386.

28. *Ibid.*, p. 454. David Lloyd's seal as Speaker of the Assembly in 1694 is illustrated in *Charter and Laws of Pa.*, p. 563.

29. MacKinney, *Votes*, I, 163-64.

30. *Col. Rec.*, I, 455-56.

31. *Ibid.*

32. MacKinney, *Votes*, I, 156-58; *Col. Rec.*, I, 456-57.

33. MacKinney, *Votes*, I, 158; *Col. Rec.*, I, 458.

34. *Col. Rec.*, I, 463.

35. MacKinney, *Votes*, I, 160; *Col. Rec.*, I, 459-60.

36. *Col. Rec.*, I, 471.

37. *Ibid.*, pp. 468, 471; MacKinney, *Votes*, I, 170.

38. *Col. Rec.*, I, 468.

39. *Ibid.*, p. 469.

40. The revenue collected from the three Pennsylvania counties in 1693 amounted to £314. David Lloyd probably included the revenue collected from the Lower Counties in his figure (Hazard, *Register*, I, 372).

41. *Col. Rec.*, I, 469.

42. *Ibid.*, p. 470.

43. *Ibid.*, p. 471.

44. *Ibid.*; MacKinney, *Votes*, I, 176.

45. Great Britain, *Calendar of State Papers, Domestic, 1547-1704, Preserved in the Public Record Office* (London: H. M. Stationery Office, 1865-1925), the volume *1694-95*, p. 261; O'Callaghan, *Doc. Rel. Col. Hist. N. Y.*, IV, 108-10.

*Chapter 7*

1. *Chester Co. Ct. Rec.*, pp. 339-40; R. N. Toppan, *Edward Ran-*

*dolph: Including His Letters and Official Papers* (Boston: Prince Society, 1898-1909), V, 112, cited hereafter as Toppan, *Randolph Papers*.

2. Markham to Lloyd, Philadelphia, [April] 7, [1695], quoted in *Martin's Bench and Bar*, p. 166.

3. *Col. Rec.*, I, 482; *Martin's Bench and Bar*, p. 166.

4. Markham to Lloyd, Philadelphia, [April] 7, [1695].

5. Queen Mary to Fletcher, Whitehall, August 21, 1694, Great Britain, Royal Commission on Historical Manuscripts, *Earl of Dartmouth MSS, American Papers* (London: H. M. Stationery Office, 1895), p. 2.

6. *Col. Rec.*, I, 472, 475, 480; O'Callaghan, *Doc. Rel. Col. Hist. N. Y.*, IV, 108-9.

7. *Col. Rec.*, I, 486.

8. *Ibid.*, pp. 492-95.

9. Penn to Lloyd, Arthur Cook, John Simcock, Carpenter, Goodson, Samuel Richardson, Turner, Pemberton, Bristol, November 5, 1695, Gratz Collection, Governors of Pennsylvania, Case 2, Box 33a, HSP.

10. Fletcher to the Lords of Trade and Plantations, New York, June 10, 1696, O'Callaghan, *Doc. Rel. Col. Hist. N. Y.*, IV, 158-59.

11. *Col. Rec.*, I, 520.

12. *Ibid.*, pp. 502, 505; Watson, *Annals*, I, 57; MacKinney, *Votes*, I, 188.

13. MacKinney, *Votes*, I, 188; *Col. Rec.*, I, 507-9.

14. *Col. Rec.*, I, 54.

15. The Frame of 1696 may be found in *Col. Rec.*, I, 48-55.

16. *Col. Rec.*, I, 52; Toppan, *Randolph Papers*, V, 178.

17. Remonstrance of the Inhabitants of the County of Philadelphia to Markham, March 12, 1696/97, copy, Petitions and Memorials, Box 4a, HSP.

18. Griffith Jones, Francis Rawle, Robert Turner, Arthur Cook to Penn, Philadelphia, April 9, 1697, Dreer Collection, William Penn's Letters, p. 71, HSP.

19. Lloyd, Edward Shippen, James Ffox, Caleb Pusey, John Simcock, Samuel Carpenter, Joseph Growdon, Phineas Pemberton, John Blunston, Robert Owen, Richard Hough, Bartholomew Coppock to Penn, Philadelphia, May 25, 1697, Fallon Scrapbook, Am. 0628, p. 4, HSP.

20. MacKinney, *Votes*, I, 350-52.

## Chapter 8

1. The exact date of Tommy Lloyd's birth is unknown, but, according to Deborah Norris Logan, the boy was eight years old in 1701. See Edward Armstrong (ed.), *Correspondence between William Penn and James Logan, Secretary of the Province of Pennsylvania, and others, 1700-1750* (Philadelphia: Historical Society of Pennsylvania, 1870-72), I, 41, cited hereafter as *Penn and Logan Corr*.

2. Hinshaw, *Encyclopedia of American Quaker Genealogy*, II, 583.

A picture of "Trevose" is in Eberlein and Hubbard, *Portrait of a Colonial City, Philadelphia, 1670-1838*, p. 69, and a description may be found in Henry W. Watson, "The Growdon Mansion," *A Collection of Papers Read before the Bucks County Historical Society*, II (1909), 451-56.

3. Watson, *Annals*, I, 522; *Penn and Logan Corr.*, I, 42.

4. Henry W. Watson, "The Growdon Mansion, " p. 451.

5. Toppan, *Randolph Papers*, V, 178.

6. *Ibid.*, V, 112.

7. Board of Trade to Lords Justices, Whitehall, September 7, 1696, in William Hand Browne (ed.), *Proceedings of Council of Maryland, 1689-1731* (Baltimore: Maryland Historical Society, 1905), p. 553, cited hereafter as Browne, *Proc. Council Md.*

8. *Ibid.*; Grant and Munro (eds.), *'Acts of the Privy Council of England, Colonial Series, 1613-1783*, II, 306; Toppan, *Randolph Papers*, V, 178.

9. Toppan, *Randolph Papers*, V, 178.

10. *Ibid.*

11. *Ibid.*, pp. 173, 178.

12. Declaration of the Assembly of Pennsylvania of Loyalty to the King and Fidelity to His Governor, May, 1697, Pemberton Papers, II, 143, HSP.

13. See the preface in John F. Jameson (ed.), *Privateering and Piracy in the Colonial Period: Illustrative Documents* (New York: Macmillan Co., 1923), especially p. ix, cited hereafter as Jameson, *Privateering*.

14. Lloyd and others to Penn, May 25, 1697, Fallon Scrapbook, Am. 0628, p. 4, HSP.

15. *Ibid.*

16. Browne, *Proc. Council Md.*, p. 578; Lloyd to Pemberton, Philadelphia, June 22, 1697, Pemberton Papers, II, 145, HSP; Francis Jones to Penn, November 13, 1697, Sainsbury, *Cal. State Papers, Col., 1697-98*, p. 23. Note Lloyd's use of the word "privateers. " Piracy was closely related to privateering, and even lawyers during this period made no clear distinction between them.

17. Lloyd, Carpenter, and Shippen to Penn, Philadelphia, July 4, 1698, Norris of Fairhill MSS, Family Letters, I, 112, HSP.

18. *Col. Rec.*, I, 548-49.

19. Great Britain, *The Statutes of the Realm . . . (1101-1713)* (London, 1810-28), VII, 103, cited hereafter as Great Britain, *Stats.*

20. *Charter and Laws of Pa.*, p. 272.

21. Great Britain, *Stats.*, VII, 105.

22. John Moore to Francis Nicholson, Philadelphia, July 1, 1698, Sainsbury, *Cal. State Papers., Col., 1697-98*, pp. 395-96.

23. Lloyd, Carpenter, and Shippen to Penn, Philadelphia, July 4, 1698, Norris of Fairhill MSS, Family Letters, I, 112, HSP.

24. *Ibid.*

25. Robert Quary to Nicholson, Philadelphia, July 9, 1698, Sainsbury, *Cal. State Papers, Col., 1697-98,* pp. 394-95.

26. Quary to Board of Trade, Philadelphia, September 6, 1698, *ibid.,* p. 415.

27. Quary to Nicholson, Philadelphia, July 9, 1698, *ibid.,* pp. 394-95.

28. Randolph to Board of Trade, New York, August 25, 1698, Toppan, *Randolph Papers,* V, 189-90.

29. Winfred T. Root, *The Relations of Pennsylvania with the British Government, 1696-1765* (Philadelphia: University of Pennsylvania, 1912), p. 352.

30. Quary to Board of Trade, Philadelphia, September 6, 1698, Sainsbury, *Cal. State Papers, Col., 1697-98,* p. 415.

31. *Col. Rec.,* I, 103.

32. Quary to Board of Trade, Philadelphia, September 6, 1698, Sainsbury, *Cal. State Papers, Col., 1697-98,* p. 415; *Col. Rec.,* I, 544.

33. *Col. Rec.,* I, 545.

34. *Ibid.,* p. 603.

35. *Ibid.* Lloyd's allusion was to the tax levied in England in 1636 for the construction of ships for the royal navy. The practice of levying such a tax on inland towns had been initiated during the Tudor era and was an extension of the medieval practice of taking ships from coastal cities when needed for the defense of the country. In 1636 Charles I extended this tax to the whole country, although England was not then at war, and he thereby aroused a storm of protest. The ensuing controversy resulted in the famous case of ship money, or Hampden's Case, in 1637, in which the principle was laid down that an emergency cannot be created by the allegation of the King that the country is in danger; if he is so allowed, then he is given the power to do what he pleases, and a bad King will act without restraint. The implication was that the prerogative of the King must be restrained so that it might not encroach upon the rights and liberties of the people (W. S. Holdsworth, *A History of English Law* [London: Methuen and Co., 1903-24], VI, 52-54).

36. Robert Snead to Sir John Houblon, [1698], Sainsbury, *Cal. State Papers, Col., 1697-98,* p. 182; John Locke, Lexington, Ph. Meadows, Abr. Hill to the Lords Justices, Whitehall, August 4, 1699, Pennsylvania Miscellaneous Papers, Penn and Baltimore, pp. 56-57, HSP.

37. Grant and Munro (eds.), *Acts of the Privy Council of England, Colonial Series, 1613-1783,* II, 341; Locke, Meadows, Hill, and John Pollexfen to Penn, Whitehall, September 12, 1699, Penn Papers, Official Correspondence, I, 17, HSP.

38. The account of this hearing, based on archival sources in the Public Record Office, London, is told in Root, *The Relations of Pennsylvania with the British Government, 1696-1765,* p. 101.

39. William III to Penn, Kensington, February 10, 1699/1700, Penn

Papers, Additional Miscellaneous Letters, I, 13, HSP; *Col. Rec.*, I, 591; MacKinney, *Votes*, I, 224; Great Britain, *Calendar of State Papers, Domestic, 1700-2*, p. 111.

40. Quary to Lords of Admiralty, Philadelphia, March 6, 1699/1700, Great Britain, Royal Commission on Historical Manuscripts, *House of Lords MSS, new series, 1693-1710* (London: H. M. Stationery Office, 1900-23), IV, 324, cited hereafter as *House of Lords MSS*.

41. *Col. Rec.*, I, 604.

42. Penn to Board of Trade, 1700, Sainsbury, *Cal. State Papers, Col.*, *1700*, p. 208.

43. *Col. Rec.*, I, 575.

44. Isaac Norris to Thomas Lloyd (the younger), October 4, 1700, Norris Letter Books, I, 81, HSP.

45. *Ibid.*; James Logan to William Penn, Jr., September 25, 1700, *Penn and Logan Corr.*, I, 18.

46. Norris to Thomas Lloyd, October 4, 1700.

47. Logan to Penn, Jr., September 25, 1700; *Col. Rec.*, I, 595; MacKinney, *Votes*, I, 318; Penn to Logan, September 14, 1705, *Penn and Logan Corr.*, II, 68.


*Chapter 9*


1. Logan to Penn, Jr., Philadelphia, September 25, 1700, *Penn and Logan Corr.*, I, 18.

2. Gabriel Thomas, *An Historical and Geographical Account of the Province and Country of Pensilvania and of West-New-Jersey in America* (London, 1698), p. 5, cited hereafter as Thomas, *Pensilvania*.

3. Fletcher to the Lords of Trade and Plantations, New York, June 10, 1696, O'Callaghan, *Doc. Rel. Col. Hist. N. Y.*, IV, 158-59.

4. Charles P. Keith, "The Founding of Christ Church, Philadelphia," *Pa. Mag. Hist. & Biog.*, LIV (1930), 308.

5. Ezra Michener, *A Retrospect of Early Quakerism; Being Extracts from the Records of Philadelphia Yearly Meeting and the Meetings Composing It to which Is Prefixed an Account of Their First Establishment* (Philadelphia: T. Ellwood Zell, 1860), p. 52; Watson, *Annals*, III, 204.

6. Lothrop Withington, "Pennsylvania Gleanings in England," *Pa. Mag. Hist. & Biog.*, XXVIII (1904), 463.

7. William Nelson (ed.), *Calendar of Records in the Office of the Secretary of State, 1664-1703. Documents Relating to the Colonial History of the State of New Jersey* (Paterson, N.J.: Press Printing and Publishing Co., 1899), XXI, 496.

8. H. Frank Eshleman, "The Birth of Lancaster County," *Historical Papers and Addresses of the Lancaster County Historical Society*, XII (1908), 10-15; H. Frank Eshleman, "The Great Conestoga Road,"

*ibid.*, p. 219; Julius F. Sachse, "Penn's City on the Susquehanna, "
*ibid.*, II (1897), 233-36; *Col. Rec.*, I, 557.

9. Lloyd, Carpenter, and Shippen to Penn, Philadelphia, July 4,
1698, Norris of Fairhill MSS, Family Letters, I, 112, HSP.

10. Turner to Penn, Philadelphia, April 15, 1697, typescript, Society Collection, HSP.

11. Lloyd, Carpenter, and Shippen to Penn, Philadelphia, July 4,
1698, Norris of Fairhill MSS, Family Letters, I, 112, HSP.

12. Thomas, *Pensilvania*, pp. 20-25; *Col. Rec.*, I, 610; Penn to
Robert Harley, *[ca.* 1701], Great Britain, Royal Commission on Historical Manuscripts, *The Manuscripts of His Grace the Duke of Portland, Preserved at Welbeek Abbey* (London: H. M. Stationery Office,
1892-1931), IV ("Harley Papers"), 31; Curtis P. Nettels, *The Money
Supply of the American Colonies before 1720* (Madison, Wis.: University of Wisconsin, 1934), pp. 121-23; *The Harleian Miscellany; or,
a Collection of Scarce, Curious, and Entertaining Pamphlets and Tracts,
as Well in Manuscript as in Print, Found in the Late Earl of Oxford's
Library, Interspersed with Historical, Political, and Critical Notes*
(London, 1810), X, 381.

13. Lloyd and others, Representation to Penn in behalf of the town
of Philadelphia, October, 1700, Logan Papers, III, 11, HSP.

14. *Ibid.;* Watson, *Annals*, III, 175.

15. *Penn and Logan Corr.*, II, 403.

16. J. T. Mitchell and S. Flanders (eds.), *Statutes at Large of Pennsylvania, 1700-1790* (Harrisburg: State Printer, 1896-1908), II, 119-
20, cited hereafter as *Pa. Stats. at Large.*

17. Statement of William Penn's agreement with Philip Ford, about
1705, Penn Papers, Ford vs. Penn, p. 7, HSP; Philip Ford's deed of
Pennsylvania to Penn, dated April 10, 1697, copy, *ibid.*, p. 3.

18. Norris to Philip Ford, May 3, 1700, Norris Letter Book, I,
77, HSP.

19. Lloyd, "The Speaker's Vindication against James Logan's In-
vectives . . . ," November 22, 1709, *Penn and Logan Corr.*, II, 404.

20. *Ibid.*

21. Norris to Daniel Zachary, December 8, 1700, *Penn and Logan
Corr.*, I, 22.

22. Lloyd, "The Speaker's Vindication . . . ," *ibid.*, II, 404.

23. Penn to Logan, S. Galloway's, June 11, 1701, *ibid.*, I, 41; Norris to John Askew, June 2, 1701, Norris Letter Book, I, 88, HSP.

24. Penn to Logan, Pennsbury, July 14, 1701, *Penn and Logan Corr.*,
I, 45.

25. Penn to Logan, Pennsbury, August 13, 1701, *ibid.*, p. 52.

26. Penn to Logan, Pennsbury, September 6, 1701, *ibid.*, p. 53.

27. Penn to Logan, Pennsbury, September 8, 1701, *ibid.*, p. 54.

28. Penn to Logan, Pennsbury, August, 1701, *ibid.*, p. 50; Joseph
Wilcox to Penn, Philadelphia, August 1, 1701, Penn-Physick Papers,

I, 15, HSP; Joseph Growdon to David Lloyd, May 24, 1702, Streper Papers, Bucks County, p. 49, HSP; *The Friend,* XXXIX (1865), 93, 99; Thomas Lower to Growdon, London, March 26, 1699, *ibid.*, pp. 98-99; Lower to Grace Lloyd, London, September 26, 1700, *ibid.*, pp. 99-100; David Lloyd to Lower, Philadelphia, March 17, 1701, *ibid.*, p. 100; Penn to Logan, Pennsbury, September 8, 1701, *Penn and Logan Corr.*, I, 54.

29. Great Britain, *Calendar of State Papers, Domestic, 1694-95,* p. 276; Lords of Treasury to Penn, March 27, 1701, William A. Shaw (ed.), *Calendar of Treasury Books Preserved in the Public Record Office, 1700-1,* p. 235.

30. *Col. Rec.*, II, 35.

31. MacKinney, *Votes,* I, 285.

32. Petition of the Inhabitants of Philadelphia to the Assembly, September 17, 1701, Logan Papers, III, 20, HSP.

33. *Ibid.*

34. *Ibid.*, p. 23.

35. *Ibid.*, p. 21.

36. MacKinney, *Votes,* I, 284-85; Penn to Logan, May 10, 1705, *Penn and Logan Corr.*, I, 17; Report on petition of the inhabitants of Philadelphia to the Assembly, September 18, 1701, Logan Papers, III, 24, HSP.

37. *Col. Rec.*, II, 40.

38. *Ibid.*, p. 35.

39. MacKinney, *Votes,* I, 292-95, 304-5.

40. Loyd, *The Early Courts of Pennsylvania,* p. 72.

41. In December, 1686, a court of equity was held at Chester by the justices of the Chester County Court of Common Pleas, who were, however, called Commissioners in Chancery for that court. *Martin's Bench and Bar,* pp. 61-62.

42. *Pa. Stats. at Large,* II, 156-57.

43. *Charter and Laws of Pa.*, p. 311.

44. Penn to Lords of Admiralty, Philadelphia, December 10, 1700, *House of Lords MSS.*, *1699-1702,* IV, 348-49.

45. *Charter and Laws of Pa.*, p. 311.

46. *Ibid.*, p. 315.

47. Sir Edward Coke, *The Third Part of the Institutes of the Laws of England: Concerning High Treason, and Other Pleas of the Crown, and Criminal Causes* (London: W. Clark and Sons, 1817), p. 75.

48. The fiction of ejectment, the most popular of fictitious actions in England, was a personal action for the recovery of damages for loss of the term of tenancy or possession of lands. An action of this nature was instituted by the fictitious allegation of eviction. For example, A, claimant of the title, delivered to B, tenant in possession, a declaration of ejectment. In this declaration John Doe and Richard Roe, fictitious persons, are respectively plaintiff and defendant. Doe declares

on a fictitious lease of the lands from A to himself for a term of years and alleges that during this term he was ousted from possession by Roe. Thus, the title of the action is *John Doe* v. *Richard Roe.* To the declaration is annexed a notice signed by Roe and directed to B, advising B to appear in court as defendant in Roe's stead, otherwise Roe would suffer judgment to be entered by default and B would be turned out of possession. If B failed to appear, judgment would be entered by default against Roe. If B appeared, he would be substituted for Roe as defendant. If B, however, failed to appear on trial and confess lease, entry, and ouster, the plaintiff was necessarily nonsuited because the fictitious lease, entry, and ouster could not be proved. This was the shortcoming of the method, and it often resulted in prolonged litigation. Ejectment was opposed in Puritan New England because every word in the declaration by which such an action commenced was untrue. For a good discussion of the fiction of ejectment see Arthur G. Sedgwick and Frederick S. Wait, "The History of the Action of Ejectment in England and the United States," in Association of American Law Schools, *Select Essays in Anglo-American Legal History* (Boston: Little, Brown and Co., 1907-9), III, 611-45.

49. *Charter and Laws of Pa.*, pp. 313-15.

50. For a study of common-law reception in the colonial period see Richard B. Morris, *Studies in the History of Anglo-American Law, with Special Reference to the Seventeenth and Eighteenth Centuries* (New York: Columbia University Press, 1930), pp. 41-47.

51. *Charter and Laws of Pa.*, p. 314.

52. *B. C. & M. R. R.* v. *State of Connecticut* (1885), quoted in Morris, *Studies in the History of Anglo-American Law*, pp. 46-47.

53. *Charter and Laws of Pa.*, p. 314.

54. *Ibid.*, p. 100.

55. *Ibid.*, p. 314.

56. *Ibid.*, pp. 311-19.

57. *Ibid.*, pp. 318-19. Lloyd recognized Penn's prerogatives in the establishment of seignory courts, but no such courts existed in Pennsylvania anyway.

58. MacKinney, *Votes*, I, 318-19.

59. *Ibid.*, p. 322.

60. *Charter and Laws of Pa.*, p. 311; MacKinney, *Votes*, I, 296, 299, 306, 308, 314, 318, 356.

61. Edward Channing wrote that the authorship of the Frame of 1701 "is uncertain and always will be owing to the imperfect state of the records." William R. Shepherd indicated that the Frame was the work of both the Assembly and Penn, but chiefly of the Assembly, because Penn never liked it. Herbert L. Osgood also showed that the Frame was the product of both Penn and the Assembly, but he credited Penn, without documentation, with excluding the Council from the legislative authority.

Lawrence H. Gipson made no attempt to assign authorship of the Frame of 1701, but he said that Penn signed the Frame "under some compulsion." Charles H. Andrews wrote that the Assembly accepted and amended the draft of the Frame written by Penn, after Penn had rejected the Frame drawn up by the Assembly. Edward Channing, *A History of the United States* (New York: The Macmillan Co., 1927), II, 322; Osgood, *The American Colonies in the Seventeenth Century,* II, 276; Lawrence H. Gipson, *The British Empire before the American Revolution*(Vol. III; Caldwell, Idaho: Caxton Printers, 1936), p. 193; Charles M. Andrews, *The Colonial Period of American History* (New Haven: Yale University Press, 1937), III, 319.

62. MacKinney, *Votes,* I, 389.

63. *Col. Rec.,* II, 54; MacKinney, *Votes,* I, 320, 323-27.

64. *Col. Rec.,* II, 62; William Penn, The Proprietor's Agreement about the Charter for the Lower Counties, New Castle, October 31, 1701, *Penn and Logan Corr.,* I, 58-59.

65. *Col. Rec.,* II, 62.

66. David Lloyd, Charter of Property of Pennsylvania, October 28, 1701, Penn MSS, Assembly and Provincial Council, Large Folio, p. 14, HSP.

67. *Ibid.*

68. MacKinney, *Votes,* I, 391.

69. See p. 41 and p. 90 above.

70. From 1718 to 1732 the great majority of settlers who took up land in the back country were squatters who did not trouble to take up legal title to the land. By 1726 there were about 100,000 squatters. Percy W. Bidwell and John I. Falconer, *History of Agriculture in the Northern United States, 1620-1860* (Washington, D.C.: Carnegie Institute of Washington, 1925), p. 72. A study of settlement in the Pennsylvania back country prior to 1718 is needed.

71. William Penn, "The Proprietor's Agreement . . . ," New Castle, October 31, 1701, *Penn and Logan Corr.,* I, 58-59.

72. *Ibid.*

73. William Penn's commission to James Logan, May 26, 1701, Maria Dickinson Logan Papers, HSP.

74. Charter of the Corporation of Philadelphia, 1701, HSP; Charter of the Borough of Chester, 1701, HSP.

75. Diffenderffer, "Early Local History as Revealed by an Old Document," pp. 5-10; Eshleman, "The Birth of Lancaster County," pp. 10-15; Eshleman, "The Great Conestoga Road," p. 219.

76. David Lloyd and Isaac Norris to Penn, New Castle, October 29, 1701, with endorsement by Penn, George W. Norris Papers, HSP.

77. Penn to Logan, Pennsbury, September 8, 1701, *Penn and Logan Corr.,* I, 53.

78. Penn to Logan, Shipboard, November 3, 1701, *ibid.,* p. 59.

79. Logan to Penn, Philadelphia, December 2, 1701, *ibid.*, p. 67; Logan to Penn, Philadelphia, February 1701/2, *ibid.*, pp. 80-81.

80. Logan to Penn, Philadelphia, December 2, 1701, *ibid.*, p. 67; David Lloyd, "The Speaker's Vindication . . . ," *ibid.*, II, 404.

81. David Lloyd, "The Speaker's Vindication . . . ," *ibid.*, II, 404.

82. Penn to Logan, Kensington, January 4, 1701/2, *ibid.*, I, 75.

83. Penn to Logan, Kensington, February 3, 1701/2, *ibid.*, p. 78.

*Chapter 10*

1. David Powell to Logan, February 1, 1700/1, Logan Papers, I, 37, HSP; 1702 accounts in Miscellaneous Papers of the Philadelphia Monthly Meeting, Friends Bookstore, Philadelphia, Pa.; Egle, *Old Rights*, III, 83; Egle, *Minutes*, XIX, 324, 330, 346, 406.

2. Stevenson W. Fletcher, *Pennsylvania Agriculture and Country Life, 1640-1840* (Harrisburg: Pennsylvania Historical and Museum Commission, 1950), p. 302; Logan to Penn, Philadelphia, December 2, 1701, *Penn and Logan Corr.*, I, 67; Logan to Penn, Philadelphia, May 7, 1702, *ibid.*, p. 98.

3. Logan to Penn, Philadelphia, May 7, 1702, *Penn and Logan Corr.*, I, 94-95; Logan to Penn, Philadelphia, October 2, 1702, *ibid.*, p. 137; Grant and Munro (eds.), *Acts of the Privy Council of England, Colonial Series, 1613-1783*, II, 441-42.

4. Logan to Penn, Philadelphia, May 7, 1702, *Penn and Logan Corr.*, I, 99.

5. Penn to Logan, London, June 21, 1702, *ibid.*, p. 113.

6. Sainsbury, *Cal. State Papers, Col.*, *1702*, p. 329.

7. *Martin's Bench and Bar*, p. 8; Logan to Penn, Philadelphia, October 2, 1702, *Penn and Logan Corr.*, I, 139; Quary to Board of Trade, March 31, 1702, Sainsbury, *Cal. State Papers, Col.*, *1702*, p. 182; John Moore to Nathaniel Blakiston, Philadelphia, April 21, 1702, *ibid.*, pp. 487-88. Moore was primarily interested in obtaining a suitable salary from the Crown.

8. Logan to Penn, Philadelphia, July 9, 1702, *Penn and Logan Corr.*, I, 120-21; Logan to Penn, Philadelphia, May 7, 1702, *ibid.*, pp. 94-95.

9. Logan to Penn, New Castle, May 28, 1702, *ibid.*, p. 105; Norris to James Mills, July 15, 1699, Norris Letter Book, I, 70, HSP; Logan to Penn, Philadelphia, May 7, 1702, *Penn and Logan Corr.*, I, 94; Joseph Growdon to Lloyd, May 24, 1702, Streper Papers, Bucks County, p. 49, HSP.

10. Charter of the Corporation of Philadelphia, 1701, HSP; Logan to Penn, Philadelphia, October 2, 1702, *Penn and Logan Corr.*, I, 137-38, 139, 140.

11. Loyd, *The Early Courts of Pennsylvania*, p. 113; Thomas Story, "The Journal of the Life of Thomas Story, A Minister of the Gospel in the Religious Society of Friends," *Friends Library*, X, 245.

12. *Col. Rec.*, II, 66-67; Logan to Penn, Philadelphia, October 2, 1702, *Penn and Logan Corr.*, I, 137-39.

13. Charter of the Corporation of Philadelphia, 1701.

14. *Col. Rec.*, II, 66-67; Logan to Penn, Philadelphia, October 2, 1702, *Penn and Logan Corr.*, I, 137-39.

15. Logan to Penn, Philadelphia, December 1, 1702, *ibid.*, p. 148.

16. Logan to Penn, Philadelphia, October 2, 1702, *ibid.*, p. 139.

17. Quoted in Watson, *Annals*, I, 84.

18. Logan to Penn, Philadelphia, October 18, 1702, *Penn and Logan Corr.*, I, 144; Penn to Logan, London, July 28, 1702, *Pa. Mag. Hist. & Biog.*, XXXVI (1912), 306.

19. *Martin's Bench and Bar*, p. 29; Logan to Penn, Philadelphia, October 2, 1702, *Penn and Logan Corr.*, I, 139.

20. Logan to Penn, Philadelphia, October 2, 1702, *Penn and Logan Corr.*, I, 138-39.

21. *Ibid.*, p. 138.

22. Proud, *Pennsylvania*, I, 442.

23. MacKinney, *Votes*, I, 392.

24. Logan to Penn, Philadelphia, October 18, 1702, *Penn and Logan Corr.*, I, 143.

*Chapter 11*

1. Logan to Penn, Philadelphia, October 18, 1702, *Penn and Logan Corr.*, I, 143; MacKinney, *Votes*, I, 392.

2. Watson, *Annals*, II, 485; Logan to Penn, Philadelphia, June 18, 1702, *Penn and Logan Corr.*, I, 107.

3. Logan to Penn, Philadelphia, October 18, 1702.

4. *Ibid.*

5. *Col. Rec.*, II, 75-82; MacKinney, *Votes*, I, 362-71; Logan to Penn, Philadelphia, December 1, 1702, *Penn and Logan Corr.*, I, 154.

6. MacKinney, *Votes*, I, 371; *Col. Rec.*, II, 83.

7. MacKinney, *Votes*, I, 372; *Col. Rec.*, II, 83.

8. Logan to Penn, Philadelphia, December 1, 1702, *Penn and Logan Corr.*, I, 153-54.

9. MacKinney, *Votes*, I, 372-75; *Col. Rec.*, II, 83-86.

10. Logan to Penn, Philadelphia, May 2, 1702, *Penn and Logan Corr.*, I, 88.

11. David Lloyd, "The Speaker's Vindication . . . ," *ibid.*, II, 404; Logan to Penn, Philadelphia, December 1, 1702, *ibid.*, I, 150.

12. Logan to Penn, Philadelphia, December 1, 1702, *ibid.*, I, 150; Logan to Penn, Amboy, April 29, 1703, *ibid.*, p. 186; Shaw (ed.), *Calendar of Treasury Books, 1703*, pp. 254, 354.

13. *Col. Rec.*, II, 105-6; MacKinney, *Votes*, I, 375-77; Logan to Penn, Philadelphia, September 29, 1703, postscript [October 1, 1703],

*Penn and Logan Corr.*, I, 246; Logan to Penn, Philadelphia, December 5, 1703, *ibid.*, p. 253.

14. Logan to Penn, Philadelphia, September 29, 1703, postscript [October 1, 1703], *Penn and Logan Corr.*, I, 246.

15. Logan to Penn, Philadelphia, December 5, 1703, *ibid.*, p. 253.

16. Lower to David Lloyd, March 30, 1703, quoted in *The Friend*, XXXIX, 106.

17. *House of Lords MSS, 1702-4*, V, 313.

18. *Col. Rec.*, II, 105, 109.

19. MacKinney, *Votes*, I, 381-82, 389; *Col. Rec.*, II, 110-11.

20. *House of Lords MSS, 1702-4*, V, 314.

21. *DAB*, VI, 214; *Col. Rec.*, II, 115; Penn to Logan, London, March 10, 1703/4, *Penn and Logan Corr.*, I, 272.

22. *Col. Rec.*, II, 119.

23. *Col. Rec.*, II, 126; Logan to Penn, Philadelphia, February 15, 1703/4, *Penn and Logan Corr.*, I, 267.

24. Logan to Penn, Philadelphia, April 3, 1704, *Penn and Logan Corr.*, I, 282.

25. See Robert W. Johannsen, "The Conflict between the Three Lower Counties on the Delaware and the Province of Pennsylvania, 1682-1704," *Delaware History*, V (1952), 129-30.

26. *Col. Rec.*, II, 125.

27. *Ibid.*, p. 126.

28. *Ibid.*

29. Provincial Assembly to the Representatives of the Lower Counties, April 13, 1704, Logan Papers, III, 77, HSP.

30. *Col. Rec.*, II, 129-30, 134, 136.

31. *Ibid.*, p. 139.

## Chapter 12

1. MacKinney, *Votes*, I, 404-6, 416.

2. *Ibid.*, pp. 412, 415, 416, 418, 419, 422, 426, 427, 429, 432, 434.

3. Grant and Munro (eds.), *Acts of the Privy Council of England, Colonial Series, 1613-1783*, II, 419-20.

4. Logan to Penn, Philadelphia, September 11, 1703, *Penn and Logan Corr.*, I, 239; Logan to Penn, Philadelphia, June 24, 1703, *ibid.*, p. 196; Moore to Quary, Philadelphia, September 7, 1703, Sainsbury, *Cal. State Papers, Col.*, *1702-3*, pp. 740-41; Logan to Penn, Philadelphia, September 7, 1703, *Penn and Logan Corr.*, I, 236.

5. MacKinney, *Votes*, I, 413-14.

6. Penn to Nathaniel Puckle, London, April 8, 1704, Penn Papers, Domestic and Misc. Letters, p. 92, HSP.

7. MacKinney, *Votes*, I, 427.

8. Lloyd to G[eorge] W[hitehead], W[illiam] M[ead], T[homas] L[ower], Philadelphia, October 3, 1704, Logan Papers, I, 52, HSP.

9. Logan to Penn, Philadelphia, February 15, 1703/4, *Penn and Logan Corr.*, I, 268.

10. *Col. Rec.*, II, 144-45.

11. *Ibid.*, pp. 144-46.

12. Address of the Assembly to Penn, May 26, 1704, Penn MSS, Assembly and Provincial Council, Large Folio, p. 19, HSP.

13. MacKinney, *Votes*, I, 411.

14. *Ibid.*; Penn to Puckle, London, April 8, 1704, Penn Papers, Domestic and Misc. Letters, p. 92, HSP.

15. *Col. Rec.*, II, 139.

16. MacKinney, *Votes*, I, 414, 416.

17. Logan to Penn, Philadelphia, March 14, 1703/4, *Penn and Logan Corr.*, I, 278.

18. Logan to Penn, Philadelphia, July 14, 1704, *ibid.*, p. 303.

19. Logan to Penn, Philadelphia, February 15, 1703/4, *ibid.*, p. 268.

20. Logan to Penn, Philadelphia, September 28, 1704, *ibid.*, p. 317; MacKinney, *Votes*, I, 415.

21. See above p. 74.

22. *Col. Rec.*, II, 149; MacKinney, *Votes*, I, 424, 429.

23. *Col. Rec.*, II, 157; MacKinney, *Votes*, I, 425.

24. MacKinney, *Votes*, I, 423.

25. *Col. Rec.*, II, 157; MacKinney, *Votes*, I, 425.

26. *Col. Rec.*, II, 158.

27. *Ibid.*

28. MacKinney, *Votes*, I, 389.

29. *Col. Rec.*, II, 114.

30. Logan to Penn, Philadelphia, February 15, 1703/4. *Penn and Logan Corr.*, I, 268; MacKinney, *Votes*, I, 423.

31. *Col. Rec.*, I, 19.

32. MacKinney, *Votes*, I, 423.

33. *Col. Rec.*, II, 149.

34. Logan to Penn, Philadelphia, July 14, 1704, *Penn and Logan Corr.*, I, 299.

35. Penn to Logan, July 22, 1704, *ibid.*, p. 308.

36. Logan to Penn, Philadelphia, July 14, 1704, *ibid.*, p. 304; Charter of the Corporation of Philadelphia, 1701; *Martin's Bench and Bar*, p. 59. Martin erroneously listed Lloyd as having been the city recorder in 1702.

37. MacKinney, *Votes*, I, 419.

38. *Ibid.*

39. *Ibid.*, p. 418.

40. *Ibid.*, p. 419.

41. "Money is so scarce that many good farmers now scarce ever see a piece of eight of their own throughout the whole year; what there is . . . is in town, and, therefore, neither rents nor other pay can be had in money, and wheat for two years past has been worth very little"

(Logan to Penn, Philadelphia, October 3, 1704, *Penn and Logan Corr.*,
I, 325).

42. MacKinney, *Votes*, I, 420.

43. *Ibid.*

44. *Ibid.,* p. 433.

45. *Ibid.*, p. 419.

46. *Ibid.*, pp. 422, 430.

47. *Ibid.*, p. 421.

48. Quoted in Watson, *Annals*, I, 84.

49. *Col. Rec.*, II, 157.

50. MacKinney, *Votes*, I, 428.

51. *Ibid.*, p. 432.

52. Biles, Wilcox, Morris, Wood, Jones, Norris, and Richardson.

53. David Lloyd, "The Speaker's Vindication . . . ," *Penn and Logan
Corr.*, II, 407-8.

54. Logan to Penn, Philadelphia, December, 1704, *ibid.*, I, 349-50.

55. Cf. MacKinney, *Votes*, I, 467.

56. *Ibid.*, p. 433.

57. *Ibid.*

58. The final draft of the "Remonstrance" has not been found.

59. MacKinney, *Votes*, I, 433. See Thomas Hobbes, *Leviathan* (London: J. M. Dent and Sons, 1931), Part I, XV, 78, and John Locke, *An
Essay Concerning the True Original, Extent and End of Civil Government*, II, 13. The idea was really an old one. Andrew of Isernia, a
thirteenth-century commentator on the constitution of the kingdom of
Naples, wrote in his *Peregrina: "Non erit dominus judex in causa sua,"*
"A lord cannot be judge in his own case" (quoted in R. W. and A. J.
Carlyle, *A History of Medieval Political Theory in the West* [New York:
Barnes and Noble, Inc., n.d.], V, 105).

60. MacKinney, *Votes*, I, 433.

61. *Ibid.*

62. Lloyd to G[eorge] W[hitehead], W[illiam] M[ead], T[homas]
L[ower], Philadelphia, October 3, 1704, Logan Papers, I, 52, HSP.
This letter, a copy, is written in the hand of Hannah Penn, William
Penn's second wife.

63. *Ibid.*

*Chapter 13*

1. Logan to Penn, Philadelphia, October 27, 1704, *Penn and Logan
Corr.*, I, 338.

2. Norris to Jonathan Dickinson, Philadelphia, September 27, 1704,
Maria Dickinson Logan Papers, HSP.

3. Quoted in Watson, *Annals*, I, 115.

4. *Col. Rec.*, II, 152, 160-62.

5. Logan to Penn, Philadelphia, October 3, 1704, *Penn and Logan*

*Corr.*, I, 322-24; Minutes ot the City Council of Philadelphia, October 3, 1704, in Watson, *Annals*, I, 58.

6. Logan to Penn, Philadelphia, October 3, 1704, *Penn and Logan Corr.*, I, 323.

7. David Lloyd, "The Speaker's Vindication . . . , " *ibid.*, II, 408; Lower to Lloyd, London, April 17, 1705, *The Friend*, XXXIX, 114-15.

8. *Col. Rec.*, II, 168-69; MacKinney, *Votes*, I, 442.

9. Logan to Penn, Philadelphia, October 27, 1704, *Penn and Logan Corr.*, I, 338.

10. *Col. Rec.*, II, 172, 176.

11. Logan to Penn, New Castle, November 22, 1704, *Penn and Logan Corr.*, I, 344; *Col. Rec.*, II, 174-76.

12. Logan to Penn, Philadelphia, December, 1704, *Penn and Logan Corr.*, I, 349; MacKinney, *Votes*, I, 467.

13. MacKinney, *Votes*, I, 467.

14. Logan to Penn, Philadelphia, December, 1704, *Penn and Logan Corr.*, I, 349-50.

15. Penn to Logan, London, January 16, 1704/5, *ibid.*, pp. 357-58.

16. *Ibid.*, p. 331; David Lloyd, "The Speaker's Vindication . . . , " *ibid.*, II, 405-8.

17. Logan to Penn, Philadelphia, December, 1704, *ibid.*, I, 350.

18. Penn to Logan, [1704], *ibid.*, p. 280.

19. MacKinney, *Votes*, I, 471, 481; Penn to Logan, London, January 16, 1704/5, *Penn and Logan Corr.*, I, 356. The "New Castle charter" was Lloyd's draft of a charter of property.

20. MacKinney, *Votes*, I, 471.

21. Great Britain, *Journal of the Commissioners for Trade and Plantations from April 1704, to 1728. Preserved in the Public Record Office* (London: H. M. Stationery Office, 1920), I, 77, 80, 112, 131-32, 137-43; Logan to Penn, Philadelphia, February 11, 1704/5, *Penn and Logan. Corr.*, I, 362.

22. Penn to Logan, London, January 16, 1704/5, *Penn and Logan Corr.*, I, 356-58.

23. Penn to Roger Mompesson, London, February 17, 1704/5, *ibid.*, pp. 373, 375.

24. Logan to Penn, Philadelphia, February 11, 1704/5, *ibid.*, p. 361; Logan to Mrs. Letitia Aubrey, Philadelphia, February 12, 1704/5, *ibid.*, p. 370.

25. Logan to Penn, Philadelphia, March 11, 1704/5, *ibid.*, p. 363; Logan to Penn, Philadelphia, April 5, 1705, *ibid.*, II, 9-10.

26. Penn to Mompesson, London, February 17, 1704/5, *ibid.*, I, 373; *Col. Rec.*, II, 186, 187; Penn to Logan, London, May 10, 1705, *Penn and Logan Corr.*, II, 17.

27. *Col. Rec.*, II, 190, 200-1; Logan to Penn, Philadelphia, July 4, 1705, *Penn and Logan Corr.*, II, 33.

28. *Col. Rec.*, II, 200; William Biles to Evans, Philadelphia, May, 1705, Streper Papers, Bucks County, p. 63, HSP.
29. *Col. Rec.*, II, 200.
30. *Ibid.*, pp. 200-1.
31. *Ibid.*, pp. 201-3.
32. Logan to Penn, Philadelphia, July 4, 1705, *Penn and Logan Corr.*, II, 33.
33. Logan to Penn, Philadelphia, April 5, 1705, *ibid.*, pp. 4-6; Logan to Penn, Philadelphia, July 4, 1705, *ibid.*, p. 33.
34. Logan to Penn, Philadelphia, April 5, 1705, *ibid.*, pp. 4-6.
35. Logan to Penn, Philadelphia, July 13, 1705, *ibid.*, p. 37; Logan to Penn, Philadelphia, August 22, 1705, *ibid.*, p. 41.
36. Norris to Ford, Philadelphia, August 29, 1705, Norris Letter Book, I, 123, HSP.
37. Logan to Penn, Philadelphia, October 24, 1705, *Penn and Logan Corr.*, II, 80.

*Chapter 14*

1. Logan to Penn, Philadelphia, July 27, 1706, *Penn and Logan Corr.*, II, 142.
2. Penn to Logan, London, September 14, 1705, *ibid.*, p. 71; Penn to Logan, London, February 9, 1705/6, *ibid.*, p. 107; Logan to Penn, Philadelphia, Spring of 1706, *ibid.*, p. 119; Logan to Penn, Philadelphia, July 27, 1706, *ibid.*, p. 142.
3. *Col. Rec.*, II, 227-29, 241, 243, 249-50; Proud, *Pennsylvania*, I, 468-69.
4. Logan to Penn, Philadelphia, June 12, 1706, *Penn and Logan Corr.*, II, 131-36.
5. Logan to Penn, Philadelphia, Spring of 1706, *ibid.*, p. 119.
6. [?] to the Assembly, sent to Henery Clower in Philadelphia, [1706], Logan Papers, III, 118, HSP. The letter itself is undated, but the date 1705 was added to the manuscript in pencil at a later time. The internal evidence of the letter, however, indicates that it was written in 1706. The title, "Libel on the Assembly," was also added to the manuscript at a later date.
7. *Ibid.*
8. MacKinney, *Votes*, I, 553, 556-57; *Pa. Stats. at Large*, II, 212-21.
9. Great Britain, *Journal of the Commissioners for Trade and Plantations from April 1704, to 1728*, I, 167; *Col. Rec.*, II, 251.
10. *Col. Rec.*, II, 253-54.
11. *Ibid.*, pp. 258-59.
12. Logan to Penn, Philadelphia, October 6, 1706, *Penn and Logan Corr.*, II, 171-72.

*Chapter 15*

1. *Col. Rec.*, II, 258-60; Logan to Penn, Philadelphia, March 3, 1702/3. *Penn and Logan Corr.*, I, 176-77.

2. MacKinney, *Votes*, I, 590-97, 599-600, 605.

3. *Col. Rec.*, II, 263-66; MacKinney, *Votes*, I, 594-95.

4. *Col. Rec.*, II, 261.

5. *Ibid.*, pp. 262, 271.

6. *Ibid.*, p. 275.

7. *Ibid.*, p. 266.

8. *Ibid.*, p. 278.

9. *Ibid.*, p. 270. The passage Lloyd referred to is in Sir Peyton Ventris, *The Reports of Sir Peyton Ventris Knt.*, *Late One of the Justices of the Common Pleas* (In the Savoy, 1726), Part I, p. 180. Ventris' *Reports* first appeared in 1695.

10. *Col. Rec.*, II, 281.

11. *Ibid.*, p. 292.

12. *Ibid.*, pp. 292-93.

13. *Ibid.*, p. 263.

14. *Ibid.*, p. 278. The legal historian, William H. Loyd, Jr., thought Lloyd was correct in making this assertion and cited Abbott's *Jurisdiction and Practice of the Court of Great Sessions of Wales* (1795) as supporting evidence, but he had added that the subject of equity jurisdiction in Wales has been inadequately treated by textbook writers (Loyd, *The Early Courts of Pennsylvania*, p. 174).

15. *Col. Rec.*, II, 268.

16. *Ibid.*, pp. 284-85.

17. *Ibid.*, pp. 266, 278.

18. *Ibid.*, p. 287.

19. *Ibid.*, p. 289.

20. *Ibid.*, p. 270.

21. *Ibid.*, p. 296. Also see *Charter and Laws of Pa.*, p. 84.

22. Early in 1705 Logan had advised Penn that, if the judiciary act of 1701 were repealed, he would have "the Power, by the Charter from the Crown, to erect all courts for the administration of justice by thyself or lieutenants" (Logan to Penn, Philadelphia, April 5, 1705, *Penn and Logan Corr.*, II, 4-5).

23. Lloyd and others to Whitehead, Mead, and Lower, Philadelphia, December 4, 1706, Fallon Scrapbook, Am. 0628, p. 6, HSP.

24. Norris to Richard Hill, London, May 17, 1707, *Penn and Logan Corr.*, II, 223.

25. Great Britain, *Stats.*, VII, 637.

26. George E. Reed (ed.), *Papers of the Governors, 1681-1747* (Pennsylvania Archives, 4th ser.; Harrisburg: William Stanley Ray, State Printer, 1900), I, 35.

27. *Col. Rec.*, II, 310-15.

28. *Ibid.*, pp. 315-17.
29. *Ibid.*, pp. 321, 323-25, 337-42.
30. Penn to Logan, London, June 10, 1707, *Penn and Logan Corr.*, II, 229.

*Chapter 16*

1. Articles of Impeachment against James Logan, February 25, 1706/7, Logan Papers, IV, 21, HSP.
2. *Ibid.*
3. Logan to Penn, Philadelphia, February 15, 1703/4, *Penn and Logan Corr.*, I, 268.
4. James Logan's Answer to the Assembly's Articles of Impeachment, March 4, 1706/7, Logan Papers, IV, 35, HSP.
5. *Ibid.*; Articles of Impeachment against James Logan, *ibid.*, p. 21.
6. James Logan's Answers to the Assembly's Articles of Impeachment, *ibid.*, p. 35.
7. Articles of Impeachment against James Logan, *ibid.*, p. 21.
8. James Logan's Answers to the Assembly's Articles of Impeachment, *ibid.*, p. 35.
9. *Ibid.*; Articles of Impeachment against James Logan, *ibid.*, p. 21.
10. *Ibid.*
11. James Logan's Answers to the Assembly's Articles of Impeachment, *ibid.*, p. 35.
12. *Col. Rec.*, II, 356.
13. *Ibid.*, pp. 358-59.
14. *Ibid.*, pp. 364, 366.
15. *Ibid.*, pp. 372-73, 377-78.
16. *Ibid.*, pp. 374-77.
17. Penn to Logan, London, June 10, 1707, *Penn and Logan Corr.*, II, 229; Penn to Logan, London, July 8, 1707, *ibid.*, p. 235.
18. *Col. Rec.*, II, 379-81.
19. *Ibid.*, pp. 398-402.
20. Quoted in Watson, *Annals*, I, 80.
21. Quoted in *ibid.*, p. 29. Cf., also, Logan to Penn, Philadelphia, June 28, 1707, *Penn and Logan Corr.*, II, 230-31.
22. Actually, Gookin's commission was dated September 3, 1708, but he did not arrive in Pennsylvania until March, 1708/9 (*Col. Rec.*, II, 427).
23. *Ibid.*, pp. 433-34.
24. *Ibid.*, pp. 444-47, 449-51, 460-64, 466-69, 477; Governor Gookin's Discourses with Members of the Assembly, March 7, 1708/9, Logan Papers, IV, 58, HSP.
25. *Col. Rec.*, II, 435; Evans to the Deputy Governor and Council

of the Province of Pennsylvania, April 12, 1704, Logan Papers, IV, 61, HSP.

26. *Col. Rec.*, II, 495-500; MacKinney, *Votes*, II, 852-55.
27. *Col. Rec.*, II, 500-2.
28. *Ibid.*, p. 504.
29. *Ibid.*, p. 506.
30. *Penn and Logan Corr.*, II, 415-16.
31. David Lloyd, "The Speaker's Vindication . . . ," *ibid.*, p. 408.
32. *Ibid.*
33. *Col. Rec.*, II, 507-8; Logan to Charles Gookin, November 28, 1709, Logan Papers, IV, 94, HSP; Gookin to Peter Evans, Philadelphia, November 28, 1709, in Proud, *Pennsylvania*, II, 41. Peter Evans, a cousin of John Evans, was the Philadelphia County sheriff.
34. Penn to the Assembly, London, June 29, 1710, in Proud, *Pennsylvania*, II, 48.
35. *Ibid.*, p. 51.
36. *Ibid.*, p. 53.
37. *Col. Rec.*, II, 516; Isaac Norris, *Friendly Advice to the Inhabitants of Pennsylvania* (Philadelphia, 1710).
38. *Col. Rec.*, II, 513-15.
39. Hazard, *Register*, IV, 29.
40. Logan to Henry Gouldney, Philadelphia, August 26, 1709, Logan Papers, IV, 80, HSP; *Col. Rec.*, II, 461; David Lloyd, "The Speaker's Vindication . . . ," *Penn and Logan Corr.*, II, 415.
41. *Col. Rec.*, II, 516.

## Chapter 17

1. Burton Alva Konkle, "David Lloyd and Chester," *Friends Historical Association Bulletin*, XXI (1932), 74.
2. Egle, *Old Rights*, III, 206, 207; Lloyd to Isaac Taylor, Chester, January 9, 1712/13, Taylor Papers, XIV, No. 2817, HSP; Henry Graham Ashmead, *Historical Sketch of Chester, on Delaware* (Chester, Pa.: Republican Steam Printing House, 1883), pp. 73, 121, 132, cited hereafter as Ashmead, *Chester*.
3. Thomas Chalkley, *The Journal of Thomas Chalkley* (New York: Samuel Wood, 1808), p. 67.
4. Lloyd also appears to have engaged in antislavery activity in the Chester Monthly Meeting of which he was a leading member (Jay Higbee, The Development of Anti-Slavery Sentiment among the Colonial Pennsylvania Quakers [Master's thesis, University of Washington, 1949]).
5. Anthony Morris to Flushing Monthly Meeting, Philadelphia, May 10, 1710, Miscellaneous Papers of the Philadelphia Monthly Meeting, preserved at Friends Bookstore, Philadelphia, Pa.; Flushing Monthly

Meeting to Philadelphia Monthly Meeting, Flushing, Long Island, New York, June 6, 1710, *ibid.*

6. Flushing Monthly Meeting to Philadelphia Monthly Meeting, Flushing, June 6, 1710, *ibid.*

7. *Ibid.*; William Burling to Philadelphia Monthly Meeting, Flushing, September 2, 1707, *ibid.*

8. In February, 1706/7, Lloyd had written: "The Real Lease Entry & Ouster is according to the Law of England, and the fictitious proceedings is a new practice, allowed only in Westminster Hall. . . ." Referring to "a Book Called the Law of Ejectments," he had stated his opinion that "the Real Lease, as at Common Law, may be rendered more certain and of less trouble and Danger to the subject here than the Late new practice . . ." *(Col. Rec.,* II, 341).

9. Hazard, *Register,* V, 255; Pennypacker, *Pa. Col. Cases,* pp. 162, 167-68, 176.

10. Pennypacker, *Pa. Col. Cases,* pp. 168, 171-78.

11. *Ibid.,* pp. 168-70.

12. Ashmead, *Chester,* p. 132.

13. Robert Raymond to the Board of Trade, December 22, 1713, signed by David Lloyd, Am. 284, p. 9, HSP.

14. William R. Shepherd, *History of Proprietary Government in Pennsylvania* (Columbia University Studies in History, Economics, and Public Law, Vol. VI [New York, 1896]), pp. 383-84.

15. Grant and Munro (eds.), *Acts of the Privy Council of England, Colonial Series, 1613-1783,* IV, 616. See also Thomas Story's account of Penn's illness in "The Journal of Thomas Story," p. 220.

16. *Martin's Bench and Bar,* p. 170.

## Chapter 18

1. Penn to Shippen, Carpenter, Hill, and Norris, December 8, 1711, Logan Papers, I, 71, HSP.

2. *Col. Rec.,* II, 541.

3. *Ibid.,* pp. 584-85.

4. *Ibid.,* pp. 585, 592, 594-95.

5. Queen Anne died July 20, 1714, and was succeeded by the Hanoverian Elector, George I, whose ministers were not as interested in buying the government of Pennsylvania as had been Queen Anne's.

6. MacKinney, *Votes,* II, 1159-62.

7. Great Britain, *Stats.,* VIII, 792-93; Board of Trade to Governor Hunter, Whitehall, February 25, 1717/18, O'Callaghan, *Doc. Rel. Col. Hist. N.Y.,* V, 500-2; Petition of Inhabitants of Pennsylvania to the Assembly, February 10, 1717/18, Petitions and Memorials, Box 3, HSP; MacKinney, *Votes,* II, 1229-30. For an account of squatters in the Pennsylvania back country see Bidwell and Falconer, *History of Agriculture in the Northern United States, 1620-1860,* p. 72, and for the

colonists' prejudice against the Palatine Germans see Francis Rawle, *A Just Rebuke to a Dialogue betwixt Simon and Timothy, Shewing What's therein to be found. Namely Levity, Perversion, and Detraction. All of which are detected in this short Examen* (Philadelphia: S. Keimer, 1726), p. 22, cited hereafter as Rawle, *A Just Rebuke*.

8. Gookin later explained that he had been ill and out of his mind when he had accused Logan of disloyalty to George I *(Col. Rec.*, III, 17).

9. Lloyd was not the Speaker of this Assembly, but he and Wilcox wrote all the legislation and messages for the Assembly during its session, and Wilcox supervised the keeping of the minutes. For their services the Assembly paid Lloyd £23.8s., and Wilcox £5--an indication that Lloyd did the lion's share of the work. No one else, except the clerk, was remunerated by the Assembly for such services (MacKinney, *Votes*, II, 1276, 1279).

10. *Ibid.*, p. 1223.

11. *Ibid.*, p. 1229.

12. *Ibid.*, pp. 1238-40.

13. *Ibid.*, pp. 1643-44, 1645-47.

14. *Col. Rec.*, III, 39.

15. *Ibid.*, p. 45.

16. For an excellent study of metropolitan development in colonial America see Carl Bridenbaugh, *Cities in the Wilderness: The First Century of Urban Life in America, 1625-1742* (New York: Ronald Press, 1938).

17. *Col. Rec.*, II, 40-41; MacKinney, *Votes*, II, 1257.

18. *Col. Rec.*, III, 41; MacKinney, *Votes*, II, 1257.

19. MacKinney, *Votes*, II, 1258, 1260-62, 1265.

20. *Ibid.*, pp. 1296, 1298-99, 1643-44.

21. *Ibid.*, p. 1290.

22. *Ibid.*, p. 1286.

23. *Ibid.*, p. 1290.

24. *Ibid.*

25. *Ibid.*, pp. 1307-9; Hazard, *Pa. Arch.*, *1st ser.*, I, 169-70. For the litigation over Penn's estate see William B. Rawle, "The General Title of the Penn Family to Pennsylvania," *Pa. Mag. Hist. & Biog.*, XXIII (1899), 60-68, 224-40, 488ff.

26. *Col. Rec.*, III, 75, 90.

27. The Assembly paid Keith an annual salary of £500 (MacKinney, *Votes*, II, 1290).

28. *Ibid.*, pp. 1329-30, 1333-35; *Col. Rec.*, III, 105; *Martin's Bench and Bar*, p. 62.

## Chapter 19

1. Jonathan Dickinson to Dr. Thomas Leigh, Philadelphia, October 28, 1718, Jonathan Dickinson Journal, Free Library of Philadelphia;

Norris and Dickinson to John Wright, Philadelphia, October 16, 1719, *ibid.*

2. Dickinson to John Askew, Philadelphia, April 6, 1719, *ibid.*

3. According to Proud, the number of writs issued in law suits increased from 431 in 1716 to 847 in 1722. Two hundred fifty writs were issued between September and December, 1722, alone (Proud, *Pennsylvania,* II, 150).

4. James Steel to Isaac Taylor, Philadelphia, May 6, 1719, James Steel's Letter Book, 1715-1732, p. 29, HSP.

5. Lloyd to Isaac Taylor, Chester, October 23, 1720, Society Collection, HSP; Lloyd to Lower, February 13, 1716/17, *The Friend,* XXXIX, 115; Lloyd to Lower, November, 1718, *ibid.;* Egle, *Minutes,* XIX, 700; Map of Survey at Uwchland, Penn MSS, Warrants and Surveys, Large Folio, p. 32, HSP; Lloyd to Isaac Taylor, Chester County. October 3, 1720, Taylor Papers, XIV, No. 2970, HSP.

6. Watson, *Annals,* I, 522; Ashmead, *Chester,* p. 75.

7. Minutes of the Chester Monthly Meeting, entries on July 28, 1718, August 25, 1718, August 11, 1718, June 29, 1719, August 31, 1719, December 28, 1719, July 25, 1720, January 30, 1720/21, October 30, 1721, microfilm copy preserved at Friends Historical Library, Swarthmore, Pennsylvania.

8. Jane Fenn Hoskens, "The Life of that Faithful Servant of Christ, Jane Hoskens, a Minister of the Gospel among the People Called Quakers," *Friends Library* (Philadelphia: Joseph Rakestraw, 1837), I, 466.

9. *Ibid.*

10. *Ibid.,* p. 468.

11. Ashmead, *Chester,* p. 121.

12. No description of the stone mansion exists. In 1862 it was leased to a Philadelphia professor for use as a pyrotechnic manufactory. One morning twenty years later fire broke out in the kitchen of the old structure, and, as firemen battled the flames, gunpowder stored in the house exploded, killing eighteen and injuring fifty-seven persons. The house was demolished *(ibid.,* pp. 112-13, 119-20).

13. Hoskens, "The Life of that Faithful Servant of Christ, Jane Hoskens . . . ," p. 471.

14. *Ibid.*; Chester County Papers, 1684-1847, p. 85, HSP.

*Chapter 20*

1. MacKinney, *Votes,* II, 1391.

2. Silver dropped in value from 9s. 2d. per ounce in 1709 to 7s. 5d. per ounce in 1723 (Proud, *Pennsylvania,* II, 174).

3. Rawle, *A Just Rebuke,* p. 17.

4. The number of vessels cleared from the port of Philadelphia dropped from 130 in 1721 to 85 in 1723 (Hazard, *Register,* V, 115).

5. Keith to the Board of Trade, Pennsylvania, December 18, 1722, Sainsbury, *Cal. State Papers., Col.*, *1722-23*, pp. 189-91.

6. Proud, *Pennsylvania*, II, 158, 169.

7. MacKinney, *Votes*, II, 1391; Rawle, *A Just Rebuke.*

8. Francis Rawle, *Some Remedies Proposed, for the Restoring the sunk Credit of the Province of Pennsylvania, with Some Remarks of its Trade. Humbly offer'd to the Consideration of the Worthy Representatives in the General Assembly of this Province, By a Lover of this Country* (Philadelphia, 1721).

9. Rawle, *A Just Rebuke*, p. 17; Keith to the Board of Trade, Philadelphia, December 18, 1722, Sainsbury, *Cal. State Papers, Col.*, *1722-23*, p. 191.

10. MacKinney, *Votes*, II, 1425.

11. Board of Trade to Keith, Whitehall, July 19, 1723, Sainsbury, *Cal. State Papers, Col.*, *1722-23*, p. 310; Proud, *Pennsylvania*, II, 151-52, 158; Shepherd, *History of Proprietary Government in Pennsylvania*, p. 412; Root, *The Relations of Pennsylvania with the British Government*, p. 189; Accusation against Sir William Keith in re-copper mine, Pennsylvania Miscellaneous Papers, Penn and Baltimore, p. 103, HSP, an unsigned, undated fragment written not earlier than the winter of 1724; *Martin's Bench and Bar*, p. 168.

12. Shepherd, *History of Proprietary Government in Pennsylvania*, p. 414; M. Carey and J. Bioren (eds. ), *Laws of the Commonwealth of Pennsylvania* (Philadelphia, 1803), I, 201; MacKinney, *Votes*, II, 1545, 1555.

13. Sainsbury, *Cal. State Papers, Col.*, *1722-23*, p. 367.

14. Proud, *Pennsylvania*, pp. 151-52, 158, 169.

15. James Logan, *The Charge Delivered from the Bench to the Grand Jury, At the Court of Quarter Sessions, held for the County of Philadelphia, the second day of September 1723. Published at the Desire of the Grand Jury. Together with Their Address* (Philadelphia, 1723), pp. 9-11; Accusation against Sir William Keith . . . , p. 103.

16. *Col. Rec.*, III, 226, 228.

17. Hamilton later distinguished himself in his brilliant defense of freedom of the press in *King* vs. *Zenger.*

18. The trustees of the General Loan Office were Samuel Carpenter, the son of Joshua Carpenter; Jeremiah Langhorne, a Bucks County Quaker; William Fishbourne, a friend of Keith; and Nathaniel Newlin, a Chester County Quaker who had long been Lloyd's partisan (Charles P. Keith, *Chronicles of Pennsylvania . . . , 1688-1748*, II, 668).

19. MacKinney, *Votes*, II, 1584-85, 1589, 1827-31; *Col. Rec.*, III, 235; Shepherd, *History of Proprietary Government in Pennsylvania*, p. 415; Anne Bezanson, Robert D. Gray, and Miriam Hussey, *Prices in Colonial Pennsylvania* (Philadelphia: University of Pennsylvania Press, 1935), p. 10.

20. MacKinney, *Votes*, II, 1591.

21. Accusation against Sir William Keith . . . , p. 103, HSP; Hannah Penn to Keith, London, May 20, 1724, MacKinney, *Votes*, II, 1621.
22. Hannah Penn to Keith, London, May 20, 1704, *Votes*, II, 1623-24.
23. Henry Gouldney and Joshua Gee to Keith, London, May 22, 1724, *ibid.*, pp. 1624-25.
24. Keith to Hannah Penn, Philadelphia, September 24, 1724, *ibid.*, pp. 1625-29.
25. *Ibid.*, p. 1597; *Martin's Bench and Bar*, p. 168.

## Chapter 21

1. MacKinney, *Votes*, II, 1620-29, 1630-42; Logan to Hannah Penn, Philadelphia, January 1, 1725/26, "Letters of William Penn," p. 347.
2. MacKinney, *Votes*, II, 1668-69.
3. A copy of this pamphlet is in the library of the Historical Society of Pennsylvania, and it may also be found in MacKinney, *Votes*, II, 1681-89.
4. James Logan, "The Antidote," *Pa. Mag. Hist. & Biog.*, XXXVIII (1914), 470-71.
5. A manuscript copy of Lloyd's *A Further Vindication* is preserved in Penn MSS, Assembly and Provincial Council of Pa., p. 34, HSP.
6. MacKinney, *Votes*, II, 1627.
7. James Logan, "A Memorial from James Logan, in behalf of the Proprietary's Family, and of himself, Servant to Said Family," in MacKinney, *Votes*, II, 1635.
8. David Lloyd, *A Vindication of the Legislative Power* (Philadelphia, 1724/25), p. 3, cited hereafter as Lloyd, *Legislative Power*.
9. James Logan, "A Memorial . . . ," p. 1637.
10. Lloyd, *Legislative Power*, p. 2.
11. MacKinney, *Votes*, II, 1659-71.
12. *Ibid.*, pp. 1630-42.
13. Lloyd, *Legislative Power*, p. 1.
14. *Ibid.* See also *Col. Rec.*, II, 146.
15. James Logan, "The Antidote," pp. 470-71.
16. David Lloyd, A Further Vindication, March 4, 1725/26, Penn MSS, Assembly and Provincial Council, p. 34, HSP.
17. *Ibid.*
18. Lloyd, *Legislative Power*, p. 2.
19. *Ibid.*, p. 3.
20. Who the "Draughts-Man" was is unknown. See Hampton L. Carson, "The Genesis of the Charter of Pennsylvania," *Pa. Mag. Hist. & Biog.*, XLIII (1918), 289-331.
21. Lloyd, *Legislative Power*, p. 4.
22. *Ibid.*
23. *Ibid.*, p. 2.
24. *Ibid.*

25. James Logan, "A Memorial . . . ," p. 1638; James Logan, *The Charge Delivered from the Bench to the Grand Jury* . . . (Philadelphia, 1723), p. 4.

26. Lloyd, *Legislative Power,* p. 3.

27. James Logan, "A Memorial . . . ," p. 1637.

28. Lloyd, *Legislative Power,* p. 3.

29. *Ibid.*

30. *Ibid.*

31. David Lloyd, A Further Vindication, March 4, 1725/26, Penn MSS, Assembly and Provincial Council, p. 34, HSP.

32. Logan, in *The Antidote,* charged that Lloyd's "Law is mis-applied, his Reasoning false" and exhorted the colonists not to listen to "designing Men, who to compass their own Ends, amuse with the charm of misunderstood Words, and empty deluding Prospects . . ." (James Logan, "The Antidote," pp. 465, 487).

33. Logan to Hannah Penn, Philadelphia, January 1, 1725/26, "Letters of William Penn," p. 348; Address of the Assembly to the Proprietors of Pennsylvania, December 7, 1725, Penn MSS, Assembly and Provincial Council, p. 33, HSP.

34. Richard West to the Board of Trade, May 10, 1725, Sainsbury, *Cal. State Papers, Col., 1724-25,* p. 370; *Col. Rec.,* II, 251.

*Chapter 22*

1. MacKinney, *Votes,* II, 1789; *Col. Rec.,* III, 257; Logan to Joshua Gee, Philadelphia, October 14, 1726, Logan Letter Books, HSP.

2. William Keith to James Logan on Occasion of Mr. Logan's having sent to Sir William a Copy of his Printed Paper called the *Antidote,* Copied from a pamphlet on Duodecimo printed at Philadelphia and sold by Andrew Bradford, 1725, Benjamin Franklin Papers, American Philosophical Society Library.

3. *Col. Rec.,* I, 548-49; II, 174-76, 310-15; *Charter and Laws of Pa.,* p. 272.

4. MacKinney, *Votes,* II, 1649.

5. Quoted in Max Savelle, *Seeds of Liberty: The Genesis of the American Mind* (New York: Alfred A. Knopf, 1948), p. 295.

6. William A. Whitehead (ed.), *Documents Relating to the Colonial History of New Jersey* (New Jersey Archives, 1st ser.; Newark, N.J.: Daily Advertiser Printing House, 1882), V, 214-30. See also Sir William Keith, *The History of British Plantations in America: The History of Virginia, with Remarks on the Trade and Commerce of that Colony* (London, 1738). A copy of this rare book is preserved in the William L. Clements Library of Americana at the University of Michigan, and it has been microfilmed as part of the American Culture Series.

7. William Keith to James Logan on Occasion of Mr. Logan's hav-

ing sent to Sir William a Copy of his Printed Paper called the *Antidote* . . . , Benjamin Franklin Papers, American Philosophical Society Library.

8. Keith obtained a copper mine under somewhat questionable circumstances and was also an active speculator in Pennsylvania iron mines. See Accusation against Sir William Keith . . . , p. 103, HSP; Keith to his friends in Philadelphia, March 22, 1728, Penn Papers, Additional Miscellaneous Letters, I, 30, HSP.

9. Depositions of Samson Davis and Thomas Parry, Philadelphia, August 6, 1728, DuSimitiere Collection, Free Library of Philadelphia.

10. Harold D. Eberlein and Cortlandt Van Dyke Hubbard, *Diary of Independence Hall* (Philadelphia: J. B. Lippincott Co., 1948), p. 26; MacKinney, *Votes*, III, 1787; Logan to Joshua Gee, Philadelphia, October 14, 1726, Logan Letter Books, IV, 126-30, HSP; Logan to John Penn, Philadelphia, October 17, 1726, *ibid.*, p. 91.

11. *Col. Rec.*, III, 257, 266, 278-79.

12. Hazard, *Pa. Arch.*, *1st ser.*, I, 188.

13. Twelve hundred Palatines arrived in Pennsylvania during the first three-quarters of 1727 (Logan to John Penn, Philadelphia, October 22, 1727, Logan Letter Books, IV, 145-50, HSP).

14. Wheat prices fell from an index peak of 142 in April, 1725, to 93.8 in October, 1727 (Bezanson, Gray, and Hussey, *Prices in Colonial Pennsylvania*, p. 10).

15. Keith to his friends in Philadelphia, Shipboard, March 22, 1728, Penn Papers, Additional Miscellaneous Letters, I, 30, HSP.

16. David Barclay to Thomas Penn, Philadelphia, October 27, 1728, Penn Papers, Official Correspondence, II, 43, HSP.

17. The Provincial Secretary at this time was Robert Charles *(Martin's Bench and Bar*, p. 167).

18. *Remarks on the Late Proceedings of Some Members of Assembly at Philadelphia: April 1728* (Philadelphia, 1728), cited hereafter as *Remarks*.

19. *Ibid.*

20. *The Proceedings of Some Members of Assembly, at Philadelphia, April, 1728, vindicated from the unfair Reasoning and unjust Insinuations of a Certain Remarker* (Philadelphia, 1728).

21. Edward Horne and others, *A Defence of the Legislative Constitution of the Province of Pennsylvania As it now stands Confirmed and Established by Law and Charter* (Philadelphia, 1728), pp. 3-6, cited hereafter as Horne, *Defence*.

22. *Ibid.*, p. 10.

23. *Ibid.*, p. 9.

24. *Ibid.*, pp. 9-10.

25. *Ibid.*, p. 2.

26. *Ibid.*

27. *Ibid.*, p. 5.

28. Depositions of Samson Davis and Thomas Parry, Philadelphia, August 6, 1728, DuSimitiere Collection, Free Library of Philadelphia.

29. *Col. Rec.*, III, 337-38.

30. *Ibid.*

31. *The Triumvirate of Pennsylvania. In a Letter to a Friend in the Country* (Philadelphia, *ca.* 1729).

32. *Col. Rec.*, III, 340.

33. *Ibid.*, pp. 341-42.

34. Address of the Assembly to Springett, John, and Thomas Penn, May 10, 1729, Penn MSS, Large Miscellany, p. 25, HSP.

35. Logan to John, Thomas, and Richard Penn, Philadelphia, April 24, [1730], Penn Papers, Official Correspondence, II, 55, HSP; *Martin's Bench and Bar*, p. 168; John Penn to Logan, London, November 11, 1728, Gratz Collection, Governors of Pennsylvania, HSP.

36. Logan to John, Thomas, and Richard Penn, Philadelphia, April 24, [1730], Penn Papers, Official Correspondence, II, 55, HSP.

37. *Ibid.*

## Chapter 23

1. Proud, *Pennsylvania*, I, 4.

2. Minutes of the Chester Monthly Meeting, November 28, 1726.

3. The full title of this book is Ellis Pugh, *A Salutation to the Britains, to Call them From the Many Things, to the One Thing needful, for the Saving of their Souls; Especially, To the poor unlearned Tradesmen, Plowmen and Shepherds, those that are of a low degree like myself, This, in Order to direct you to know God and Christ, the only wise God, which is Life eternal, and to learn of him, that you may become wiser than your Teachers.* A copy is in the Friends Historical Library, Swarthmore, Pennsylvania.

4. The first edition of Sewel's *History of the Quakers* appeared in Amsterdam in 1717 (Minutes of the Chester Monthly Meeting, November 28, 1726).

5. The first edition, compiled by a committee of the Assembly, appeared in 1714 *(Martin's Bench and Bar,* p. 186).

6. Horatio Gates Jones, "The Rev. Abel Morgan, Pastor of the United Baptist Churches of Pennepek and Philadelphia," *Pa. Mag. Hist. & Biog.*, VI (1882), 309.

7. The full title of this volume of sermons, first published in 1652 and reprinted in 1709, is *Several Sermons and Discourses of William Dell, Minister of the Gospel; Sometimes Attending both the Generals in the Army: and Now Master of Gonvil and Caius Colledge in Cambridge. Heretofore Published at Several Times, and on Several Occasions; and now gathered in One Volume, for the Benefit of the Faithful, and Conviction of the World.* On the title page the name "David" is printed inside the letter "E" and "Lloyd" in the letter "O" of the

word "Sermons." Below the word "Sermons" the signature "Now Grace Lloyd" is lined out. Below the word "Discourses" the signature "now Israel Pemberton" is lined out and printed in ink immediately below. According to entries on the flyleaf opposite the title page, the book was successively owned by Mary Pleasant, Israel Pemberton's daughter, and James Pemberton Parke. Benjamin Ferris of Philadelphia purchased it from Parke in May, 1809. The book is now the property of Friends Historical Library, Swarthmore, Pennsylvania.

8. Brooke collected a sizable library, including Italian, English, Latin, French, and Greek books. He willed his Italian books to Logan after his death in 1736. Logan's private library of about two thousand volumes later formed a substantial portion of America's first public library, the Library Company of Philadelphia (Charles P. Keith, *Chronicles of Pennsylvania . . . , 1688-1748;* II, 731).

9. Cf. Lloyd, *Legislative Power,* p. 1; David Lloyd, A Further Vindication, March 4, 1725/26, Penn MSS, Assembly and Provincial Council, p. 34, HSP.

10. Lloyd, Hill, and Jeremiah Langhorne to Patrick Gordon, June 21, 1728, Supreme Court of Pennsylvania, HSP; Lloyd to Robert Charles, Chester, January 4, 1729/30, *ibid.,* HSP.

11. Chalkley, *The Journal of Thomas Chalkley,* p. 211.

12. Hoskens, "The Life of That Faithful Servant of Christ, Jane Hoskens," p. 471; Mrs. Edith Samuel (comp.), "Index to the Deaths Mentioned in *The American Weekly Mercury,* 1724-1746," *Pa. Mag. Hist. & Biog.,* LVIII (1934), 51; *DAB,* XI, 330.

13. According to Bidwell and Falconer, there were about 100,000 squatters in the Pennsylvania back country as early as 1726 (Bidwell and Falconer, *History of Agriculture in the Northern United States, 1620-1860,* p. 72).

14. Cf. Wayland F. Dunaway, "Pennsylvania as an Early Distributing Center of Population," *Pa. Mag. Hist. & Biog.,* LV (1931), 134-64.

15. Cf. Charles Woodmason, *The Carolina Backcountry on the Eve of the Revolution: The Journal and Other Writings of Charles Woodmason, Anglican Itinerant,* edited by Richard J. Hooker (Chapel Hill: University of North Carolina Press, 1953), pp. 240-41.

16. In 1758 Richard Jackson, an English lawyer, wrote: "The Governor or Deputy [in Pennsylvania] with the Assembly have together the whole Power of Legislation.

"There is a Council composed of Persons named by the Proprietary or his Deputy, but without any Legislative Authority, being properly a Council of State, with whom the Deputy Governor is enjoyned to Advise and Consult" (Richard Jackson, "Change and Alteration," April 24, 1758, in Carl van Doren [ed.], *The Letters of Benjamin Franklin and Richard Jackson* [Philadelphia: The American Philosophical Society, 1947], p. 80).

17. E. B. Russell, *The Review of American Colonial Legislation by the King in Council* (New York: Columbia University, 1915), p. 221.

18. J. Hector St. John de Crèvecœur, *Letters from an American Farmer* (London: T. Davies, 1782), pp. 51-53.

# Bibliography

PRIMARY SOURCES

Unpublished

*Historical Society of Pennsylvania*

Attorneys General of Pennsylvania.
Blackwell Papers.
Brayton Collection.
Charter of the Corporation of Philadelphia, 1701.
Chester County Papers, 1684-1847.
Dreer Collection, William Penn's Letters.
Early Quakers, Etting Papers.
Etting Papers, Pemberton.
Fallon Scrapbook.
George W. Norris Papers.
Governors of Pennsylvania.
Gratz Collection, Governors of Pennsylvania.
Hazard Family Papers.
James Steel's Letter Book, 1715-32.
Logan Letter Books.
Logan Papers.
Maria Dickinson Logan Papers.
Norris Letter Book.
Norris of Fairhill MSS, Family Letters.
Old Manuscript Book belonging to David Lloyd.
Parrish Collection.
Pemberton Papers.
Penn MSS, Assembly and Provincial Council.
Penn MSS, Large Miscellany.
Penn MSS, Petitions, Beaver Skins.
Penn MSS, Warrants and Surveys.
Penn Papers, Additional Miscellaneous Letters.
Penn Papers, Ford vs. Penn.
Penn Papers, Official Correspondence.
Penn-Forbes Papers.

Penn-Physick Papers.
Pennsylvania Miscellaneous Papers, Penn and Baltimore.
Petitions and Memorials.
Provincial Council, Etting Papers.
Rawle Collection.
Registry of Arrivals at Philadelphia, 1682-86.
Robert Raymond to the Board of Trade, December 22, 1713, signed by
     David Lloyd.
Society Collection.
Stille Case.
Streper Papers, Bucks County.
Supreme Court of Pennsylvania.
Taylor Papers.
Vaux Papers.

*American Philosophical Society*

Benjamin Franklin Papers.
Penn Letters and Documents.

*Friends Bookstore, 302 Arch Street*
*Philadelphia, Pennsylvania*

Epistles of George Fox and Others.
Miscellaneous Papers of the Philadelphia Monthly Meeting.

*Friends Historical Library*
*Swarthmore, Pennsylvania*

Chester Monthly Meeting, Minutes. Microfilm.
Chester Quarterly Meeting, Minutes. Microfilm.

*Free Library of Philadelphia*

Jonathan Dickinson Journal.

*Library Company of Philadelphia (Ridgeway)*

Testimony from Friends & Brethren of the Quarterly Meeting, Held at
     Dolobran, in Montgomeryshire, North Wales, the 30th of the 8th mo.
     1711, Concerning Our Dear & worthy friend, Thomas Lloyd, De-
     ceased.

                              Published

Armstrong, Edward, (ed.). *Correspondence between William Penn and*

*James Logan, Secretary of the Province of Pennsylvania, and Others,
1700-1750.* 2 vols. Philadelphia: Historical Society of Pennsylvania,
1870-72, in vols. IX and X of the *Memoirs of the Historical Society
of Pennsylvania.* Logan's letters, up to 1712, are voluminous reports
on Pennsylvania life, people, and politics, and they are an indispensable source for part of David Lloyd's life.

Blackwell, John, to William Penn, Philadelphia, June 24, 1689, *Pennsylvania Magazine of History and Biography,* VI (1882), 363-64.

Browne, William Hand (ed.). *Proceedings of the Council of Maryland,
1698-1731.* Baltimore: Maryland Historical Society, 1905.

Budd, Thomas. *Good Order Established in Pennsylvania and New Jersey.* Reprinted from the original edition of 1685. Cleveland: Burrows
Bros. Co., 1902. Also preserved on microfilm in the American Culture Series.

Cadbury, Henry J., "John Hepburn and His Book Against Slavery,
1715," *Proceedings of the American Antiquarian Society,* LIX (1950),
89-160.

Carey, M., and J. Bioren (eds.). *Laws of the Commonwealth of Pennsylvania.* Vol. I. Philadelphia, 1803. A digest of the acts of Assembly passed between 1682 and 1776.

Chalkley, Thomas. *The Journal of Thomas Chalkley.* New York: Samuel Wood, 1808. A Quaker missionary who knew David Lloyd in the
late years of his life.

Colonial Society of Pennsylvania. *Records of the Court of Chester County, Pennsylvania, 1681-1697.* Philadelphia: Colonial Society of Pennsylvania, 1910.

-------. *Records of the Court of New Castle on Delaware.* 2 vols.
Meadville, Pa.: Colonial Society of Pennsylvania, 1935.

-------. *Records of the Courts of Quarter Sessions and Common Pleas
of Bucks County, Pennsylvania, 1684-1700.* Meadville, Pa.: Colonial Society of Pennsylvania, 1943. The above three groups of records
contain cases in which David Lloyd appeared sometimes as prosecutor
and sometimes as defense attorney.

Crèvecoeur, J. Hector St. John de. *Letters from an American Farmer.*
London: T. Davies, 1782.

Davis, Samson, and Thomas Parry. *Depositions, laid before the House,
9 August 1728.* Philadelphia, 1729.

"Early Letters from Pennsylvania, 1699-1722," *Pennsylvania Magazine
of History and Biography,* XXXVII (1913). 330-40. Descriptions of
Pennsylvania in the seventeenth century.

"An Early Petition of the Freemen of Pennsylvania to the Assembly,
December 3, 1692," *Pennsylvania Magazine of History and Biography,* XXXVIII (1914), 495-501.

Egle, William Henry. *Minutes of the Board of Property of the Province
of Pennsylvania.* (Pennsylvania Archives, 2nd ser.) Vol. XIX. Harrisburg: E. K. Meyers, State Printer, 1893. Contains information

about David Lloyd's land purchases and sales and about his activities as an attorney.

------- (ed.). *Old Rights, Proprietary Rights, Virginia Entries, and Soldiers Entitled to Donation Land.* (Pennsylvania Archives, 3rd ser.) Vol. III. Harrisburg: Clarence H. Busch, State Printer, 1896. Also contains some information bearing on Lloyd's land speculations.

"The First Charter of the City of Philadelphia, 1691," *Pennsylvania Magazine of History and Biography*, XVIII (1894), 504-9.

Fisher, Joshua Francis. "Narrative of Sir William Keith's Coming to the Government of Pennsylvania, with his Conduct in it (1726)," in *Memoirs of the Historical Society of Pennsylvania*, Vol. II, Part II. Philadelphia: E. Littel, 1830. An anti-Keith pamphlet.

George, Staughton, Benjamin M. Nead, and Thomas McCamant (eds.). *Charter to William Penn and Laws of the Province of Pennsylvania, Passed between the Years 1682 and 1700, preceded by Duke of York's Laws in Force from the Year 1676 to the Year 1682, with an Appendix containing Laws Relating to the Organization of the Provincial Courts and Historical Matter.* Harrisburg: L. S. Hart, State Printer, 1879. A complete compilation of the acts of the Pennsylvania Assembly passed before 1700, the frames of government of 1682, 1683, and 1696, and judiciary legislation. Also contains annotations giving the action of the King-in-Council on each act of Assembly.

Grant, W. L., and James Munro (eds.). *Acts of the Privy Council of England, Colonial Series, 1613-1783.* 6 vols. Hereford: Printed for H. M. Stationery Office, by Anthony Bros., 1908-12. Contains the texts of entries relating to colonial affairs in the Privy Council Register. Some of the entries deal specifically with Pennsylvania.

Great Britain. *Calendar of State Papers, Domestic, 1547-1704, Preserved in the Public Record Office.* 76 vols. London: H. M. Stationery Office, 1865-1925.

-------. *Journal of the Commissioners for Trade and Plantations, from April 1704, to 1728, Preserved in the Public Record Office.* 5 vols. London: H. M. Stationery Office, 1920.

-------. *The Statutes of the Realm . . . (1101-1713).* 11 vols. London, 1810-28.

Great Britain, Royal Commission on Historical Manuscripts. *1st Report.* London: Eyre and Spottiswoode, 1870.

-------. *House of Lords MSS, new series, 1693-1710.* 8 vols. London: H. M. Stationery Office, 1900-23.

-------. *Earl of Dartmouth MSS, American Papers.* London: H. M. Stationery Office, 1895.

-------. *Earl of Lonsdale MSS.* London: H. M. Stationery Office, 1893.

-------. *The Manuscripts of His Grace the Duke of Portland, Preserved at Welbeek Abbey.* 10 vols. London: H. M. Stationery Office, 1892-1931.

Hall, Clayton C., Bernard C. Steiner, J. Hall Pleasants, Raphael

Semmes, and others (eds.). *Archives of Maryland.* 65 vols. Baltimore: Maryland Historical Society, 1883-1952.

*The Harleian Miscellany; or, a Collection of Scarce, Curious, and Entertaining Pamphlets and Tracts, as Well in Manuscript as in Print, Found in the late Earl of Oxford's Library, Interspersed with Historical, Political, and Critical Notes.* 12 vols. London, 1810.

Hazard, Samuel (ed.). *Colonial Records of Pennsylvania.* 16 vols. Philadelphia: Jo. Severns and Co., 1852.

———. *Pennsylvania Archives, Selected and Arranged from Original Documents in the Office of the Secretary of the Commonwealth.* (Pennsylvania Archives, 1st ser.) 12 vols. Philadelphia: Jo. Severns and Co., 1852-56.

Hobbes, Thomas. *Leviathan.* London: J. M. Dent and Sons, 1931.

Horne, Edward, and others. *A Defence of the Legislative Constitution of the Province of Pennsylvania As it now stands Confirmed and Established by Law and Charter.* Philadelphia, 1728.

Hoskens, Jane (Fenn). "The Life of That Faithful Servant of Christ, Jane Hoskens, a Minister of the Gospel Among the People Called Quakers," *Friends Library* (Philadelphia: Joseph Rakestraw, 1837), I, 460-73. David Lloyd's housekeeper and friend during the late years of his life.

Jameson, John F. (ed.). *Privateering and Piracy in the Colonial Period: Illustrative Documents.* New York: Macmillan Co., 1923.

Keith, George. "An Exhortation & Caution to Friends concerning Buying or Keeping of Negroes," *Pennsylvania Magazine of History and Biography,* XIII (1889), 265-70.

*A Letter from a Gentleman in Philadelphia to His friend in Bucks,* signed *Philalethes, Philadelphia, September 30, 1728.* Philadelphia, 1728. Preserved at the Free Library of Philadelphia in the DuSimitiere Collection of Imprints Relating to Pennsylvania, 1660-1770.

*A Letter, Occasioned by the Perusal of a Paper lately Published, called, A Dialogue between Freeman and Trusty,* signed by A. B. *with Advertisement,* signed by A. H., *Philadelphia, April, 1728.* Philadelphia, 1728. Preserved at the Free Library of Philadelphia in the DuSimitiere Collection of Imprints Relating to Pennsylvania, 1660-1770.

Lloyd, David. "Correspondence with Thomas Lower," *The Friend,* XXXIX (1865), 93, 98-100, 105-6, 114-15.

———. *A Further Vindication of the Rights and priviledges of the People of this Province of Pensilvania.* Philadelphia, March 4, 1725/26. Manuscript copy in Penn MSS, Assembly and Provincial Council, HSP.

———. *A Vindication of the Legislative Power.* Philadelphia, 1724/25.

Lloyd, Thomas. *A Seasonable Advertisement to the Freemen of this Province etc.* Philadelphia, 1689.

Locke, John. *An Essay Concerning the True Original, Extent and End of Civil Government: Second Treatise.* London, 1690.

Logan, James. "The Antidote," *Pennsylvania Magazine of History and*

Biography, XXXVIII (1914), 463-87.

--------. The Charge Delivered from the Bench to the Grand Jury, At the Court of Quarter Sessions, held for the County of Philadelphia, the second day of September 1723. Published at the Desire of the Grand Jury. Together with their Address. Philadelphia, 1723.

--------. Remarks on Sir William Keith's Vindication. Philadelphia, 1726.

MacKinney, Gertrude (ed.). Votes and Proceedings of the House of Representatives of the Province of Pennsylvania. Pennsylvania Archives, Eighth Series. 8 vols. Harrisburg: John R. Hood, director, Bureau of Publications, Department of Property and Supplies, 1931-35.

Michener, Ezra. A Retrospect of Early Quakerism: Being Extracts from the Records of Philadelphia Yearly Meeting and the Meetings Composing It to which Is Prefixed an Account of Their First Establishment. Philadelphia: T. Ellwood Zell, 1860.

Mitchell, J. T., and S. Flanders (eds.). Statutes at Large of Pennsylvania, 1700-90. 11 vols. Harrisburg: State Printer, 1896-1908. Acts of the Pennsylvania Assembly. Volume I (1682-1700) was never published. Hence, this collection must be used in connection with Staughton George and others, Charter to William Penn, and Laws of the Province of Pennsylvania, Passed between the Years 1682 and 1700.

Myers, Albert C. (ed.). Narratives of Early Pennsylvania, West New Jersey and Delaware 1630-1707. New York: Charles Scribner's Sons, 1912.

Nelson, William (ed.). Calendar of Records in the Office of the Secretary of State, 1664-1703. Documents Relating to the Colonial History of the State of New Jersey. Vol. XXI. Paterson, N. J.: Press Printing and Publishing Co., 1899. Contains some information concerning the Thomas Lloyd estate, of which David Lloyd and Isaac Norris were the executors.

Norris, Isaac. Friendly Advice to the Inhabitants of Pennsylvania. Philadelphia, 1710.

O'Callaghan, E. B. (ed.). Documents Relative to the Colonial History of the State of New York. 14 vols. and index. Albany, N. Y.: Weed, Parsons and Co., 1853-87. Contains the Whitehall papers, a valuable source of information concerning the relations between the homeland and the colonies and intercolonial relations. It throws considerable light on the Fletcher administration in Pennsylvania.

Pastorius, Francis D. "Description of Pennsylvania, 1700, " in Old South Leaflet, No. 95. Boston: Directors of Old South Work, Old South Meeting House, n. d.

Penn, William. Coleman's Re-Print of William Penn's Original Proposal and Plan for the Founding and Building of Philadelphia in Pennsylvania, America, in 1683. London: J. Coleman, 1881. The orig-

*Bibliography* 287

inal imprint appeared in London in 1683.

------. *A Letter from William Penn, Proprietary and Governour of Pennsylvania in America, to the Committee of the Free Society of Traders . . . To which is added, An Account of the City of Philadelphia Newly laid out.* London, 1683.

------. "Letter of William Penn to James Logan, 1702," *Pennsylvania Magazine of History and Biography*, XXXVI (1912), 303-8.

------. "Letters of William Penn," *Pennsylvania Magazine of History and Biography*, XXXIII (1909), 303-18, 423-31.

Pennypacker, Samuel W. "Collection of Various Pieces Concerning Pennsylvania Printed in 1684," *Pennsylvania Magazine of History and Biography*, VI (1882), 312-28.

------. *Pennsylvania Colonial Cases: The Administration of Law in Pennsylvania prior to A. D. 1700 as shown in the cases decided and in the court proceedings.* Philadelphia: George T. Bisel Co., 1892. Contains records of important seventeenth-century Pennsylvania court trials in which David Lloyd participated.

*The Proceedings of some Members of Assembly at Philadelphia, April, 1728, vindicated from the unfair Reasoning and unjust Insinuations of a certain Remarker.* Philadelphia, 1728. Preserved at the Free Library of Philadelphia in the DuSimitiere Collection of Imprints Relating to Pennsylvania, 1660-1770.

Rawle, Francis. *A Just Rebuke to a Dialogue betwixt Simon and Timothy, Showing What's therein to be found. Namely Levity, Perversion, and Detraction. All which are detected in this short Examen.* Philadelphia: S. Keimer, 1726.

------. *Some Remedies Proposed, for the Restoring the sunk Credit of the Province of Pennsylvania, with Some Remarks of its Trade. Humbly offer'd to the Consideration of the Worthy Representatives in the General Assembly of this Province, By a Lover of this Country.* Philadelphia, 1721. Rawle, a follower of David Lloyd, was the first to advocate paper money in Pennsylvania.

Reed, George E. (ed.). *Papers of the Governors, 1681-1747.* (Pennsylvania Archives, 4th ser.) Vol. I. Harrisburg: William Stanley Ray, State Printer, 1900.

*Remarks on the late Proceedings of some Members of Assembly at Philadelphia, April, 1728.* Philadelphia, 1728. Preserved at the Free Library of Philadelphia in the DuSimitiere Collection of Imprints Relating to Pennsylvania, 1660-1770.

*A Revisal of the Intreagues of the Triumvirate, with the rest of the Trustees of the Proprietor of Pennsylvania, and also, of a Warning to the Inhabitants of the said Province, against the Guiles of the Devil and Men.* Philadelphia, 1729. Preserved at the Free Library of Philadelphia in the DuSimitiere Collection of Imprints Relating to Pennsylvania, 1660-1770.

Sainsbury, W. Noel (ed.). *Calendar of State Papers, American and*

*West Indies.* 40 vols. London: Eyre and Spottiswoode, 1893. Also known as *Calendar of State Papers, Colonial.*

Sewel, William. *The History of the Rise, Increase and Progress of the Christian People Called Quakers.* Philadelphia, 1728.

Shaw, William A. (ed. ). *Calendar of Treasury Books Preserved in the Public Record Office.* 25 vols. London: H. M. Stationery Office, 1904-52. The records of the British Treasury. They contain some items relating to Pennsylvania affairs, especially quitrents and Penn's debts to the Crown.

Shumway, Daniel B. "A Rare Dutch Document Concerning the Province of Pennsylvania in the Seventeenth Century, " *Pennsylvania Magazine of History and Biography,* XLIX (1925), 99-140. Contains a translation from the Dutch of *Detailed Information and Account for Those who are Inclined to America and Are Interested in Settling in the Province of Pennsylvania--1686,* a promotion pamphlet attributed to Robert Webb and published in Amsterdam in 1686. An excellent description of social life in seventeenth-century Pennsylvania.

Story, Thomas. *Journal of the Life of Thomas Story, containing an account of his remarkable convincement of . . . truth as held by the people called Quakers, also his travels and labours in the service of the Gospel.* Newcastle-on-Tyne, 1747. This journal may also be found in *Friends Library,* X, 1-372. Contains little about David Lloyd, but one gets from it something of the flavor of Quaker life in early eighteenth-century Pennsylvania.

Thomas, Gabriel. *An Historical and Geographical Account of the Province and Country of Pensilvania and of West-New-Jersey in America.* London, 1698.

Toppan, R. N. *Edward Randolph, Including His Letters and Official Papers.* 7 vols. Boston: Prince Society, 1898-1909. These papers throw some light on David Lloyd as an attorney general.

*The Triumvirate of Pennsylvania. In a Letter to a Friend in the Country.* Philadelphia, ca. 1729. Preserved at the Free Library of Philadelphia in the DuSimitiere Collection of Imprints Relating to Pennsylvania, 1660-1770.

"Unpublished Minutes of the Provincial Council of Pennsylvania, 1692, " *Pennsylvania Magazine of History and Biography,* XI (1887), 151-59.

Van Doren, Carl (ed. ). *The Letters of Benjamin Franklin and Richard Jackson.* Philadelphia: The American Philosophical Society, 1947.

Ventris, Sir Peyton. *The Reports of Sir Peyton Ventris Knt., Late One of the Justices of the Common Pleas.* In the Savoy, 1726.

Whitehead, William A. (ed. ). *Documents Relating to the Colonial History of New Jersey.* (New Jersey Archives, 1st ser. ) Vol. V. Newark, N. J. : Daily Advertiser Printing House, 1882.

Withington, Lothrop. "Pennsylvania Gleanings in England, " *Pennsylvania Magazine of History and Biography,* XXVIII (1904), 456-69.

Woodmason, Charles. *The Carolina Backcountry on the Eve of the*

*Revolution: The Journal and Other writings of Charles Woodmason, Anglican Itinerant.* Edited by Richard J. Hooker. Chapel Hill: Published for the Institute of Early American History and Culture at Williamsburg, Virginia, by the University of North Carolina Press, 1953.

## SECONDARY SOURCES

Allinson, Edward P., and Boies Penrose. "The Early Government of Philadelphia and the Blue Anchor Tavern Landing, " *Pennsylvania Magazine of History and Biography,* X (1896), 61-77.

Ames, Herman V., and Luther R. Kelker. "Public Archives of Pennsylvania, " *American Historical Association Annual Report for 1904,* pp. 629-49. Lists the contents of the Pennsylvania Archives.

Andrews, Charles M. *The Colonial Period of American History.* 4 vols. New Haven: Yale University Press, 1937.

Applegarth, Albert C. *Quakers in Pennsylvania.* Baltimore: Johns Hopkins Press, 1892.

Ashmead, Henry G. *Historical Sketch of Chester, on Delaware.* Chester, Pa.: Republican Steam Printing House, 1883. A collection of antiquarian researches, rather than a history. Contains descriptions of colonial buildings which were still standing during the author's lifetime.

Beers, Henry P. *Bibliographies in American History: Guide to Materials for Research.* New York: H. W. Wilson Co., 1938. Lists Pennsylvania bibliographies to 1938.

Bezanson, Anne, Robert D. Gray, and Miriam Hussey. *Prices in Colonial Pennsylvania.* Philadelphia: University of Pennsylvania Press, 1935. An analysis of price fluctuations in Pennsylvania from 1720 to 1775.

Bidwell, Percy W., and John I. Falconer. *History of Agriculture in the Northern United States, 1620-1860.* Washington, D. C.: Carnegie Institute of Washington, 1925.

Bining, Arthur C., Robert L. Brunhouse, and Norman B. Wilkinson. *Writings on Pennsylvania History: A Bibliography.* Harrisburg: Pennsylvania Historical and Museum Commission, 1946. The best of the Pennsylvania bibliographies, but limited to secondary materials.

Bolles, Albert S. *Pennsylvania, Province and State: A History from 1609 to 1790.* 2 vols. Philadelphia: J. Wanamaker, 1899. Although superseded in many ways by more recent scholarship, this is still a usable account.

Bradford, Thomas L. *The Bibliographer's Manual of American History, Containing an Account of All State, Territory, Town and County Histories Relating to the United States.* Revised by Stanley V. Henkels. 5 vols. Philadelphia: S. V. Henkels and Co., 1907-10. Contains titles of Pennsylvania town and county histories.

Braithwaite, William C. *The Beginnings of Quakerism.* London: Macmillan and Co., 1912. A social history of Quakers in seventeenth-century England.

Bridenbaugh, Carl. *Cities in the Wilderness: The First Century of Urban Life in America, 1625-1742.* New York: Ronald Press, 1938. Deals partly with early colonial Philadelphia.

Burke, Sir John B. *Burke's Genealogical and Heraldic History of the Landed Gentry, including American Families with British Ancestry.* London: Burke's Peerage, 1939. Contains the genealogy of the Lloyds of Dolobran.

Carlisle, Nicholas. *A Topographical Dictionary of the Dominion of Wales.* London, 1811. Contains a description of Manafon and surrounding country.

Carlyle, R. W. and A. J. *A History of Medieval Political Theory in the West.* 6 vols. New York: Barnes and Noble, n. d.

Carson, Hampton L. "The Genesis of the Charter of Pennsylvania, " *Pennsylvania Magazine of History and Biography,* XLIII (1918), 289-331.

Channing, Edward. *A History of the United States.* 6 vols. New York: The Macmillan Co., 1927.

Davies, Godfrey. *Bibliography of British History: Stuart Period, 1603-1714.* New York: Oxford University Press, 1928. Lists secondary accounts relating to Welsh, Quaker, colonial, and English history in the seventeenth century to 1714.

Davis, W. W. H. "Early Settlers in Bucks County, " *A Collection of Papers Read before the Bucks County Historical Society,* II (1909), 198-99.

Diffenderffer, F. R. "Early Local History as Revealed by an Old Document, " *Historical Papers and Addresses of the Lancaster County Historical Society,* II (1897), 3-27. An account of the Susquehanna Land Company.

-------. *The German Immigration into Pennsylvania through the Port of Philadelphia from 1700-1775.* (Proceedings of Pennsylvania German Society, Vol. X.) Lancaster, Pa.: Pennsylvania German Society, 1900.

Dunaway, Wayland F. "The English Settlers in Colonial Pennsylvania, " *Pennsylvania Magazine of History and Biography,* LII (1928), 317-41.

-------. *A History of Pennsylvania.* New York: Prentice-Hall, 1935. Considered the standard work on the subject. Dunaway believes that colonial Pennsylvania became a pure democracy as the result of David Lloyd's efforts.

-------. "Pennsylvania as an Early Distributing Center of Population, " *Pennsylvania Magazine of History and Biography,* LV (1931), 134-64.

Eberlein, Harold D., and Cortlandt Van Dyke Hubbard. *Diary of Independence Hall.* Philadelphia: J. B. Lippincott Co., 1948.

-------. *Portrait of a Colonial City, Philadelphia, 1670-1838.* Philadelphia, J. B. Lippincott Co., 1939.

Eshleman, H. Frank. "The Birth of Lancaster County, " *Historical*

*Papers and Addresses of the Lancaster County Historical Society,* XII (1908), 5-39. An account of the Susquehanna Land Company and of early settlement in what is now Lancaster County.

-------. "The Constructive Genius of David Lloyd in Early Colonial Pennsylvania Legislation and Jurisprudence, 1686 to 1731, " *Pennsylvania Bar Association Report,* XVI (1910), 406-61. A sketch of David Lloyd as a republican, marred by an uncritical use of source materials.

-------. "The Great Conestoga Road, "*Historical Papers and Addresses of the Lancaster County Historical Society,* XII (1908), 215-32.

-------. "The Struggle and Rise of Popular Power in Pennsylvania's First Two Decades (1682-1701), " *Pennsylvania Magazine of History and Biography,* XXXIV (1910), 129-61.

Evans, J. *The Beauties of England and Wales: or, Original Delineations, Topographical, Historical, and Descriptive, of Each County.* 18 vols. London, 1812. Contains a description of Montgomeryshire.

Fitzroy, Herbert W. K. "The Punishment of Crime in Provincial Pennsylvania, " *Pennsylvania Magazine of History and Biography,* LX (1936), 242-69.

Fletcher, Stevenson W. *Pennsylvania Agriculture and Country Life, 1640-1840.* Harrisburg: Pennsylvania Historical and Museum Commission, 1950.

Franklin, Benjamin. *An Historical Review of Pennsylvania, From its Origin, Embracing, among other subjects, the Various Points of Controversy which have arisen from time to time, between the several Governors and the Assemblies.* Philadelphia: E. Olmstead and W. Power, 1812. Originally published in London in 1759, this account is based on official records, but otherwise it faithfully represents the pro-Assembly, antiproprietary point of view. There is some unproved speculation that it was originally written by Richard Jackson under Franklin's supervision.

"George Fox's bequest to Friends of Philadelphia, and the Reasons why our city missed having the free Botanical Garden he intended for it, " *The Friend,* XXXIX (1865), 93-100.

Gipson, Lawrence H. *The British Empire before the American Revolution: Provincial Characteristics and Sectional Tendencies in the Era Preceding the American Crisis.* 9 vols. Caldwell, Idaho: The Caxton Printers, 1936 (Vols. I-III); New York: Alfred A. Knopf, 1939, 1942, 1946, 1949, 1954, 1956 (Vols. IV-IX).

-------. "Crime and its Punishment in Provincial Pennsylvania, " *Pennsylvania History,* II (1935), 3-4.

Griffin, Grace G. , and others (eds. ). *Writings on American History: A Bibliography of Books and Articles on United States History, 1906-1940.* New York: Macmillan Co. , 1908-10 (for years 1906-8); Washington, D. C. : Government Printing Office, 1911-13 (years 1909-11 in *American Historical Association Reports for 1909-11);* New Haven: Yale University Press, 1914-19 (for years 1912-17); Washington,

D. C. : Government Printing Office, 1921-42, 1949 (years 1918-40 in *American Historical Association Reports* as supplements). See also Masterson, James R. (ed. ). No volumes were published between 1943 and 1948. The 1949 volume contains the bibliography for the years 1939-40.

Hazard, Samuel (ed. ). *The Register of Pennsylvania, Devoted to the Preservation of Facts and Documents, and Every Other Kind of Useful Information Respecting the State of Pennsylvania.* 16 vols. Philadelphia: W. F. Geddes, 1828-36. Many of the documents printed here have since been published elsewhere, but Hazard's *Register* remains a useful collection of all sorts of interesting information.

Herrick, Cheesman A. *White Servitude in Pennsylvania: Indentured and Redemption Labor in Colony and Commonwealth.* Philadelphia: J. J. McVey, 1926.

Hinshaw, William Wade. *Encyclopedia of American Quaker Genealogy.* 6 vols. Ann Arbor, Mich.: Edwards Bros., 1936-50. A useful compilation of genealogical materials gleaned from Quaker meeting records.

Holdsworth, W. S. *A History of English Law.* 7 vols. London: Methuen and Co., 1903-24.

Johannsen, Robert W. "The Conflict Between the Three Lower Counties on the Delaware and the Province of Pennsylvania 1682-1704, " *Delaware History,* V (1952), 96-132.

Johnson, Allen, and Dumas Malone (eds. ). *Dictionary of American Biography.* 21 vols. New York: Charles Scribner's Sons, 1928-44. Contains a thumbnail sketch of David Lloyd's life and suggestive references.

Johnson, William Thomas. "Some Aspects of the Relations of the Government and German Settlers in Colonial Pennsylvania, 1683-1754, " *Pennsylvania History,* XI (1944), 81-102. 200-7.

Jones, Horatio Gates. "The Rev. Abel Morgan, Pastor of the United Baptist Churches of Pennepek and Philadelphia, " *Pennsylvania Magazine of History and Biography,* VI (1882), 300-10.

Jones, Rufus M. *The Quakers in the American Colonies.* London: Macmillan and Co., 1911. A standard history. The chapters on Pennsylvania were written by Isaac Sharpless.

Jorns, Auguste. *The Quakers as Pioneers in Social Work.* Translated from the German by Thomas K. Brown, Jr. New York: Macmillan Co., 1931.

Keith, Charles P. *Chronicles of Pennsylvania from the English Revolution to the Peace of Aix-la-Chapelle, 1688-1748.* 2 vols. Philadelphia: Patterson and White Co., 1917. An annalistic work which lacks interpretation, this is the product of considerable research in primary sources and is replete with factual information. Unfortunately, it is unsuitably documented.

-------. "The Founding of Christ Church, Philadelphia; " *Pennsyl-*

*vania Magazine of History and Biography*, LIV (1930), 307-14.

———. *The Provincial Councillors of Pennsylvania Who Held Office between 1733 and 1776, and Those Earlier Councillors Who Were Some Time Chief Magistrates of the Province, and Their Descendants*. Philadelphia, 1883. Contains a genealogical account of the Lloyds of Dolobran.

Konkle, Burton Alva. "David Lloyd and Chester, " *Friends Historical Association Bulletin*, XXI (1932), 71-74.

———. David Lloyd and the First Half Century of Pennsylvania. Unpublished manuscript preserved at Friends Historical Library, Swarthmore, Pennsylvania.

———. "David Lloyd, Penn's Great Lawmaker, " *Pennsylvania History*, IV (1937), 153-56. Konkle offered the theory that David Lloyd and William Penn secretly conspired to establish a democratic republic in Pennsylvania. Unfortunately the theory was inadequately documented.

Leonard, Sister Joan de Lourdes. "The Organization and Procedure of the Pennsylvania Assembly, 1682-1776, " *Pennsylvania Magazine of History and Biography*, LXXII (1948), 215-39, 376-412.

Levick, James J. "The Early Welsh Quakers and Their Emigration to Pennsylvania, " *Pennsylvania Magazine of History and Biography*, XVII (1893), 385-413.

Lewis, Lawrence. "The Courts of Pennsylvania in the Seventeenth Century, " *Pennsylvania Magazine of History and Biography*, V (1881), 141-90. Contains a brief, but unilluminating, sketch of David Lloyd's life.

Library of Congress. *American and English Genealogies in the Library of Congress*. Washington, D. C. : Government Printing Office, 1919. Contains a list of genealogies on the Lloyds of Dolobran.

Lowe, Rachel J. *Farm and Its Inhabitants, with Some Account of the Lloyds of Dolobran*. Privately printed, 1883.

Loyd, Jr., William H. *The Early Courts of Pennsylvania*. Boston: Boston Book Co., 1910.

Martin, John Hill. *Martin's Bench and Bar of Philadelphia*. Philadelphia: Rees Welsh and Co., 1883. Useful listing of courts, judges, and lawyers in Philadelphia and Pennsylvania.

Masterson, James R. (ed. ). *Writings on American History*. Washington, D, C. : Government Printing Office, 1952-56 (years 1948-51 in *American Historical Association Reports* as supplements). Continues the work of the late Grace G. Griffin. Volumes for the years 1941-47 have not yet been prepared.

Morris, Richard B. *Studies in the History of Anglo-American Law, with Special Reference to the Seventeenth and Eighteenth Centuries*. New York: Columbia University Press, 1930. The outstanding study in a much-neglected field.

Myers, Albert C. *Immigration of the Irish Quakers into Pennsylvania,*

*1682-1750, with their Early History in Ireland.* Swarthmore, Pa.:
    The Author, 1902.
Nettels, Curtis P. *The Money Supply of the American Colonies before
    1720.* (University of Wisconsin Studies in the Social Sciences and
    History, No. 20.) Madison, Wis.: University of Wisconsin, 1934.
Osgood, Herbert L. *The American Colonies in the Seventeenth Cen-
    tury.* 4 vols. New York: Columbia University, 1904.
Peare, Catherine Owens. *William Penn: A Biography.* Philadelphia:
    J. B. Lippincott Co., 1957.
"A Penn Rarity," *Quakeriana Notes,* No. 1 (1933), p. 3.
Pennsylvania Historical Commission. *Pennsylvania Bibliography: Ar-
    ticles Published by Societies Belonging to the Pennsylvania Federa-
    tion of Historical Societies.* Harrisburg: Pennsylvania Historical
    Commission, 1933. Lists articles on town and county history in local
    historical society collections and transactions.
Pennsylvania, Historical Society of. *Guide to the Manuscript Collec-
    tion in The Historical Society of Pennsylvania,* 2nd ed. Philadelphia:
    Historical Society of Pennsylvania, 1949. A descriptive guide to 1,611
    collections containing more than 4,000,000 manuscripts. It also con-
    tains a name and subject index.
Pomfret, John E. "The Proprietors of the Province of West New Jersey,
    1674-1702," *Pennsylvania Magazine of History and Biography,* LXXV
    (1951), 117-46.
Proud, Robert. *The History of Pennsylvania, in North America, from,
    the Original Institution and Settlement of that Province, under the
    first Proprietor and Governor William Penn, in 1681, till after the
    Year 1742. . . .* 2 vols. Philadelphia: Zachariah Poulson, Jr., 1797-
    98. Based on the archives of which David Lloyd was one of the cus-
    todians, this work is still serviceable because it contains much ma-
    terial not available elsewhere.
Rawle, William B. "The General Title of the Penn Family to Penn-
    sylvania," *Pennsylvania Magazine of History and Biography,* XXIII
    (1899), 60-68, 224-40, 464-82.
Rees, Thomas. *History of Protestant Nonconformity in Wales, from
    Its Rise in 1633 to the Present Time.* 2nd ed. London: John Snow and
    Co., 1883. Contains information about the Welsh Quakers of David
    Lloyd's boyhood, including the Lloyds of Dolobran.
Rhys, John, and David Brynmor-Jones. *The Welsh People: Chapters
    on Their Origin, History, Laws, Literature, and Characteristics.*
    New York: Macmillan Co., 1900.
Rodney, Richard S. "Early Relations of Delaware and Pennsylvania,"
    *Pennsylvania Magazine of History and Biography,* LIV (1930), 209-40.
Root, Winfred T. *The Relations of Pennsylvania with the British Gov-
    ernment, 1696-1765.* Philadelphia: University of Pennsylvania, 1912.
Russell, E. B. *The Review of American Colonial Legislation by the
    King in Council.* New York: Columbia University, 1915.

Sabin, Joseph A. *Bibliotheca Americana: A Dictionary of Books Relating to America from its Discovery to the Present Time.* 29 vols.
New York: Bibliographical Society of America, 1868-1936. Particularly useful for older works. Items on Pennsylvania are listed, XIV,
327-444; on William Penn, XIV, 311-24; on Philadelphia, XIV, 524-82,
XV, 9-54.

Sachse, Julius F. "Penn's City on the Susquehanna, "*Historical Papers
and Addresses of the Lancaster County Historical Society,* II (1897),
223-37.

Samuel, Mrs. Edith (comp.). "Index to the Deaths Mentioned in *The
American Weekly Mercury,* 1724-46, " *Pennsylvania Magazine of History and Biography,* LVIII (1934), 37-60.

Savelle, Max. *Seeds of Liberty: The Genesis of the American Mind.*
New York: Alfred A. Knopf, 1948.

Sharpless, Isaac. *A History of Quaker Government in Pennsylvania.*
2 vols. Philadelphia: T. S. Leach and Co., 1898-99. A standard work
by a leading Quaker historian.

-------. *Political Leaders of Provincial Pennsylvania.* New York: The
Macmillan Co., 1919. Contains a biographical sketch of David Lloyd.

Shepherd, William R. *History of Proprietary Government in Pennsylvania.* (Columbia University Studies in History, Economics and Public Law, Vol. VI.) New York: Columbia University, 1896.

-------. "The Land System of Provincial Pennsylvania, " *American
Historical Association Annual Report for 1894,* pp. 117-25.

Smith, Culver H. "Why Pennsylvania Never Became a Royal Province, "
*Pennsylvania Magazine of History and Biography,* LIII (1929), 141-58.

Smith, H. F. Russell. *Harrington and His Oceana: A Study of a 17th
Century Utopia and Its Influence in America.* Cambridge: Cambridge
University Press, 1914.

Stille, Charles J. "Religious Tests in Provincial Pennsylvania, " *Pennsylvania Magazine of History and Biography,* IX (1885), 365-406.

Thayer, Theodore. "The Quaker Party of Pennsylvania, " *Pennsylvania
Magazine of History and Biography,* LXXI (1947), 19-43.

Tolles, Frederick B. *Meeting House and Counting House: The Quaker
Merchants of Colonial Philadelphia 1682-1763.* Chapel Hill: University
of North Carolina Press, 1948. The Quaker merchants of colonial
Philadelphia and their mores. Tolles wrote that under the leadership
of David Lloyd and James Logan "two Quaker parties arose in Pennsylvania, drawing their strength respectively from the country and
the city, and that between them they divided the Whig heritage, the
one cherishing liberty above all things, and the other, property" (p.
16).

Turner, Edward R. "Slavery in Colonial Pennsylvania, " *Pennsylvania
Magazine of History and Biography,* XXXV (1911), 141-51.

Wainwright, Nicholas B. "Governor John Blackwell." *Pennsylvania
Magazine of History and Biography,* LXXIV (1950), 457-72.

Walton, Joseph S. "A Sketch of David Lloyd's Life," *Journal of the Friends' Historical Society*, Vol. III (1906), nos. 2-3.

Watson, Henry W. "The Growdon Mansion," *A Collection of Papers Read before the Bucks County Historical Society*, II (1909), 451-56.

Watson, John F. *Annals of Philadelphia and Pennsylvania in Olden Times*. 3 vols. Philadelphia: J. M. Stoddart and Co., 1881. An ill-arranged, but invaluable, collection of original materials, the result of diligent antiquarian researches, and accounts gathered from interviews with surviving contemporaries of David Lloyd when he was an old man.

Westcott, Thompson, and John T. Scharf. *History of Philadelphia: 1609-1884*. 3 vols. Philadelphia: L. H. Everts, 1884. A storehouse of factual information about colonial Philadelphia.

Wilson, James G., and John Fiske (eds.). *Appleton's Cyclopedia of American Biography*. 12 vols. New York: D. Appleton and Co., 1887-89, 1918-31. Contains a brief sketch of David Lloyd's life.

Winsor, Justin (ed.). *Narrative and Critical History of America*. Boston: Houghton Mifflin and Co., 1884.

Works Progress Administration. *Inventory of the County Archives of Pennsylvania, Delaware County, No. 23*. Philadelphia: The Historical Records Survey, 1939.

Zimmerman, Albright G. "Daniel Coxe and The New Mediterranean Sea Company," *Pennsylvania Magazine of History and Biography*, LXXVI (1952), 86-96.

# Index